SAGE was founded in 1965 by Sara Miller McCune to support the dissemination of usable knowledge by publishing innovative and high-quality research and teaching content. Today, we publish over 900 journals, including those of more than 400 learned societies, more than 800 new books per year, and a growing range of library products including archives, data, case studies, reports, and video. SAGE remains majority-owned by our founder, and after Sara's lifetime will become owned by a charitable trust that secures our continued independence.

Los Angeles | London | New Delhi | Singapore | Washington DC | Melbourne

Marketing Planning and Strategy

Marketing Planning and Strategy

A Practical Introduction

John Dawes

Professor of Marketing at UniSA Business and an Associate Director of the Ehrenberg-Bass Institute for Marketing Science, University of South Australia

SAGE | TEXTS

Los Angeles | London | New Delhi
Singapore | Washington DC | Melbourne

Originally published in 2021 by

SAGE www.sagepublishing.com
Los Angeles | London | New Delhi | Singapore | Washington DC | Melbourne

The South Asian adaptation published in 2022 by

SAGE | TEXTS

SAGE Publications India Pvt Ltd
B1/I-1 Mohan Cooperative Industrial Area
Mathura Road, New Delhi 110 044, India
www.sagepub.in

Published by Vivek Mehra for SAGE Publications India Pvt Ltd. Typeset in 10/12 pt ITC Century by Zaza Eunice, Hosur, Tamil Nadu, India.

Library of Congress Control Number: 2022936334

ISBN: 978-93-5479-482-7 (PB)

Contents

PART II READINGS AND KNOWLEDGE BASE

Detailed Contents

Praise for the Book

The book is sophisticated, challenging and contemporaneously relevant. It systematically integrates empirical generalisations, research methodology, as well as concepts involving consumer motivation into the market planning process. The text logically progresses from there into innovative marketing strategy formulation for real-world problems. Pedagogical aids inspire instructional creativity and effectiveness, and provide an excellent platform for lectures, discussion and assignments.

Melvin Prince, PhD, Professor of Marketing, Southern Connecticut State University, USA

Marketing Planning and Strategy is a very well-written textbook which combines a complex mix of academic excellence and practitioner relevance. It blends the traditional formal planning approach with an underpinning of empirical generalisations. The book approaches the subject in a very accessible way, using contemporary case studies. The style and approach are attractive from both an academic and a practitioner point of view.

Professor Dr Stefan Roth, Professor of Marketing, University of Kaiserslautern, Germany

If constructing a marketing plan was easy, then there would be no need for any of the many books available to help the marketing manager/business owner. The problem with most of the existing texts, especially those aimed at practitioners, is that they tend to comprise rhetorical checkboxes limited to just description. John Dawes demonstrates that it is possible to go beyond the mundane and has produced a volume which delivers on the claim 'to project a view of open-mindedness, coupled with a healthy dose of scepticism'. It is refreshing to see critical evaluation of sacred cows such as segmentation; Porter's competitive advantage; Net Promoter Score and Marketing Return on Investment, and their limits in the planning process.

Professor Philip Stern, University of Exeter Business School, UK

Professor John Dawes, of the world-leading and myth-busting Ehrenberg-Bass Institute for Marketing Science, does it again! Another example of his thoughtful and insightful work that's based on scientific principles of being evidence-based and independently replicated in varied contexts. Professor Dawes offers a refreshing take on the subject, packed with solid insight from the Institute and elsewhere, which makes his work supremely relevant to today's marketers. Based on decades of experience and reflection, terabytes of real data from the world's leading brands and a fearless willingness to slay some of marketing's dragons (or sacred cows?) based on reasoning and data, this book on strategy and planning belongs on every marketer's bookshelf.

Dr John Williams, Senior Lecturer, University of Otago, New Zealand

Planning is difficult, especially about the future. While planning is a fundamental function of management, many marketers are reluctant to plan because they see it as a stifling, bureaucratic process and activity, often hemmed in by business school lessons from the past, no longer relevant today. John Dawes' book on writing the marketing plan is a *simple* one in the very best sense of the word: 'easily understood or done; presenting no difficulty; plain, basic, or uncomplicated in form, nature, or design; without much decoration or ornamentation'. It is exactly what today's marketing practitioner needs to be guided through a simple but robust planning process that will result in good implementable marketing plans. While academically and theoretically rigorous, it also avoids an overemphasis on archaic strategic marketing thinking from the past. John Dawes cuts through the clutter, and provides simple but hardy guidelines to marketing planners and management students alike. By following these the reader will be able to craft a marketing plan that will fit the requirements of today's marketplace.

Professor Leyland Pitt, Dennis F. Culver EMBA Alumni Chair of Business and Professor of Marketing, Beedie School of Business, Simon Fraser University, Canada

Marketing Planning and Strategy offers several advancements that I'm sure will appeal to both educators and practitioners.

First and foremost, refreshingly, it adopts an evidence-based approach drawn from John's extensive experience consulting to many organisations, ranging from some of the most successful multinationals right through to small businesses, and hence the guidance provided can be broadly applied to various contexts.

Secondly, while the book follows the expected conventions of strategy development incorporating internal analysis/environment analysis and SWOT, all guiding strategic development, it is also underpinned with a narrative drawn from the Ehrenberg school of empirical generalisations informing the strategic process, and thus adding further rigour to the guidance throughout the book.

Thirdly, there is a practical underpinning that makes the book readily comprehendible and able to be applied, and also includes support for those not as conversant in the business vernacular. A case study on small business is woven throughout the book, creating an opportunity for associated assessment to be developed, and a step-by-step guiding template provides further scaffolding for the learner.

As a leader of learning innovation, I find these elements are what sets the book apart from others, and in an era of increasingly complex business models, highly competitive markets and ever evolving technologies, such support will be critical for all audiences. *Marketing Planning and Strategy* is certainly a valuable and timely contribution.

Professor Sandra Luxton, Dean (Learning Innovation),
Swinburne University of Technology, Melbourne, Australia

Preface

Why Another Book on Marketing Planning and Strategy?

There are several reasons for writing this book. First, while there are numerous textbooks on marketing planning and strategy, many of them have shortcomings that this book endeavours to avoid. One is that the book avoids using out of date concepts like BCG matrix type analysis, or Porter's 1980's generic strategies that are still being recommended in books written recently. This book does briefly discuss these tools in some readings, just to be informative. But it also explains their severe limitations.

Second, the book is written with an eye on facts, and what happens in the real world. Unfortunately, many books on marketing planning feature elaborate, abstract or impractical concepts, and an absence of a real-world lens. This book contains a lot of evidence to back up its points. It provides numerous data examples that students can use to solidify their learning. The book is also up to date, covering many issues pertaining to digital marketing and mobile commerce that do not feature in older books on marketing plans.

Next, the book also does not include redundant content that occurs in many other marketing planning texts (i.e. a lengthy introduction to basic marketing concepts, but with 'planning' tacked on). The emphasis is on the planning process, the structure of a plan and the knowledge needed to create a practical plan.

The book provides detail on each section of a marketing plan, and the reasons for using the prescribed structure and content. Specific questions at the end of each section allow readers or students to self-test their understanding.

A theme of this book is that while the marketing plan itself is important, the process of discovery that goes into creating the plan is just as important. Asking and answering questions about the business is a route to its improvement.

A second theme is the logical process one goes through to construct a plan. The objectives and strategy need to link to the analysis findings. In short, the writer of the plan needs to say something along the lines of: 'we're going to do this ... *because* of this outcome, or this research finding, or this trend'.

The book is clearly structured, which makes it easy to comprehend how a marketing plan is put together and in what order the components should follow.

The book also presents a realistic picture of what the marketing team usually does and doesn't do, in terms of setting the direction for a business. For example, some marketing texts strongly imply the marketing team directs the whole business, deciding how much be sold, to whom and for how much. That isn't a realistic picture. A market-oriented philosophy – in which a business thinks a lot about what the market wants, and whether and how it can deliver it (Chad, 2013; Narver & Slater, 1990) – can direct the business, but that's not the same as the marketing department directing the business.

The book is titled *Marketing Planning and Strategy*, and so it presents a sizeable section on strategy concepts. This section canvasses a comprehensive series of strategy concepts, from economies of scope to network effects and threshold effects. These give the reader an enhanced ability to interpret strategy outcomes, as well as giving insight into the nature of the market one operates in. Moreover, a succinct checklist of questions is supplied that allow managers to identify if they are acknowledging or applying strategy concepts that apply to either the firm itself, the market, or the decisions the business is making.

Another unique aspect of the book is a series of insights into writing style. A marketing plan is a communication device, which works better if the writing is appropriately business-like and clear. The book provides examples of common errors in writing style based on MBA student work, to show how they can be improved. This feature allows instructors to specify that a marketing plan be written as the major assignment, including a 'report' or 'plan' writing style, along with examples of what that actually entails.

There is also a chapter on how to effectively use tables and charts to communicate key points in the plan. Students and practitioners can use Chapter 12 to ensure they create tables and charts that support the various analyses done in the plan.

RUNNING CASE STUDY

The book contains a running case study about a small physiotherapy business in a regional UK city. At the end of each chapter of the book, there is a short part of the case that matches the content just covered. This allows for a semester-long assignment, that students can construct week by week. The case ensures students understand the content by making them apply it to a realistic small-business case situation. The case features some elementary business numeracy, and an Excel file is provided for students (via the supportive online resources) to use to identify some aspects of the firm's performance. Instructor resources are also provided for these short Excel tasks.

At the end of Part I, there are also three mini cases that allow instructors to set some additional reading or tasks to ensure students are able to apply the material. These three cases present common marketing scenarios for small businesses or not-for-profits and can be the basis of class discussions. Discussion notes for these cases are also available in the instructor manual.

PRACTICE, THEN SOME THEORY

The first part of the book focuses on constructing a marketing plan; and within it, a marketing strategy. This is the practical part. But it's not enough simply to learn a cookbook-style list of to-dos. Therefore, the second part of the book covers some theory, including the contemporary resource-based theory of competitive advantage and how it links to marketing strategy, as well as:

Ethics: ethics is increasingly recognised as an important facet of business life, and indeed is often required to be covered in business education. This book canvasses ethical issues and presents a series of potential ethical dilemmas in which students consider what they personally would do.

Popular tools: prominent marketing concepts and tools such as Ansoff and BCG are dissected.

Empirical generalisations: this section summarises a suite of empirical generalisations, along with their marketing implications. Knowing about and using these generalisations means the marketing plan can be evidence-based. Most of these generalisations come from the work of Andrew Ehrenberg and colleagues, and my colleagues at the Ehrenberg-Bass Institute.

Managerial biases: a series of managerial blind spots and cognitive biases are identified and discussed; along with recommendations as to what managers can do to minimise their effects.

Acknowledgements

Thanks to those who kindly reviewed previous versions: Emeritus Professor David Corkindale, Dr Charles Graham, Dr Zach Anesbury and Dr Carl Driesener. Professor Philip Stern reviewed an early version of the Remedy physiotherapy clinic case study. Thanks also to Matthew Waters from SAGE who supported the project and gave valuable input on earlier drafts of the book.

About the Author

John Dawes is a Professor of Marketing at UniSA Business and an Associate Director of the Ehrenberg-Bass Institute for Marketing Science.

John has a long-standing interest in buyer behaviour and brand performance metrics, customer loyalty, pricing, as well as how knowledge about buyers and competitors translates into competitive strategy.

John has conducted research projects for global corporations including HSBC, Mars Inc., Unilever, Brown-Forman, Glaxo SmithKline and Gustav Paulig. He co-authored a wide-ranging review of pricing practices commissioned by the UK Office of Fair Trading.

John has published research in leading journals including *Journal of Retailing*, *Journal of Service Research*, *Journal of Business Research*, *European Journal of Marketing* and *Marketing Letters* among others.

Follow John on Twitter, @John_G_Dawes.

Online Resources

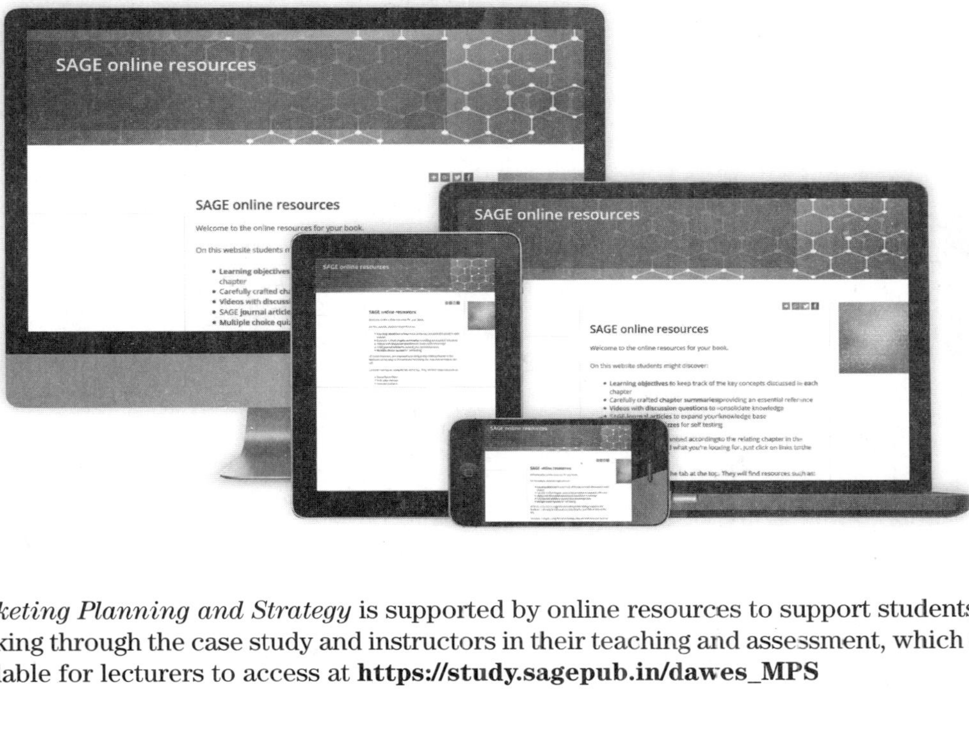

Marketing Planning and Strategy is supported by online resources to support students in working through the case study and instructors in their teaching and assessment, which are available for lecturers to access at **https://study.sagepub.in/dawes_MPS**

FOR INSTRUCTORS

- **An instructor's manual** will provide summaries of chapter content, answers to the end of chapter self-test questions, calculations for the running case study as well as a guide to the main talking points of the case to **support students' understanding of the text.**
- **PowerPoint slides** prepared by the author will allow you to seamlessly **incorporate the chapters into your weekly teaching.**

FOR STUDENTS

- **An additional data file** will help you **work through and analyse the 'Remedy Physiotherapy'** case study and other tasks in the book.

PART I

Constructing the Plan

This first part of the book outlines why a formal approach to marketing planning benefits the firm. It illustrates these benefits using the example of a new entrant into the financial services industry, Starling Bank. Part I then presents each step of the marketing planning process in detail. Also included in Part I is a running case study that allows the reader to develop their marketing planning skills.

CHAPTER 1 Planning Introduction: Is It Good to Do Formal Planning?

Before reading a book on marketing planning, or indeed studying a course on the subject, it's worthwhile to stop for a second and ask, is it a good thing to do? It might seem intuitively obvious that writing a formal marketing plan is desirable. But not necessarily to everyone! Take people who have run a small business for many years, perhaps without a formal or written marketing plan – it might seem unnecessary or even detrimental. For argument's sake, someone could say that undertaking a formal planning process – a marketing plan, or a business plan, or trying to follow a written plan, is too restrictive. Perhaps conditions change, and so some of the assumptions, forecasts or identified trends from the plan fail to materialise in the future. In which case, following such a plan might indeed seem counterproductive. Or perhaps some businesspeople have not ever embraced the idea of marketing, at least what their idea of it is – perhaps they think it means gimmicks, hard selling or being synonymous with television advertising and dealing with smartly dressed people from advertising and media agencies.

So, are there some sound arguments that marketing planning is a good thing to do? Or even better, is there empirical evidence that marketing planning is valuable? Evidence to support doing a marketing plan would be either:

- findings showing businesses that do it are more successful than those that do not; or
- there are identified benefits relating to various parts of the planning process, even though there might not be a clear planning–performance relationship.

Before looking at the logic and evidence, let's be clear about what is involved in marketing planning.

WHAT IS INVOLVED IN MARKETING PLANNING?

Doing a marketing plan, or engaging in what would be called 'formal marketing planning', will involve:

1. Time taken out of normal day-to-day activities.
2. A plan that covers a time span of a year or more.

3. A process of thinking and considering the issues facing the business (not merely filling in a form or template).
4. Discussion and consultation with others, obtaining various points of view.
5. A written document outlining an analysis of the current situation, specific objectives a strategy for achieving them, a budget and a forecast outcome for a time period.

Taking time out of normal day-to-day activities doesn't necessarily mean a fortnight out of the office to write the plan. It is often done in a 'drip-feed' fashion, in spare scraps of time, or possibly out of hours. This is because the pressures of day-to-day work don't relent. But the important fact is that some time, either a lump or a series of small bits, is taken from normal duties to think about the future direction of the business. Many businesses have an annual planning cycle, whereby at the same time each year marketing managers present their plans. A typical example is to have a plan ready at the end of summer in the UK for the following commercial year. The months leading up to this period are often studded with working late nights, getting the plan finished!

There is a specific reason for point 3 above, namely that there is a process for thinking and considering the issues facing a business. This is because some large organisations have 'planning templates' that they issue to various departments. The heads of those departments do an annual exercise that is called strategic planning or marketing planning but what it really involves is just filling in forms, oftentimes using slightly modified content from the years before! This isn't proper planning for the future.

ARGUMENTS FOR FORMAL PLANNING – EITHER A MARKETING PLAN OR A BUSINESS PLAN

Coping with the External Environment

The external environment impacts all businesses. Factors like government decisions, changes to the economy, competitor entry or activity and so on, impact entire industries and the firms that compete within them. Therefore, a business needs a formal approach to appraise how these factors in the external environment are going to impact it. This approach should then allow the business to capitalise on favourable trends, while hopefully minimising the impact of unfavourable circumstances.

But What If There Are Severe, Unpredictable Events?

Of course, sometimes the external environment changes dramatically, in quite unpredictable ways. The Covid-19 pandemic is an obvious recent example. Before that there was the much smaller SARS epidemic, which caused approximately 800 deaths and localised disruption to travel between some countries. In 2008, there was a global economic meltdown – the GFC (global financial crisis) – caused by the collapse of some large US banks. There were significant increases in unemployment and bankruptcy in many countries in its aftermath.

Situations like these can hardly be expected to factor into most businesses' plans. Such events cannot really be planned for, because by definition they are unexpected. Indeed, the severity of the Covid-19 crisis in 2020–21 caused some people to question whether businesses can really use formal plans anymore. That is, to question how a plan can be useful when the world is thrown into turmoil. The answer is: indeed, many industries were completely upended by the pandemic. In particular, firms like restaurants faced oblivion from being forced to close; airlines were grounded in many countries; hotel chains that normally accommodated international tourists were empty. However, business carried on, albeit not 'business as usual', for others. Many businesses adapted their strategies and arguably were able to do so, because they had already done a good job of understanding their competitive environments, their strengths and weaknesses, their customers. And those with a track record of environmental scanning and responding to the environment, being more practised at adaptation, were likely to be better able to read the new situation and react accordingly.

It Is Desirable to Assemble Relevant Facts

A business or other organisation almost always faces challenges, in the form of competition, regulation, shortages of resources, or difficulties in its internal operations. Often, a firm's management will have some idea of what these challenges are, but might not understand their full extent, whether they are expected to get better or worse, or what other forces might lie behind them. And the business environment is complex – there can certainly be more events and circumstances affecting the business than can be simply held in one's head. A marketing plan will necessarily gather all the relevant facts and assemble them in a coherent pattern or sequence so that the management of the business has the necessary fact-base. They can stop guessing or assuming, and actually know what the situation is. Moreover, this fact-base can be re-used (with amendments and updates) in the future. It is likely to be the case that the act of starting to plan makes the business realise how much it doesn't know – which is a good thing. As Donald Rumsfeld suggested, known unknowns are better than unknown unknowns. Moreover, plans should be kept as a kind of historical document or organisational memory. One's successors in years to come would find it useful to see what goals, trends and strategies were canvassed in the past. Indeed, not only keeping the plan but documenting the sources of information used to create the plan is incredibly valuable. For example, the first time a business writes a marketing plan might involve 100 hours of trawling around for information. If the sources of all that information are documented in the appendices of the plan, the second time a plan is created the information search might take only 20 hours.

As a Management Socialisation and Co-operation Mechanism

Businesses often have multiple managers who run specific aspects of the business – marketing, accounting/finance, human resources (HR), production or operations, the general manager. Understandably, these people are primarily interested in their own sphere of operations and much less interested in the others. Indeed, sometimes managers of one part of the business don't necessarily have a lot of empathy for the problems or issues faced by their counterparts in the other areas of the business. The process of formal planning is likely to involve soliciting the views of at least some of these managers in each other's plans, or the plans for the business as a whole. Interaction, and listening to the goals, strategies and problems being encountered by others, allows managers in one part of the business to better appreciate what their colleagues are experiencing. This experience can help managers understand why their colleagues are taking certain courses of action. Overall, the process can therefore create a more co-operative, mutually supportive management environment.

To Develop a Common Direction

Businesses usually have one chief executive or general manager but will have a team of senior managers (or perhaps, partners in the case of many professional services firms). It may be these people have their own ideas about the direction or priorities of the business. For argument's sake an architectural business might have one partner who thinks it should focus on boutique, upscale renovations for inner-city living; while another thinks it should pursue public-funded high-rise housing projects. It would be difficult for the business to progress with these competing priorities, or without at least some mutual agreement about the relative emphasis given to them both. Engaging in a formal planning process would make these different preferences in long-term direction more apparent, so they could be discussed and reconciled.

Knowledge Sharing

The planning process can bring about the benefit that there is more sharing of knowledge inside the business. Many large businesses not only have different management functions, but have different teams working on marketing, in quite different parts of the organisation. And this separation can mean that learnings acquired in one part of the business are not known about, or used, in other parts of the business. And this situation could persist unless a process of marketing planning, involving the whole business, is undertaken. To illustrate, let's take the example of the global bank HSBC. HSBC is a multifaceted bank. It offers consumer or retail banking: and has a retail banking marketing team. It also offers SME (small to medium-sized enterprise) banking and has a marketing team dedicated to small business clients. Recognising that big businesses have different needs in terms of products and servicing, HSBC also has a corporate banking marketing team. Lastly, HSBC recognises that wealthy individuals represent a distinct and valuable market segment. Moreover, HSBC knows that to successfully pursue this specific segment or market it needs staff who are knowledgeable about it; hence it has a premium banking marketing team. In sum, the one organisation has five different marketing teams, working on different types of markets and clients. All of them operate to some extent independently to the others, of course with senior management co-ordination. And this scenario is not unique to HSBC. Any of the big global banks, or indeed large services organisations, will have multiple marketing teams organised by client type or perhaps geography.

Next, it is easy to imagine that one team in such a big organisation could do some research or derive some really valuable marketplace learning that could be beneficial to the other teams – but it might not be shared. This is because the teams see themselves as semi-independent of each other; they all have their own issues, opportunities and goals. This lack of knowledge sharing might persist, unless there is a marketing planning process for the business as a whole, that pulls together insights from these various parts.

As a Way to Improve the Business's Performance

Consider a business that has been performing reasonably well over the past three to five years. Perhaps it has been growing at a modest rate of 2 per cent per year, and earns a fair return on investment of 5 per cent. How could such a business markedly improve? If it keeps doing exactly the same thing, we would guess its performance would stay at about the same level. Therefore, to get more pronounced improvement, it would need to identify a factor such as:

- Is there a high growth part of the market we are not present in?
- Are there potential new products we could launch, that would capture a lot of sales?
- Are there some aspects of our marketing mix on which we underperform, such as old range, poor staff skills, over-priced products, poor advertising?

The only reliable way to identify these factors is to go through a thorough process of reviewing what the business does, to identify areas that it could do better in. As a side-note, in some cases this reviewing can benefit from the use of an external party. One thing the author has noted from working with our Marketing Clinic clients over the years is that many marketing people do not notice really obvious avenues for improvement, because they live with them every day. However, these factors can often be quickly identified by outsiders. Indeed, our student teams in the Marketing Clinic usually see them as glaringly obvious. One example is a small business that failed to notice several of its key website links ('enquire here') didn't work! Another was a small software development company that had on its site a link to a former client – but this link highlighted that the client had unanimously negative reviews! While the client was a separate company, these bad reviews made the software developer look very bad by association. But it had failed to pick up this fact.

Addressing Internal Issues

Preparing a plan necessarily involves some appraisal and thinking about the performance and components of the business: including internal factors that are good or bad. In the normal course of events, some managers perhaps put up with sub-par resources, skills, activities and so on. Creating a written plan necessarily forces a business, or at least provides the vehicle, to identify and confront these factors.

Dealing with Complexity

Managing a business, indeed managing the marketing activities of even a small business, is complex. There can be so many things to do that attempting to work without a plan will result in activities not being completed, or even started. One aspect of this complexity is the fact that one activity might not be able to commence until a preceding activity is complete, which itself might need input from some other activity … which could take three months to do. Therefore, going from 'we want to do x' to actually seeing it done might take months or years. If the business has many such tasks or activities to be done, they need to be mapped out with anticipated starting and completing times and assigned resources. Otherwise there is simply too much complexity on to be managed without a formalised plan of action.

It is often the case that a business or organisation works on a series of medium-to long-term plans – for future periods of five to even ten years. These are often intended to radically change the organisation over that upcoming period. To promulgate such serious change, these plans need to be carefully constructed involving lots (months, years) of preparation, planning and consultation. The final product – a strategic plan – is even given its own name in many instances, for example a higher education institution launching a ten-year plan might call it 'making the future' or 'crossing the horizon' or 'outward bound' – with the name seeking to signal that the plan will bring about serious change. Of course, these large-scale endeavours would not be possible without carefully documenting what will be done and why; so that the multiple stakeholders who will be affected can find out what exactly will occur so they can anticipate its effects and give viewpoints on its chance of success.

Partners of the Business Can Work Better if They Know the Broad Direction of the Business

Business partners (e.g. suppliers, channel distributors, vendors such as ad agencies) can support the business better if they know in broad terms what its goals and strategies are for the upcoming period. Business books and articles refer to these partners as stakeholders. There is evidence that stakeholders offer higher levels of co-operation with the implementation of a plan if they have had some say in its formulation.

Another important point is that some channel partners simply need to know what the firm's plan is for the coming year. For example, large supermarket retailers will be very interested to know the broad plans of their major suppliers (the corporations like Mars, Kellogg's, Cadbury, Reckitt-Benckiser, Colgate, etc.) and would be offended if they were not shared. The Australian Tourism Commission would be very interested to know about Qantas' plans for the coming year and vice versa, since they have such mutual interests. There has to be a plan in existence for such information sharing to occur, so this is another rationale for engaging in a formal planning process.

Setting Objectives Has Value in Itself

Formal planning usually involves specifying objectives. There is evidence that employees working to specific objectives are more productive than those who are given more general or vague guidelines (Armstrong, 1982). Also, it seems sensible to think that unless a business actually sets certain objectives, it is unlikely to reach a level of sales (or some other criterion) that fulfils those objectives. Arguably, while it sounds trite, setting an objective is the first step to reaching it. That said, some research points to the negative side-effects of unduly focusing on specific objectives or goals. For example, Ford suffered badly from over-emphasising lower production cost for its cars, and as a consequence had widespread product recalls. Some businesses which heavily emphasise staff achieving sales targets often find those staff engage in aggressive or ethically dubious conduct. Schwepker and Good (2007) found that having very difficult-to-reach sales goals imposed by senior management can induce sales managers to turn a blind eye to unethical conduct.

Therefore, a range of objectives should be set, as well as stressing to staff they should not abandon common sense or ethical practices in pursuing company objectives.

Decisions Impact on Other Decisions

Without a formal plan it is likely the business will be making decisions without much consideration, and without thinking how one decision affects other factors. Whereas a formal plan encompasses a multiplicity of issues and decisions, and allows one to make decisions about each issue, taking into consideration the impacts on the other issues. Therefore, it seems reasonable that a formal plan will result in a higher quality strategy.

A simple example to illustrate this point is that over the course of a year, a business might want to have an emphasis on different parts of its product range. Take a multi-product company like Glaxo SmithKline (GSK) – it makes and sells brands such as Panadol, Sensodyne, Voltaren and Nicabate, among others. These brands cover quite separate consumer goods categories – pain relief, toothpaste for painful teeth and gums, and nicotine replacement. While GSK would obviously want to achieve high performance on each of these brands, all the time, it may want to have particular periods of time when there is a concentrated effort on advertising and sales promotion for a specific brand. For argument's sake, GSK might choose to focus on Panadol in the winter months coinciding with the cold and flu season (during which time those illnesses induce aches and pains), Sensodyne in some other two or three month period of the year, Nicabate in another period – perhaps in the new year when people make resolutions such as quitting smoking. This demarcation of effort makes it possible for the sales force to go to channel partners to get them excited about what the business has planned for these brands in a specified time period (so that the retailers support the idea, allocate valuable in-store space to the specific GSK brand, buy more stock and perhaps advertise the brands themselves). The key point is this strategy has to be planned out in advance so that the business knows when things will happen, how much resources need to be allocated to make them happen, and so that other activities don't 'get in the way'.

Knowing How Well the Business Should Be Doing

Some businesses perform very well, others perform poorly. The question arises as to how well a business *should* be doing, in terms of sales, margins or profit. Writing a marketing plan is a way of assembling various pieces of information together so that the management team is in a position to know how well the business is doing and should be doing. For example, a firm might conclude its current annual sales revenue of $2.0 million and growth of 3.5 per cent per year is very good, but the marketing plan might reveal that given the buoyancy of the industry, or given the firm's excellence in product design or service, for example, it could be doing much better.

As an Ongoing Reference Point

The advantage of having a written plan is that it acts as a reminder, or re-enforcer of the priorities and intended strategy of the business. It is fair to say that sometimes staff forget why they are doing certain activities, or why they are supposed to be doing things a certain way. The written plan can be used as a reminder – 'remember, our plan calls for ...'. While a senior marketer is not going to stand up at a meeting and wave the plan to staff like a flag, they can certainly reiterate to junior managers and staff what the main points of the plan are, and why those decisions were made – and signal that future actions need to be consistent with the plan.

HOW SOUND PLANNING CAN PAY OFF – THE CASE OF STARLING BANK

Before we plunge into the actual process of writing a marketing plan, let's consider why a sound plan is so important. A marketing plan involves a thorough analysis of the business itself, as well as the external world – relevant trends, occurrences or events that impact on the business. These external events – what we formally call 'environmental forces' – shape what the business needs to do to succeed. Therefore, identifying trends in the external environment and figuring out what they mean for the business, and what should be done about them, is paramount. Doing this well means the business is better able to capitalise on opportunities presented by the outside world, and better equipped to minimise potential threats. We now consider the fascinating case of a new, technologically savvy bank in the UK, Starling Bank – and how its launch and success were inextricably linked to understanding, and using, a series of environmental changes.

Starling Bank: How It Built on a Sound Understanding of Marketplace Changes

The framework for a marketing plan is built on understanding external events or trends, and how they relate to the businesses' own strong and weak points. A marketing plan is basically about how to deploy one's resources in order to capitalise on favourable occurrences, sidestep the negative trends, and identify how one can remedy or make up for weaknesses.

This framework can be used to analyse any sort of business, from a traditional 'old school' firm to a new, technology-enabled player such as Starling Bank in the UK. Starling was founded by a very experienced ex-bank executive, Anne Boden. She decided she wanted to run her own bank! In the space of four or five years, Starling went from being just an idea, to having over a million consumers as customers. And then it moved into small-business banking, quickly carving out over 2 per cent of the market for SME customers in the UK. The name was chosen to represent a bank that was 'fast, effortless, sociable and agile' (Boden, 2020).

Let's try to understand Starling's success. We can do this by dissecting all the environmental trends and changes occurring that would work in its favour. Of course, success didn't just fall into Starling's lap – it figured how to harness these changes to its benefit. And, to build the resources and capability needed to compete in the banking market.

Consumer Behaviour and Technology

First, there are some long-term trends in consumer behaviour that presented an opportunity for a new bank like Starling. Over decades, the advent of ATMs, credit cards and debit cards meant consumers didn't have to go inside a bank branch like they used to. Then came EFTPOS (electronic funds transfer at point of sale) technology, which meant people could pay for goods and services in stores, which meant they didn't need cash as much. Less need for cash means less need for banks. Then, money transfers via the internet meant people could manage their funds and bank accounts themselves, at home. This meant over a long period of time, people got used to not having much personal contact with their bank. The arrival of smartphones and 'apps' meant it became even easier to manage money quickly and easily, using bank-supplied technology, but embedded in an easy interface. Therefore, consumers had been slowly primed for many years to use internet and smartphone technology for their banking. By the time Starling was launching, the notion of using the internet and smartphone to manage money wasn't scary, as many consumers had been doing it for years. But Starling offered a far superior user experience and as-yet un-dreamed of options.

The founders of Starling used this backdrop to argue to investors that a new, mobile only bank would be a winner. They certainly made a good impression on the billionaire fund manager Harald Pike, who invested £48 million – he is now a major shareholder. This funding allowed Starling to start seriously building a team and the technology to work towards launch.

Competition and Government Interventions

Despite these technological and consumer trends, the major banks in countries like the UK still held the lion's share of business. Retail banking had shown itself to be a very tough market to break into. At the time, the top six UK banks accounted for around 80 per cent market share. They had overwhelming advantages in awareness and branch coverage. As well as that, competition was being dampened because doing things like switching from one bank to another is difficult. If someone has their income and certain payments automatically linked to their bank account, it is time-consuming to switch to another bank because all those payments need to be re-directed. But the UK government was keen to open up competition in the sector. The government believed that more competition would spark innovation and create new banking providers and products that would grow the entire sector. A strong, growing banking sector was seen to be extremely positive for the

UK economy. To this end, the government launched several interventions into the sector. First, it told the UK banking regulator to be favourable to new banking licence applications. This helped Starling actually get its licence to become a bank (not normally an easy feat!). Second, the government launched the 'current account switch guarantee' (Current Account Switch Service, 2020). This meant people could switch from one bank to another and all their linked payments would automatically transfer.

In a marketing plan we would classify these government interventions in the banking industry as a *political-legal trend*. For Starling, this trend represented an *opportunity* – that is, an external occurrence that was potentially favourable to the new bank. If it becomes easier to switch accounts or open new accounts, that's great news for a new start-up bank. A third political-legal event was that the UK government made grant money available to help new banks enter the sector. Starling made a convincing case to be awarded this support, and received a £100 million grant in 2019 (Starling Bank, 2019). This cluster of changes in the environment helped Starling get started.

Other Trends Harnessed in Starling's Favour

Another long-term *socio-cultural trend* is the rapid growth in smartphone ownership in the UK. In 2008, 17 per cent of adults had a smartphone; by 2019 that figure had leaped to 79 per cent. And ownership is even higher among 16–24 year olds at 96 per cent, and among wealthier people at 87 per cent compared to 66 per cent of those on lower incomes (Statista, 2021). This trend suited a new bank start-up like Starling. It meant Starling's plan, namely, to launch a branch-free mobile bank that consumers used on their phones, would be accessible by almost everyone. And particularly, it would be attractive to younger people, and wealthier people. This trend was favourable to Starling because younger people are somewhat more embracing of new brands and new technology, and wealthier consumers are attractive to have as customers because they simply have more money to manage. Banks make more money from people who have more money.

There were many other trends and events that Starling leveraged. One of them was that the European Union, like the UK, wanted to stimulate competition in the banking sector. It created a directive that banks needed to share their data (Browne, 2018). The end result was that smart technology players, like Starling, could offer a service that allowed consumers to view all their bank accounts in one application. It also made it much easier for consumers to compare deals between providers. The UK built on the EU initiative by launching 'Open Banking' (Manthrop, 2018) – encouraging banks to share information, as well as encouraging consumers to download and use apps to view their finances across all the banks or credit unions they used.

This EU and UK government initiative meant that third-party developers could use data from the big banks to develop new products to help consumers manage their money. For example, bank data tells a lot about how people spend their money, and the costly mistakes they make (paying too much on overdrafts, keeping money in accounts that give zero interest or have high fees). New banking apps can show people how to save better, what they spend their income on, how to work to budgets and so on. Or, for example, when someone applies for a loan it would make it easy to show the lender their income and spending history straight from the app, rather than having to assemble documents (Cossor, 2019).

For Starling, these political-legal changes represented a massive opportunity. They meant that right from the start it could offer smart accounts, enabling Starling customers to 'see' their spending and income in an informative way, and view all of their banking information presented together. Starling was ahead of the Big 6 banks on deploying this technology. The big banks' size worked against them, they were not quick or nimble enough to develop these new ways of banking. For example, Starling was the first bank to offer Apple Pay (Fingas, 2017) on its platform. And the ability to offer this 'whole view of banking' technology meant Starling was a low-risk decision for buyers, because consumers who banked with a big bank like Barclays or HSBC could still see those accounts easily, in their Starling smartphone app. Lastly, research shows that people view apps as safer than websites, so Starling's whole proposition to consumers was very desirable (Cossor, 2019).

There were other external events that Starling leveraged. A major one related to proof of identity and opening accounts. A factor that had always worked in the favour of the big banks – keeping them big – was the hassle in opening a new bank account. Traditionally, someone would need to go to a bank branch with proof of their identity to open their new account. This dampened consumers' enthusiasm to either switch banks, or to have multiple accounts. But again, a change in the market occurred which Starling was able to capitalise on. The UK government changed the rules for identity provision. It became much easier to prove one's identity by simply taking a photo of a passport or driver's licence, along with a selfie video and send these to the bank. This change meant it was very easy for new customers to open their account with Starling. The strong uptake Starling achieved would have been impossible in the past without an extensive network of branches, if the identity rules had not changed.

All these changes in banking rules, technology and society meant Starling got off to a very quick start. It rapidly gained 500,000 customers within just a couple of years. This early success meant it was a very attractive proposition to invest in. Consequently, Starling was able to secure even more funding, £205 million in 2019 (Boden, 2020) for a total of over £300 million from its inception. With more money available it could hire more people, spend more money on advertising, and develop even more mobile banking solutions.

Branches – An Innovative Solution

Traditionally, a branch network has been a massive advantage for incumbent banks – such as Barclays, Lloyds, HSBC and so on. It seemed impossible to be a big bank without having many hundreds of branches. Of course, all banks shed huge numbers of branches since 2000 onwards, but the bigger banks still had many more than the smaller ones. However, commentators noted that for new players like Starling, not having a branch network was an advantage in the sense that it was not 'capital intensive' – in other words, it didn't have billions of pounds tied up in brick and mortar branches like the big banks (Cossor, 2019). And this meant that Starling was running off a lower cost base than the bigger banks and could be very profitable for its size. In fact, Anne Boden's original idea for Starling came from noticing that existing banks could not properly invest in digital, because they had to spend so much money on their branches.

The business did, though, come to realise that a lack of branches would place a limit on how big Starling could get, or at least slow its growth. Physical branches make it possible to do things like deposit or withdraw cash, which many people need to do at some time.

Small businesses often need to bank cash, and the SME segment was one that Starling wanted to develop further. So, Starling plugged this gap by forming an alliance with the UK post office, which has over 10,000 branches. This gave it a massive boost in 'physical availability', which is an essential ingredient for brand growth (Romaniuk & Sharp, 2016).

Of course, a new business can't succeed purely based on external changes and events – it needs resources and capabilities that match the opportunities present in the environment. And Starling had these or acquired them. To begin with, Starling's founder Anne Boden had 30 years of experience in the sector. This background provided essential knowledge about what would be needed for success and simply 'how things worked' in this complex, competitive market. Given the whole concept of Starling was mobile banking powered by technology, Anne hired two formidable IT talents, John Mountain and Steve Newson. They assembled a talented in-house software development team. In 'IT speak', Starling built a capability to create new software 'builds' very quickly, allowing it to rapidly deploy newer and better interfaces with consumers (Macaulay, 2018).

Marketing at Starling Bank

Of course, the bank didn't rely just on technology; marketing issues were central. One important marketing factor was that from the outset, Starling benefited from a lot of online exposure. Given the widespread publicity surrounding open banking, many people were interested to know just a little bit about the benefits. There was considerable online content and advice around using Starling from finance blog sites.

But the bank also hired marketing talent. An early hire was Terry McParlane, who had extensive bank marketing experience at Lloyds. And then later, Rachael Pollard – who had in-depth knowledge and capability in digital marketing, having headed up Just Eat (an online intermediary between takeaway food outlets and customers) and comparethemarket.com. Starling commenced with digital advertising, using paid campaigns on Facebook and Instagram. This allowed it to do a lot of initial testing to see which types of ads worked, which targeted groups were more responsive, and to keep spending at a fairly low level (Simpson, 2018).

Branding aspects such as logos have obviously been known to be important since the advent of trading, thousands of years ago. But marketers are increasingly realising they are even more strategically valuable, based on the work of researchers such as Romaniuk (Romaniuk, 2018). Starling obviously realised this point and developed a *very* distinctive logo using a stylised S and the colour purple. This colour is not associated with any other bank in the UK. Moreover, it made sure the logo featured prominently in its ads. This prominence helped make its advertising more likely to actually be linked to the brand (often, less than half of the people who have seen an advertisement can say which brand it is for). In sum, the logo's distinctiveness – and its prominent use – helped Starling's advertising to be more effective.

Once Starling had become established, it turned to broader-scale brand building via TV advertising (McCarthy, 2019). A campaign was devised to develop memory links around the brand's name. The campaign featured flocks of Starlings. Showing these birds in flight was designed to communicate the idea of 'fast, effortless, sociable and agile' – what Starling wanted to be, and be known for. These four descriptors are what are known as brand attributes. The campaign did communicate well the idea that Starling is a new, customer-oriented bank offering a great banking experience. And the ads inextricably linked the brand's name to the content of the ad (the Starlings). Moreover, the ads were very well branded – it was very obvious which bank they were for.

However, the attributes focused on in that campaign were not necessarily what Sharp and Romaniuk would call 'Category Entry Points' (Romaniuk & Sharp, 2016). The concept of Category Entry Points (CEPs) is that there are varied situations in which the category is in the mind of a buyer, and advertising should endeavour to link the brand to those CEPs. Starling's next campaign appeared to utilise this concept.

The next campaign was called 'Bank anywhere with Starling Bank'. It cleverly used a range of situations in which the Starling banking app could be used. It showed vignettes such as two people splitting a bill at a restaurant, a person who appears to have forgotten to bring cash or a credit card on an outing, a woman sitting in a cafe looking at her recent spending, checking a card balance at home, booking something online, or putting some money aside for an anticipated event. The question arises, how did Starling or its agency know to use these situations? The answer is, it would come from doing a basic part of the marketing plan – customer analysis. Customer analysis is about knowing the who, what, where and when of your customers and their buying situations. This campaign showed the effective use of customer analysis and how it could form the basis of good advertising.

Another aspect of marketing is creating partnerships. Starling has a philosophy of co-operating with other entities. In line with that aim, it formed partnerships with numerous other players in financial services. It started what it called the Starling Bank Marketplace, which allows Starling customers to freely use a plethora of new, innovative financial software from independent software developers or vendors. An example is its collaboration with FreeAgent, an accounting software company. This partnering allows Starling SME customers to use the FreeAgent software app, which allows them to analyse client transactions in real time (Cossor, 2019). The app allowed a small business to easily identify factors such as what the client's spending was for, the time of transaction and the identity of the client. Before this sort of app arrived, a small business owner might have had to wait weeks to get such information. Another collaboration example is Churchill Insurance. Starling customers can apply for insurance from Churchill within the Starling app, which dramatically streamlines the process of buying insurance.

This planned sequence of creating partnerships reinforces the idea that relationships with external parties can be valuable assets. They allow the firm to offer better products than it otherwise would, and allow it to potentially reach and sell to buyers it otherwise would not be able to access. As we will see in Chapter 3, in the early stages of the marketing plan one examines which strategic relationships the business has, and identifies which additional ones are needed to be forged to implement the strategy.

Will competition catch up with Starling? Perhaps. Existing banks are trying hard. For example, RBS, one of the Big 6 UK banks, has already tried to launch its own version of Starling, called Bo. Unfortunately, it failed. This was due to a combination of unfavourable circumstances. The economic downturn from the Covid-19 pandemic stopped Bo's growth in its tracks; adverse business conditions also meant large, existing banks like RBS had no appetite for costly new experiments and so Bo was killed off quickly.

Summary: Lessons Learned from Starling

To summarise, this case illustrates the importance of:

- noticing and responding to external circumstances and events
- harnessing the power of new technology, but deploying it in a customer-oriented way and making its benefits to buyers very clear
- developing distinctive branding, and harnessing customer insights about buying situations to create effective advertising
- building strategic partnerships, without which it would be difficult to construct and offer competitive products

The case also shows us how digital technology has presented opportunities for new firms to overcome barriers that would have once stopped them from seriously entering a market.

Starling Questions

1. Why do you think it was particularly important that Starling did a lot of ad or campaign testing at the start?
2. Why would it be useful to show a range of buying or usage situations in which the Starling app could be used?
3. Do you think that Starling had certain advantages over established banks in achieving what it did in its first couple of years?

Lastly, the Starling case shows that big, incumbent players in an industry, with stable market shares, can start to be displaced by new players with different ways of offering goods and services. As mentioned, all the big banks are working on launching and improving their mobile banking offerings. But what they're finding is that it can be very difficult for a big player – which often means bureaucracy and inertia – to adapt, when what is needed is agility and responsiveness in a new competitive arena created by technology.

A REALITY CHECK BEFORE WE GO FURTHER – COMPETITIVE ADVANTAGE?

This book has an emphasis on practicality. It endeavours to project a view of open-mindedness, coupled with a healthy dose of scepticism. One of the big ideas or concepts we're going to talk about here – and present a reality check on – is the notion of having a *competitive advantage.*

Porter (1985) built on concepts from Industrial Organisation economics (e.g. Bain, 1965, 1967, 1968) to write a runaway best-selling book on competitive strategy, and the concept of competitive advantage. He defined the concept like this:

> The basis for above average performance in the long run is sustainable competitive advantage. Though a firm can have a myriad of strengths or weaknesses vis-à-vis competitors there are two basic types of competitive advantage a firm can possess: low cost or differentiation. (Porter, 1985: 14)

Differentiation is defined as when: 'a firm seeks to be unique in its industry along some dimensions that are widely valued by buyers. It selects one or more attributes that many buyers perceive as important, and uniquely positions itself to meet those needs. It is rewarded for its uniqueness with a premium price' (Porter, 1985: 14).

Cost leadership is fairly self-explanatory, Porter defined it as when: 'a firm sets out to become the lowest cost producer in its industry ... the firm has a broad scope and many segments ... breadth is often important to its cost advantage. The sources of cost advantage ... may include ... economies of scale, proprietary technology, preferential access to raw materials' (1985: 12). Porter also included a third strategy called focus, which meant the business concentrated on the needs of a narrow market or segment.

The term competitive advantage therefore appears to be about earning higher margins than competitors, i.e. via selling a product for more or less the same price as competitors but with lower costs, or earning a higher price than competitors and therefore enjoying high margins.

Since the publication of Porter's books on competitive strategy and competitive advantage in the 1980s, literally thousands of other books and papers have adopted the idea that the objective of a firm or the outcome of a strategic plan or a marketing plan is to achieve a competitive advantage. It's also worth noting that every business discipline, from HR to IT has numerous textbooks claiming that they offer the route to competitive advantage.

Challenging the Concept

This book takes a sceptical view on the concept of competitive advantage. First, the whole idea implies that a business *can* have a competitive advantage over its rivals. Furthermore, the phrase competitive advantage implies a business really has something unbeatable, and its rivals are far behind. For many firms in many industries, this whole idea is more aspirational than practical. Take the international hotel industry: hotel chains like Accor with brands such as Swissotel, Raffles and Sofitel; the Marriot chain with brands including Westin, Le Meridien and Sheraton; and Intercontinental with brands like Crowne Plaza, Holiday Inn and Candlewood. They all have great hotels in great locations, they have very good systems for recruiting and training staff, they offer great customer service with probably isolated exceptions, and they all have ample marketing budgets and access to talented advertising agencies. Does one of them have a competitive advantage over the others? It would be doubtful; or at least the magnitude of advantage that one might have over another would probably be fairly small.

Second, the concept of a competitive advantage can be inappropriate or fanciful for most small businesses. Imagine a proprietor of a restaurant, an accountancy firm, an HR consultancy or a small transport company – they hire a consultant who promises to write a plan to give them a competitive advantage over rivals. Their firm – not the hundreds of other businesses in the industry – is going to be able to outperform every other player in the industry. How likely is this? Not very. Also consider in any industry there are many competitors. Imagine every year the management team of those competitors devote some time to writing their strategic plans and/or marketing plans. Furthermore, imagine in each of, say, 16 competing businesses the marketing director is writing a plan – based on Porter or the battalions of academics and consultants who use his ideas – so that they will achieve a sustainable competitive advantage. Plainly this can't happen, they can't all have a competitive advantage over each other. Indeed, there can't realistically be room for more than one or two firms to, in theory at least, have a competitive advantage. The concept becomes meaningless if we think ten businesses in an industry have a competitive advantage.

Then we have the non-profit sector, such as sporting clubs or charities – these entities engage in marketing, but the concept of a competitive advantage just doesn't translate well into this sector. A competitive advantage over which other player?

Third, the concept of differentiation, as presented by Porter, is that the business is perceived as unique and superior along certain key attributes. We know a lot about whether this occurs for brands, at least – from research on buyer behaviour and perceptions about brands. We know that buyers buy multiple brands over a time period in categories like consumer packaged goods (Dawes, 2016b; Ehrenberg, 2000), but also in contexts like financial services (Dawes, 2014) and hospitality (Lynn, 2013b). If buyers see certain brands as having unique or superior attributes, why would they buy one brand on one occasion (because it has unique features?) and then buy a competitor brand on another occasion? So multi-brand buying implies that brands aren't bought because they are necessarily seen as unique or superior.

Perhaps buyers buy brand A for one situation because it has unique, superior qualities and a competitor brand B – with other unique features – for some other situation. This seems a bit fanciful, because the other factor about multi-brand buying is that buyers share their brands with competitors in line with the size (market share) of those competitors. This pattern is so strong it is known as the duplication of purchase law (see, for example, Lees & Wright, 2009; Lynn, 2013a; Mansfield & Romaniuk, 2003; Wilson et al., 2019). This strong pattern of sharing buyers in line with brand size seems very inconsistent with the idea of brands being bought only for specific situations or occasions.

Buyers also tend not to perceive brands as unique or different. One study across several categories showed brands are rarely perceived as the only one having a particular attribute (Romaniuk & Gaillard, 2007). That is, few people think the only 'rebellious' shoe brand is Nike, or the only 'German engineering' car is Mercedes. Another study showed that few buyers think the brands they buy are *unique* (Romaniuk et al., 2007). Therefore, the idea that the route to competitive advantage is to build unique and superior features (and these features are the reason buyers will buy) is rather shaky.

Take, for example, the huge usage of (consumer) social media platforms – Facebook, Instagram, Snapchat, Pinterest and others. All these platforms essentially do extremely similar things. Users do not use any particular platform because they perceive it to be unique, or that there is a distinct advantage in using it. They use it because it's in the news, it's easy and their friends are using it.

Next, we note that inherent in Porter's notion of competitive advantage is a price premium. The concept of a price premium sounds simple at first glance. A firm creates some value-added feature to its offering which allows it to earn a higher price. But just about all firms do this in one way or another. Let's revisit the international hotels example from earlier. We all know a hotel room in an inner-city location is priced according to location, room size, room features (décor, view, furnishings), the general quality of the hotel (modernity, pool, visual appeal of the reception area). All these hotel chains sell a small room cheaper than a medium-sized room which is cheaper than a suite, a room with a sea view sells for more than one with a city view. And so on. Therefore, it is rather difficult to see that one chain or hotel brand could create a feature that allows it to earn a price premium over all the others. They all sell budget, normal, superior and luxury rooms. And have standard and luxury brands.

We could say the same about car brands. The biggest car brands – Toyota, Ford, Volkswagen, Mazda and so on – all sell entry level cars, family sedans, SUVs, people carriers. And all of them come with dozens of options (leather seats, premium trim, sunroof, mag wheels, etc.) that customers can choose from according to their individual tastes. The idea that one car brand 'sells at a price premium' is illogical in this market. If, say, a Toyota family sedan sells for a higher price than a Ford or Mazda it will be mostly due to it having certain physical features that are somewhat better than those of other brands – which in turn probably incur some additional manufacturing costs. Indeed, it may be the case that Toyota cars tend to sell for a somewhat higher price than comparable brands, on the basis they have a slightly superior reputation for quality and longevity. But that's hardly the same as concluding Toyota has a competitive advantage. Rather, it just reflects a very long-term commitment to product quality and engineering (which may mean that Toyota has spent more money making its cars than its rivals, and continues to do so). And this is hardly a marketing decision.

Are there some brands that really do have a competitive advantage? There must be some. To say it's impossible to achieve would be obtuse. Perhaps Harvard University has a competitive advantage? After all it has a $37 billion endowment fund, so it certainly has an edge in getting philanthropy. And the Harvard Law School is a ridiculously desirable destination for prospective students, as is Harvard Medical School, with many more students clamouring to get in, even with very high fees. Maybe we could also say famous cities like London, Paris and New York have a level of fame that gives them a competitive advantage over almost every other city in the world as tourist destinations. And there may well be some businesses or brands that could accurately be said to have a real, marked advantage in the market; they are not necessarily the biggest in terms of market share but they are able to earn a noticeably higher rate of return for their owners. In many cases these circumstances can arise from smart investments in advertising and securing distribution over decades. But these are likely to be exceptions. So, the idea that in general terms marketers should approach the task of writing a plan with a view to creating a competitive advantage seems misguided. In fact, in decades of working with marketing people this author can't recall the term ever being mentioned by a marketer.

Therefore, the viewpoint presented in this book is that marketing planning can help a firm to improve its competitiveness, and can help it to become more efficient and effective at marketing. But not necessarily to achieve a competitive advantage – that could be over-promising in many cases.

The book does present a synopsis of the widely written about resource-based theory of competitive advantage, but presents some qualifications about it.

WORDING IN A MARKETING PLAN – DOS AND DON'TS, WITH EXAMPLES

Before we dive into the construction of a marketing plan it is a good idea to highlight what the language in a plan should be like. The most basic ingredient, especially for students who may not have written any sort of plan before is: write it as if you work in the business or you own the business. Use language like 'ours', 'us', or 'the business'. Don't talk about the business or organisation as 'they', or 'their'.

These are excerpts from MBA students' marketing plans written as part of a major assignment. They show five common flaws in plan writing that we can learn from:

Issue 1: Don't write the plan as if it is someone else's responsibility.

Example: As a result of new customer acquisition, the growth rate was stable. But there was a drop in both growth and acquisition rate in 2020 and 2021, which deserves some attention by management group.

Problem: The passage reads as if this is someone else's problem. A marketing plan should be written as if the writer is taking responsibility for it.

Solution – write as if you are taking responsibility for the plan: As a result of new customer acquisition, the growth rate was stable. However, there was a drop in both growth and acquisition rate in 2020 and 2021. We identify that this drop was caused by _______. Our plan for 2022 will remedy this shortcoming by doing ________.

Example: This marketing plan provides a roadmap that allows them to go from 1 per cent of market share to 6 per cent, by focusing on fixing their business weaknesses …

Problem: Because it uses 'them' and 'their' this sentence sounds like it was written by a passive observer, not someone with an active interest in the plan, and the business.

Solution – write in more active voice: This marketing plan provides a roadmap that will take the business from 1 per cent of market share to 6 per cent, by focusing on fixing two key weaknesses …

Issue 2: Avoid vagueness, be specific.

Actual writing (as part of a SWOT): Strength: Bank X has a long history, founded in 1930.

Problem: We don't know why this is a strength, or indeed if it is actually a strength.

Solution – explain why something is a strength: Bank X has a long history, founded in 1930. Consumers perceive Bank X has been in the market for a long time and that this imparts a sense of solidity and safety. These are desirable attributes (if there is research that actually supports this conclusion).

This now explains a rationale for why the bank's history is a strength. Of course, you don't just make up a rationale, it has to be based on some evidence or sound logic.

Actual writing (written as part of a marketing strategy section): The business should advertise more.

Problem: The statement is far too vague. It doesn't say why the business should do this, it doesn't say what media should be used, and it doesn't give any indication of how much, or the level of activity.

Solution – re-write with more specific details: The business currently does very little advertising and therefore has low awareness. Our analysis indicates local news media, and search, both offer low cost per thousand reach of category buyers. Therefore, we recommend increasing advertising spending. Investing $X per year on each of these media will allow us to accomplish the reach required to build awareness, and stay within the budget limit.

Of course, such a statement doesn't have to be written exactly like this, the idea is simply to provide enough detail so that a reader understands the rationale and what exactly is proposed.

Issue 3: Don't write generic 'this is a good thing' type statements.

Actual writing: Advertising is a good method of increasing a brand's mental availability and making more people aware of the brand. As a small financial corporation based in the local community, X Bank must increase its rate of media exposure as well as its word of mouth among …

Problem: This is a generic statement, merely stating a particular marketing mix tool is 'good'. Such statements are usually not appropriate for a marketing plan. Also, the word 'based in the local community' is redundant and vague – all businesses are based somewhere, so they are all in some sort of community. And the information from which this statement originated had no mention of word of mouth, so there was no justification for specifically highlighting it in the plan.

Solution – be factual and explain why you recommend certain courses of action: X Bank currently has a small market share. In order to grow it needs to increase mental availability, and to do that, it must increase its media spend.

Issue 4: Don't identify businesses using descriptors that are appropriate for people, specifically don't use 'them', 'they' or 'their' when talking about a business or brand.

Actual writing: Bank X have a number of good qualities to help them grow and succeed.

Problem: This writing is referring to a business as a person, not an entity.

Solution – use 'has' not 'have': Bank X has a number of good qualities to help it grow and succeed.

Actual writing: JPMorgan launched their new cash management product …

Problem: This writing is referring to a business as a person, not an entity.

Solution – use 'its' not 'their' when referring to a business: JPMorgan launched its new cash management product ...

Issue 5: Don't raise points and leave the reader questioning if they will be addressed.

Actual writing: Customer acquisition was quite good in 2020 but fell by 5 per cent in 2021. [proceeds to next section]

Problem: The writer has identified a problem but has left the reader hanging, not knowing if the reason for this problem will be identified, or whether the plan will formulate a solution.

Solution – identify the problem and signal that it will be addressed: Customer acquisition was quite good in 2020 but fell by 5 per cent in 2021. Our analysis finds this was caused by poor client follow-up by the sales team, discussed in section 4. The marketing strategy section outlines how we will avoid this in 2022.

Let's now take a quick look at the components of a marketing plan – or what we can call the 'roadmap' for one. Table 1.1 shows the structure and contents. Basically, we start with an examination of the business itself, we then look at what's going on in the outside world – generally, and more specifically in our market. We then see how the internal factors of our business stack up when considering all those external trends and events. Following that we can make informed choices about objectives, formulate a strategy, devise detailed plans of action relating to what we offer, our pricing, the ways in which we make our goods or services available to buyers and, of course, what forms of advertising and other communications we will use and how we will portray our company or brand in it. Lastly, we map out what metrics we'll use to guide progress and what research we might need to do in the following year.

TABLE 1.1 *Roadmap: The Contents of a Marketing Plan*

Component	Content
Executive summary	A 1/2 page summary of key points. A 'selling' piece for the plan
Internal Analysis	Examine the businesses: its resources, capabilities and past performance. Then conduct an audit of its products, pricing, channels, advertising and business relationships.
Global Environment Analysis	Start examining how the external world is impacting the business, paying attention to demographic, economic, socio-cultural, technological, environmental-natural resources and political-legal circumstances and trends.
Market Environment Analysis	Continue to examine how the external world is impacting the business, specifically: the market it operates within, customers and competitors.
SWOT Analysis	Summarise the conclusions from the business, global and market environment analyses. Classify key aspects of the business as strengths or weaknesses, and key aspects of the external environment as opportunities or threats.
Objectives and Assumptions	Show what the plan is designed to achieve. Rationale for the objectives. List assumptions that the objectives are based on.

Component	Content
Marketing Strategy	Detail the approach by which objectives will be achieved. Address how opportunities will be capitalised on and weaknesses will be addressed; how strengths will be used and improved, and how weaknesses will be addressed; how insights about buyers and competitors will be capitalised on; choice of market segments if applicable; how the brand will be portrayed, and what efforts will be made to preserve or improve mental and physical availability; what channel strategy will be used, i.e. direct to buyers or via distributors, or both.
Marketing Programme and Budget: Communications, Product, Pricing, Distribution Actions	Describe the set of co-ordinated actions that will occur in the planning time period. For example, the programme of marketing communication activity, product launches, price changes, new distribution arrangements. This section should also indicate the personnel responsible for the activity, costs of the actions and anticipated revenue.
Metrics; Market Research	Indicate how one will know the plan is progressing. For example, how often and when will progress towards budget figures be reviewed? What key metrics will be obtained and reported? How and when will any change in strengths and weaknesses be measured?
Bibliography/ Information Sources	List out key information sources. Summarise where information came from to write the plan, so a reader can check original sources if needed.

CHAPTER 2 The Front-End of a Plan: The Executive Summary

The first section of a marketing plan is the executive summary.

This is a short, half- to one-page explanation of what the plan is about, what the principal issues are, and how the plan will address those issues. The executive summary should be interesting! It is aimed at senior management who have competing priorities, so it should capture their attention and paint a picture of a desirable future for the organisation. The executive summary should function a little bit like a good advertisement – it should showcase the rest of the plan. Other managers should expect the marketing department to produce a readable, clear plan – since marketers are meant to be communications experts.

The executive summary should identify the principal challenges facing the business and what the plan is to tackle them.

The executive summary should be written last, after the rest of the plan is completed. That way, the executive summary is complete and can encapsulate the plan's entire scope.

The executive summary (indeed the whole plan) needs to be written in the *active voice.* An example of active voice is: 'This marketing plan identifies two key opportunities for the business, namely growth in the premium end of the market, and high numbers of inbound tourists. It then formulates a strategy, which comprises …'.

By contrast, trying to say the same thing using the *passive voice* might be along the lines of: 'Identification of two key opportunities has been undertaken, pursuit of these may be the basis of a strategy …'. This style is boring and distracting – it reads as if the writer is writing about circumstances that they are not taking ownership of or responsibility for. This style should not be used in a plan – instead, use the *active voice.*

The executive summary must also be written in a report style, not an essay style. Many students, and less experienced practitioners, may have become used to writing in the academic essay style while studying at school and university. But an academic style is not appropriate for this type of document.

An example of a report style introductory sentence is:

> 'This document sets out Lulu Vegetables marketing plan for the 2022 year. The plan identifies Lulu's major marketing challenges to be (1) increased discounting in the sector and (2) retailers prioritising their own private label packaged vegetables'.

Whereas an essay style might start off like this:

> 'Marketing planning is an explicit process for determining ...' or 'Research shows that a sound appraisal of the external environment is an important step in creating a ...'.

These two sentences are not the appropriate writing style for a plan. While a plan should cite the sources of certain facts, its purpose is to outline a plan of action, not to review what academic literature has to say about the topic, or make general statements about the usefulness of planning. In general, references are not needed for a marketing plan unless the plan makes statements about certain facts, such as 'GDP growth was 2.7 per cent last year [insert reference]'. Likewise, a plan should not be studded with academic references, especially definitions of concepts.

The sequence of points in an executive summary could be written like this:

1. An opening statement of who/what the plan is for.
2. The way in which the principal objective will be accomplished.
3. A description of the key features of the business, and if there are any major changes to those features in the foreseeable future.
4. Who the client base of the business is, the major environmental factors that are relevant to the business, and the overall way in which the business will compete for sales.
5. How major opportunities or threats will be dealt with in conjunction with leveraging strengths, addressing weaknesses, or altering past strategies.
6. The way in which the business will portray itself, and the principal way in which it will reach and communicate with buyers.
7. A statement explaining the logic of why the proposed plan of action will work.

Next, we take a look at the second section of the marketing plan, namely the analysis of the business and its environment. That section starts with the internal analysis of the business.

CHAPTER 3 The Internal Analysis

The internal analysis is a review of the current situation faced by the firm. It should first include a *context statement* – a short (two to three sentences) summary of the nature of the business and what its major issues are.

The internal analysis looks inside the business to assess its performance and key characteristics. It comprises these sections: resources and capabilities audit, previous performance; then a product audit, channel audit, pricing audit, advertising audit of both media and content, business relationships audit; and lastly, a section on key issues in which any other important points that do not fit neatly into the other sections can be canvassed.

While there is a focus on the business itself, some aspects of the external world still need to be incorporated, in order to provide context to the analysis. For example, the advertising media audit examines how the business currently communicates to buyers and in what media, but it also necessarily considers what media *could* be utilised, which is an aspect of the external world.

After the internal analysis, the focus turns to what is going on outside the firm – we call this its 'environment'. We look at the environment at two levels – the 'global' environment (comprising six factors) and the 'market' environment (comprising three factors). Note that there may be some duplication in terms of major points in the context statement about the business, and in the external analysis. For example, if a major issue facing the business is a dramatic lowering of prices of competing imported products, then this will obviously feature in the context statement as well as the external environment analysis. The latter might be along the lines of, say, exchange rate changes or new sources of competition leading to lower prices. But the context statement is very brief, so the extent of duplication from this section and the external analysis is not high.

WHAT IS THIS ANALYSIS FOR?

It could be easily the case that a business has certain problems that are causing poor performance, but it is not sure what those problems are. Therefore, it might be doing things like juggling with the mix of products the business sells, picking a different advertising agency, or perhaps even firing the marketing director and finding a new one. But these will only treat symptoms. Therefore, a key purpose of these analyses, or audits, is to figure out what the firm's real problems are, as well as identifying promising new avenues for the future. Another major purpose of the internal and external audits is to lay the groundwork for making informed decisions on the firm's strategy: it will choose certain courses of action because of what it identified in the internal and external audits.

The internal analysis starts off by considering the organisation's resources and capabilities. The goal of doing this analysis is to identify (a) some aspects of the business upon which the marketing strategy can be based; (b) some other aspects that need to be improved.

RESOURCES AND CAPABILITIES AUDIT

Resources are things the organisation has or has control of, such as knowledgeable staff, systems, information resources (databases, market knowledge), or perhaps production technology. Capabilities are things the organisation can *do* with its resources. Examples are: the business has a high-level capability to develop new products; or is excellent at conducting training seminars to clients, or perhaps a food catering business has a superior capability to produce gourmet food in a fairly short timeframe to a high standard. Another example might be a rural services company that has staff who are expert at dealing with farmers and know all about the rural business context.

Note that in this section we are not specifically looking at products or services offered, the idea is to look at what lies behind them. We want to understand the factors that make it possible for the business to offer those goods or services: the resources and capabilities that the organisation has. One should list resources and capabilities that are strong, but also identify things that are lacking. For example, a business might have marketing people who are fabulous with analytics but collectively poor in terms of client management skills.

A danger here is that one ends up with a simple list including variables such as:

Resources: great staff, good branding, good product quality.

The business has 87 staff and five managers.

The business has a head office in the centre of the city.

A simple list like this will not be very useful to base a strategy on, because it has not identified relevant factors that can either be employed to grow (Valentin, 2001) or that need to be strengthened for the future. In order to identify relevant resources and capabilities you should use one of these two logic link statements:

1. 'Which means that ...'. This phrase is a device that forces you to think about how the organisational feature, or resource or capability, is relevant for the marketing plan.
2. 'Relative to competitors'. It seems reasonable that an organisational feature, or resource or capability, should be evaluated relative to competitors. For example, if a business has a wide range of products, but it is no wider than competitors have, it probably does not sound as if it will be the underpinning of the firm's strategy.

While the idea of assessing resources relative to competitors seems very sensible, one has to consider the likelihood that some businesses just will not have any resources or capabilities that are superior relative to competitors. Many small businesses or not-for-profits will fall into this category. In these situations, all they can do is identify what they do have and what they can improve over time. Moreover, perhaps some businesses simply have to accept their resource base isn't better, but they can base their strategy on telling their message better than competitors. The old line about Avis and 'We try harder' wasn't based on Avis actually trying harder than competitors or having a superior human resource base. It was just a memorable message.

Next, in order to get value from the planning process, the writer of the plan has to spend time thinking and look behind the obvious. For example, suppose a business has excellent customer service. The question should turn to, *why* does it have good customer service? The intuitive answer is that it has good quality staff, but that would be just re-defining service as staff. Is it something to do with the experience of the staff, or the firm's training systems, or some sort of effect from a few leaders in the organisation who act as role models for others? Or are there some other systems inside the organisation (information systems, policies in relation to customer follow-up)?

In summary, the key thing is to ask the question 'Why?' to uncover the organisational resources or capabilities that underpin a firm's visibly good features.

Market-based Assets – An Important Resource

An important factor to note is that resources are not only those that exist inside the firm. There are other assets that exist outside the firm – out in the market. These are called *market-based assets* (Sharp, 1995; Srivastava et al., 1998). Key market-based assets are, broadly: mental availability and physical availability. These are built up over time, from simply selling and satisfying customers, advertising, and building relationships with distributors.

Note that the internal analysis has a specific section titled the channel audit, and channels are synonymous with physical availability. Likewise, there is an advertising audit, and this obviously relates closely to the building of market-based assets like brand mental availability. However, market-based assets are really important and deserve a dedicated section in their own right.

Mental Availability

As a starting point, does the business have any evidence about how readily buyers link its brand to the product or service category that it is in? For example, has research been done to identify the brand's awareness? This could take two parts: unaided (does the brand get mentioned by people when asked to 'name some brands that offer pain relief') or aided ('have you heard of Blythe's headache tablets?'). Awareness is a limited proxy for the broader concept of mental availability – it is simply the link that buyers have between the brand and the name of the category.

More broadly, what we want to know here is the extent to which buyers link the brand to various usage or buying cues (Romaniuk & Sharp, 2004). This is an important distinction to the narrower concept of awareness, because many buyers 'enter' the category via need or usage situations that don't necessarily involve explicitly naming or thinking about the category. For example, a couple considering a short holiday to escape the winter blues might think 'sunny beaches and not too far away' – what destinations are linked in their minds to this mental picture? Mental availability for a brand or business would be derived from a market research survey. Romaniuk and Sharp (2016, Ch. 4) provide details of how such a survey would be constructed.

Physical Availability

Here we would assess how present the brand (or business) is in terms of being easy to access and buy from (Nenycz-Thiel, Romaniuk, & Sharp, 2016; Sharp & Sorensen, 2017). Examples of physical availability are:

- The business has a location that attracts many passers-by, in the form of car traffic or shoppers, and is accessible to them.
- The business, if it has a physical premises, is easily seen from a distance.
- The business has resources that enable it to be easy to buy from or use. For example, a local restaurant has home-delivery service, which enables people to buy from it who cannot or do not want to travel. Another example is a school that has a fleet of buses to make it easy for children who live far away to attend it.
- The brand is sold or present in many places. A common measure of physical distribution prevalence is called ACV or All Category Volume. This measure means, essentially, the brand is present or available to be bought in the places that account for a certain percentage of all the sales in the category. For example, 'Brian's Organic Dog Food' is sold in a range of pet food stores and supermarkets, which collectively account for 40 per cent of all the dog food sold in the market. Brian's, therefore, has 40 per cent ACV.
- A brand that appears in online search (as opposed to one that doesn't, or one that appears deep down in a long list of brands).
- A brand or business that features in many online resellers. For example, a restaurant that is on The Fork, Zomato and Trip Advisor has more physical availability than one that doesn't.

The physical availability audit will need some comparisons with competitors to be useful. We obtain this by examining some competitors or comparable organisations. That way, we can better interpret our results as either good or bad relative to our firm's sales revenue. An important point to take into consideration is that a big factor separating large firms from smaller competitors is the bigger players have more physical availability. This arises almost inevitably because:

- The way they got to be bigger was by building physical availability. For example, Trader Joe's in the US has been growing steadily for 20 years – in large part because it has been building new stores every year.
- Since they're bigger, they can afford the widespread physical availability. A retail business like Kmart is known by everyone, it can have stores everywhere. A big food

manufacturer like ConAgra can afford to employ hundreds of sales representatives and merchandisers to service its retail channel partners.

This close link between size and physical availability means we need to be careful who we compare to. Ideally, we would select one larger competitor, one smaller competitor and perhaps one the same size as ourselves. And while overall, a larger firm will likely have greater levels of physical availability, we will gain valuable insight into how well we perform on specific aspects of it. For example, we might find that we are very strong in terms of physical location(s) and online search, but far weaker in terms of delivery capabilities and presence on reseller sites.

Recognition of the Brand's Distinctive Assets

Brands usually incorporate what are called *brand elements* – non-brand-name elements that serve to identify the brand. Examples are logos, stylised colours, or characters such as the Michelin Man or Kinder's Pingui. The more that the brand's elements are known, and linked to the brand itself, the more valuable they are as market-based assets (see Romaniuk, 2018). More specifically, these brand elements are an aspect of physical availability because they make the brand easier to notice; but they are also an aspect of mental availability because they help the brand's advertising be noticed and correctly attributed.

To illustrate the worth of distinctive assets, imagine a bank brand, such as HSBC. It has a unique, stylised logo of a box with folding flaps in red and white: known as the 'hexagon'. Imagine if this logo was shown to 100 potential buyers in a particular country, be they consumers or businesspeople, and only 20 per cent correctly say, 'that is HSBC's logo'. This means, arguably, that HSBC has to educate the market that this is its logo! If a much higher figure of 70 per cent correctly identified it, that would mean this logo is a much more valuable asset to HSBC, because when people see advertising for it, they are far more likely to recognise it as being for HSBC; and when they're vaguely thinking about a financial need and they see the hexagon, they link that to HSBC and to its presence in banking.

In relation to conducting the internal audit of resources and capabilities, consider that your brand elements, or what are also called brand assets, are a resource. The question is, how much of a resource are they? How well do buyers recognise your brand assets as yours, and no other brand's: what Romaniuk (2018) calls fame and uniqueness. This information requires a buyer survey. Obviously mounting a significant survey is more feasible for larger businesses. Smaller firms can at least attempt to use their own judgement to consider if they employ brand elements that help them stand out in the market.

PREVIOUS PERFORMANCE

This section of the internal analysis details the recent trends and sales performance of the business overall. For example, what has the company's growth rate been over the past five years? If there have been 'bad' years, is there some explanation for them? Has the business lost more customers lately than is usual – if so, why?

In this section we can discuss factors such as our total number of customers, the customer acquisition rate, the customer retention rate, as well as profitability. For a services business it is usually possible to distinguish between a new customer and an (old) existing one; for example, a bank generally knows when a person signs up to become a customer and so it is possible to calculate the acquisition rate: if we had 30,000 clients last year and in the past 12 months we have had 1,000 new customers join up then our acquisition rate is 1,000 divided by 30,000 or 3.3 per cent. Likewise, we could look at how many customers ceased being customers each year. This is called the attrition rate or loss rate (it's presumptuous to call it the defection rate because we don't know if those lost customers have defected to a competitor or just stopped buying from us).

Market Share

Market share is a metric that would often be included in this section on previous performance. However, it might be the case that in an extremely fragmented market the market share of any small provider is so small it is hardly worth calculating. To use the example of a small accountancy practice gain, it might only have a turnover of, say, $2 million, whereas the total market in its geographic area would be hundreds of millions. In this case it would hardly seem worthwhile to calculate the firm's market share and one could alternatively just say the business is very small in the context of the entire market. Note that it is important to get your market definition right to correctly assess your market share. For example, if we sell tyres to consumers, our market definition would likely be retail sales of passenger car tyres in a specified geographic market. We would not count sales to commercial businesses with fleets of cars (that need new tyres) or trucks, or buses and so on.

The following sections cover other aspects of the business and so there is an emphasis on the business itself, but we do also have to consider the external world to contextualise what we uncover about the business. For example, we can look at the various communications channels the business uses to talk to buyers, but we also need to consider what other communication channels there are realistically available to the business.

Note that in the product audit, discussed next, we examine the performance of particular products or service.

PRODUCT AUDIT

This section examines the products or services that are offered by the business. For example, an accounting practice might look at the major services it offers: tax returns for private individuals, investment advice, bookkeeping for small businesses; as well as more complex services for businesses such as business setup, audits and compliance work. The examination would consider factors such as sales levels of each 'product', market share information if available or relevant, price levels and profitability. The reasons for doing this audit of current offerings or products are to ascertain whether the current range is adequate, which parts of the range or suite of offerings should be prioritised or perhaps culled, to identify possible gaps in the range, and whether there is a need for new offerings and what they should be.

Commencing the process of listing and discussing current offerings will straightaway identify questions and issues that can be pursued further.

Key Questions for the Product Audit

- What are our biggest sellers, and what proportion of total sales do they comprise?
- Are there some product offerings that used to be popular, but are less popular now? If we confirm that is the case, we can then ask – why?
- Does the business have a lot of products that hardly sell – and if so, why does it still have them in its range?
- Are there some products that depend on others? For example, are there products that people buy as their first purchase from the business, then they buy others later?
- Are there some products that are 'traffic builders' for a store, that attract buyers who then buy other things?
- Do we have some products that have high margins and others that we hardly make money on? If so, is there a good reason to keep the lowest-margin products? Perhaps there is a good reason, maybe they help provide the sales volume needed to keep unit costs down – but this needs to be confirmed.

Product Audit: Example

We now look at an example of how to construct a product audit. The example uses general insurance for consumers. It summarises a range of factors into a simple table.

The example also highlights that in many cases the product audit, which is overall part of an internal analysis, necessarily looks for some external information for context. An example is that the firm's price levels (an internal factor) are only meaningful when considered compared to competitor's (an external factor).

The example uses a firm called Hallowell, which is a small provider of insurance to consumers in a geographic market of two million people.

This is an example of a services business. Therefore, its product audit factors relate to factors from which the demand for insurance is derived. In this case, the demand for car insurance is derived from the number of cars on the road. If we were a business that sells physical goods, such as wine, we might include the number of wine drinkers or number of consumers in our market, rather than the number of products or objects from which demand is derived.

Product Audit Self-test Questions

1. Which products are performing well at Hallowell?
2. Are there some products that Hallowell could be more successful with?
3. Which products does Hallowell appear to under-price and which ones does it seem to over-price? Note, under-pricing would be charging less than what the quality of the product suggests, over-pricing is the opposite.

(Continued)

TABLE 3.1 *Example Product Audit Structure: Hallowell Insurance Services Ltd*

	Products (Insurance Policies for ...)							
Product Audit Factors (Rows)	**Vehicle**	**Building**	**Contents**	**Renters**	**Travel**	**Income Protect**	**Boat**	**Pet**
Buyer Profile	**Adults/ Partners 18+ with Own Vehicle**	**Adults Almost All 24+**	**Adults Almost All 24+**	**Property Owners Who Rent a Home to Others**	**Adults 18+ Who Travel (Airline Flight) in a Year**	**Higher Income Adults, Usually 30+**	**Boat Owners, Usually 30–60 yrs**	**Pets with Owners, Usually Adults 30+***
N of products/objects potentially insurable in our geographic market	1,000,000	350,000	350,000	50,000	62,000	300,000	10,000	150,000
Our sales (N policies sold last 12 months)	3,400	958	1,145	57	236	210	40	120
Growth rate last 2 yrs – this product – Hallowell	3	1	1	0	2	1	1	1
Growth rate last 2 yrs – this product – National	2	1	1	0	2	1	1	3
Profit margin** (%)	35	35	35	30	40	32	45	35
Claims per year % of policyholders	8	1	2	4	4	3	2	6
Quality of our policies relative to market leader – = less expensive, 0 = no difference, + = more expensive	+	0	0	–	+	+	0	–

(Continued)

(Continued)

	Products (Insurance Policies for ...)							
Product Audit Factors (Rows)	**Vehicle**	**Building**	**Contents**	**Renters**	**Travel**	**Income Protect**	**Boat**	**Pet**
Dependency with other products we sell			50% are in conjunction with building cover				70% are in conjunction with vehicle cover	
Average premium value per year	$700	$800	$400	$1200	$200	$300	$400	$500
Hallowell price vs leading competitor/similar policy – = less expensive, 0 = no difference, + = more expensive	0	+	+	+	+	+	+	–
% of product buyers who buy this as their first policy with us	22	18	22	4	10	5	1	2

*This is the profile of people who take out pet insurance, not pet owners.

**Profit margin is the average revenue minus the average cost per policy arising from claim incidence and magnitude, expressed as a percentage.

(Continued)

4. Are some products more important to Hallowell than others, if so which ones?
5. Is there a product of Hallowell that looks like it could be usefully 'bundled' with another?
6. Why does the internal audit need to incorporate some amount of external information as well?

CHANNEL AUDIT

Many businesses have distribution channels – the network of intermediaries by which buyers buy the product. For example, insurance companies sell direct to consumers and businesses, many of them also sell via insurance brokers as well as financial services providers such as banks. Big banks such as HSBC or Barclays in the UK, or Bank of America in the US, sell insurance policies, but those policies are 'made' or 'manufactured' for them by big insurance companies. The banks are therefore extremely important selling outlets for the insurance makers. A sound appreciation of how the various channels in your industry work, which ones you are present in, and how well you are performing is important for making informed marketing planning decisions.

Note that a distribution channel doesn't have to be physical. Selling online is a distribution channel, and if the business sells direct to buyers via traditional means such as a factory outlet, its own physical premises, then having its own online 'store' is an additional distribution channel because it means buyers don't have to physically go to the firm's premises to buy. And indeed, a business could have multiple online or non-physical distribution channels. One might be via its own website, as well as via retail stores. Or a pet food business could sell its product via petonly.ca, an online pet food and products retailer. For some businesses, we can consider the ways in which clients can buy or enquire as 'channels.' For example, a small hairdressing boutique – does it have an online booking system, or do clients need to call or email to book in? Or does it offer both? More ways in which buyers can enquire or buy is better.

An important type of distribution channel takes the form of what is called affiliate marketing. What this means is that the firm makes an agreement with another business – the affiliate – to advertise the firm's products on its website. The affiliate receives a commission for every buyer or visitor that is directed from its site to the firm's site. Examples of affiliate marketing are the well-known accommodation sites: Expedia, HotelsCombined, Booking.com, TripAdvisor and so on. If someone clicks on or makes a booking through one of these sites, that affiliate site earns a commission from the property. A desirable aspect of affiliates is that they are essentially commission-based: the firm only pays for what is actually sold from them. A potential shortcoming of affiliates is that the sales derived through them – for which a commission needs to be paid – might have occurred anyway. Arguably, affiliates act as advertising channels for the business too, but since they allow buyers to actually purchase one's goods, they are better considered as a distribution channel.

More distribution sounds better at face value, and it usually is. However, we do need to consider if the support we get from one set of channel members depends on what we do, or don't do, with other channels. For example, perhaps we are a cosmetics brand that enjoys a particularly good relationship with a retail chain, which accounts for 20 per cent of our revenue. In part, this favourable arrangement is because we have traditionally not sought to sell via other retail format types, nor have we sold directly to consumers. In other words, they support us because our brand is not available via their competitors.

In this section of the plan, you evaluate each channel to ascertain which of them offer the most opportunity for growth; and what combination of channels will work best for the firm. The overarching question to be addressed is whether the business is making the most use of the various distribution channels potentially available to it.

Key Questions for the Channel Audit

- What is the size of each distribution channel in our market and its current rate of growth?
- Which channels are we present in – that is, which ones do we sell our product via?
- What is our performance (sales, share) in each channel?
- Are there channels we wish to be present in but are not – if so, what is the reason?
- Which channels offer us the ability to sell to incremental buyers – i.e. those who don't buy us now?
- Are there key features of various channels that require differences in the marketing mix, such as the size of the product, packaging or returns policy?
- Are there any downsides from pursuing additional distribution channels or partners?

Channel Audit: Example

Here is an example of a small brewery that sells via its own premises as well as through several other channels. The brewery is a small business in a geographic area of two million people, being a city with several surrounding towns. It sells $1,200,000 of beer a year. It sells the majority of its beer at its own premises or 'cellar door', mostly on weekends when locals and tourists come to sample and drink the beer and enjoy tasting plates (bread, dips, meat, cheese, antipasto). The list of channel audit factors is not meant to be exhaustive, but to convey the essential ideas of doing an audit – which is to ask sensible questions about the business so that decisions are fully informed.

This simple arrangement of the key channel factors reveals some useful facts. First, we see that the business is much more dependent on own-premises sales than other players in the category. This might already be known in general terms, but it's good to formally set out the extent of this over-dependence. We can also relate our growth in each channel with how the channel itself is growing: BrewHaus' own-premises sales are growing faster than category-wide own-premises sales; but it's online sales are growing slower. Table 3.2 also shows BrewHaus is growing comparatively quickly in small local alcohol retailers, as well as restaurants and pubs in its own region – which suggests whatever it is doing for those channels is working and perhaps investment in those should be increased. Online sales are attractive from the point of view of margins and is a growth channel in the industry

TABLE 3.2 *Example Channel Audit: BrewHaus Brewing Company*

Channel Audit Factors	Cellar Door/Our Premises	Online Sales via Own Website	Alcohol Retailers: Large National Chains	Alcohol Retailers: Small Local Stores/ Chains in Our Region**	Restaurants (in Our Region)	Pubs (in Our Region)
BrewHaus dollar sales last 12 months	732,000	180,000	–	96,000	96,000	96,000
% of our sales through this channel	61	15	0	8	8	8
% of total category sales to each channel	10	2	53	15	8	12
Avg. annual growth rate, BrewHaus last 2 years (%)	2.5	6	n/a	4	4.5	4.5
Avg. annual growth rate national last 2 years* (%)	6	7.5	1.5	2.5	1	1
% Profit margin on sales made via this channel	50	50	25	30	30	30

*Growth rate may depend on the category definition: a narrower definition could be 'craft/premium beer' and a broader one simply 'beer'. Here we use craft/premium beer for the sake of simplicity. Example is hypothetical.
**Share of craft/premium beer in the brewery's local region.

generally, but apparently at the present time, this firm is highly dependent on cellar door sales. Additional contextual knowledge is that it would be very difficult to grow cellar door sales faster than what has been occurring, and the business should ideally reduce its dependence on that channel anyway. Collectively these facts point to the need for BrewHaus to adjust or invest more in its online strategy.

Channel Audit Self-test Questions

1. Large alcohol retailers account for the bulk of sales in this category. Should BrewHaus try to secure distribution in one of the large chains?
2. Is one of these channels dependent on one of the others?
3. Which channel offers the best growth prospects to BrewHaus?
4. What benefit would further 'spreading' of BrewHaus sales across multiple channels have to the company, aside from the potential increase in sales itself?

PRICING AUDIT

This audit examines the prices the business obtains for what it sells. As part of this audit, we consider things like discounting structures, and price levels relative to competitors. As with the other components of the internal audit, this one is based around a series of questions. The objectives of asking these questions are: (1) to get the business thinking about these issues – which will likely generate additional questions and tasks; and (2) to provide a basis for recommending if certain prices be changed, and how the process of setting prices could be improved.

Key Questions for the Pricing Audit

- How do we actually set prices? Do we base prices mostly on what costs are, or on customer perceived value?
- Which departments or people in the business set and change prices?
- Do we monitor the prices that competitors charge for similar products to ours?
- How *do* our prices compare to those of competitors?
- If we sell products at different quality or feature levels, are the prices we set for them commensurate with their different quality levels?
- Do we have a good idea of the value that customers place on various features or extra services?
- Do we offer different prices on the same products to different customers – either end-users or distributors? Is there a clear rationale for when this should occur?
- Are we under a lot of pressure to offer lower prices? Why?
- What proportion of our total sales revenue comes from discounted prices?

- How do we ensure that discounts or other price concessions are appropriate?
- Do we vary prices according to factors such as demand or seasonality?
- Do we/can we respond quickly enough to competitors' price changes or offers?
- Do we offer price bundles – a price for a series of products bought together that is less than the sum of the individual prices? How are the prices for these bundles determined, and is there any evidence this practice is effective for us?
- Do we offer trading term discounts or other allowances, and if so, have we reviewed them in the last two years to determine if they are structured properly? An example of a trading term discount is a 2 per cent discount paid to clients who pay their accounts within 30 days. The idea is to trade-off a lower price for prompt payment, which helps cash flow. Cash flow for a business refers to the movement of money in and out. A business doesn't want too much time to pass by between spending its money and receiving money it is owed. A business can be selling lots of product but can go bankrupt if its cash flow is poor because it won't have enough money to pay its debts. Businesses prefer money that's in their actual bank account rather than money that's owed to them by their clients.

A New Tool: Dynamic Pricing

Dynamic pricing is a new way of pricing which continuously updates the prices of goods and services based on demand. It is often implemented using custom software. This is because it is too difficult to do manually if one has a wide range of products, or very high demand. The essential idea is that if demand begins to accelerate, prices for items not yet sold are increased. If demand starts to drop, the business starts lowering prices for goods not yet sold, to try to get demand back up again. A simple way to illustrate this is a hotel with, say, 100 rooms. Its standard room rate is £100 per night for simplicity. A crucial business metric for a hotel is its occupancy rate – the proportion of rooms that are booked over a period such as a week or month. Hotels are usually comfortable with about 90 per cent occupancy, that is, when guests are in around 90 per cent of their rooms at the present time. They also look ahead in time and consider the booking levels, or occupancy rate, for the next few months. And they would usually like to see that they have, for instance, 40 per cent of their rooms booked four weeks in advance, 30 per cent booked six to eight weeks in advance and so on. Suppose it is March and a hotel looks ahead to May – and so far, only 20 per cent of rooms have been booked. The hotel might then drop the

Dynamic Pricing Self-test Question

Could the principle of dynamic pricing apply to a small business? Suppose you are a marketer working for a chain of hairdressing salons. How could you successfully use dynamic pricing to obtain a better outcome in terms of sales revenue, customer numbers and ensuring there is capacity to meet demand at all times, for the business?

prices of rooms for May until the occupancy rate is, say, 30 per cent. It will then bring prices back to normal (for new bookings for the month of May). This practice is one reason why different people can end up paying different prices for the same hotel room. The basic idea of dynamic pricing is to use pricing to increase or decrease demand, so as to (a) ensure we reach sales targets, and (b) balance demand that might otherwise fluctuate a lot, especially if we have limited capacity at any point in time.

ADVERTISING AUDIT

The word advertising is used to cover all aspects of marketing communications including publicity. We create two advertising audits: first, the media – i.e. the ways in which we communicate; second, the content of our advertising.

The main focus is communication to customers or potential customers, but communication to other stakeholders such as distributors could also be incorporated.

The over-arching theme in the advertising media audit is that communications can only influence the people whom it reaches. Therefore, we are looking to see how efficiently we can expend resources to reach potential buyers.

Key Questions for the Advertising Media Audit

- What media are we using to reach our audience(s)?
- How much is being spent on each – in terms of paid media space for advertising; and in terms of staff costs in relation to earned media/social media?
- What reach are we achieving in each media, and to what extent do they duplicate each other, or result in incremental reach? Incremental reach means reach over and above what the other media are achieving. For example, if we achieve 30 per cent reach using Facebook ads and 20 per cent reach using Instagram, how much above 30 per cent is our total reach across the two media. An advertising medium is more valuable if it can help achieve incremental reach.
- How many category buyers who *don't* currently buy from us are we reaching, or are we mostly hitting our existing buyers or clients?
- What channels of communication are realistically available to us? Take for example a small business in a regional town. The locale has a newspaper, a local radio station, there is the option to use external signage either on street-front or in locations such as sports venues. Local sporting clubs offer sponsorship to businesses, which provides some exposure at their premises or sports grounds. In addition, there are options such as being able to geographically target via broad-based social media advertising in Instagram and Facebook. The advertising audit would consider which of these are cost-effective or appropriate options.
- Do we have an idea of the extent to which each media we use generates some short-term response in terms of enquiries or purchases?
- Do we have a rationale for frequently communicating with our current (or intending) customer base in terms of answering questions, keeping them updated with events or news about us? If yes, this is a significant reason for maintaining a social media presence on Facebook and so on.

- Do we benefit, or would we benefit, from having a communications channel through which buyers or other interested stakeholders can give us feedback?
- Is demand for our product seasonal? If so, to what extent do we focus spending on the times of the year when demand (or information search) is high?

Finally, we make some conclusion or judgement about what the firm is doing in relation to media – is it underspending in some areas, overspending in others, or perhaps failing to use certain media that appear to offer good value? But we don't start making decisions about future media use here, that comes later in the strategy.

Advertising Media Audit: Example

One useful way the advertising media audit can be summarised is to assemble the various media the business employs into a simple table. The table should show the spending on each media, the reach they achieve and any other information about response. For example, for adwords spending, we would summarise how many clicks and estimated sales it generates, as well as views – since a view is an impression or 'reach' to one person, however fleeting. An example is shown below of a bridal wear retailer located in a mid-sized town. As we can see, this business should ideally get more quantification of the reach and effects of some of its media used.

Advertising Media Audit Self-test Questions

1. Is there more information that Marianne's should gather about any of these media/channels?
2. Which one of these channels appears to give the best value for money to Marianne's?

The second part of the advertising audit pertains to content.

Key Questions for the Advertising Content Audit

A series of fairly straightforward questions forms the basis of the advertising content audit.

- Does our advertising convey the key brand attributes we want to communicate?
- Do our marketing communications prominently feature our distinctive brand assets – i.e. non-brand-name elements that identify the brand – logos, characters, colour schemes and so on (see Romaniuk, 2018).

TABLE 3.3 *Media Use Summary: Marianne's Bridal Wear*

Media	Amount of Media Used	Cost in Last 12 months	Reach (How Many People Reached in a Time Period)	What are the Broader End Results?
Colour 'lifestyle' magazine insert in local newspaper that is published once per month	4 x ½ page ads per year	£500	8,000 as per magazine publisher stats each edition	Many clients comment they learned about us from the magazine ads
Google adwords	Keywords: bridal wear, wedding dress, + location	£500	3,000 views per month but difficult to identify unique views	20–50 visits to website per month from this source
Facebook page	Monthly posts featuring brides and wedding party	Staff cost, 3–5 hours per week	Currently 2,371 people like our page, and we have 2,226 followers	Clients tell us they check updates on Facebook quite regularly (while in the pre-wedding phase)
Facebook paid ads	Locally targeted ads each month April–June	£200	1,500 each month over the three months	10–20 visits to website or Facebook page from this source
Instagram influencers	We sponsor two UK wedding-wear influencers	£400	Not ascertained	Anecdotally our brand is noticed by many people via this source

- Does our advertising reflect typical or common usage or buying situations? We know advertising largely works through memory: linking a brand to various cues. If we highlight or use those cues it is logical the ad should better link the brand in memory to relevant situations.
- Do we employ a consistent theme or look and feel, across our various pieces of communication? Many businesses fail to integrate the visual components of their various pieces of communication (such as video, static graphics, online and printed, outdoor). This can make it less effective because the various pieces do not fully support each other.
- Is our advertising consistent over time? A logical test for this is whether last year's advertising would still be helping buyers recognise this year's advertising as being for us. Consistency is desirable – since buyers are very good at not noticing things, especially things that are unfamiliar to them, keeping one's advertising consistent over a long time period is a way for it to work more effectively.

If the answers to these questions are no, then the marketing strategy section should state how the business will revise its advertising content.

BUSINESS RELATIONSHIPS AUDIT

No business exists in isolation. A business or organisation exists within a network of other businesses that it depends on to source goods or services, or to which it supplies goods or services, in other words, channel partners. In this section we consider businesses that our firm has an important relationship with, but who may not be clients. Clients are discussed later, in the customer audit.

In this section the plan lists out the important partners the business has, and evaluates its relationships with them. For example, are there key suppliers who are important for the business to successfully market its goods or services, and how well-established and favourable is the firm's relationship with them? Examples might be, does the marketing department have a good relationship with a trusted, intelligent market research agency and advertising agency?

Many businesses are themselves an actor in a larger distribution channel, therefore their ability to service clients depends on particular suppliers. A simple example is a garage door installer, who makes appointment times to install new doors or undertake repairs. The installation or repair depends on the delivery of the product on an agreed day, so there could be two crucial suppliers that impact on the installer – the manufacturer, and the transport company that delivers the door or spare part. One could argue that transport and delivery are not a marketing issue, but if the reliability of deliveries via these suppliers directly affects customer service and satisfaction, it would seem to be marketing-related. Therefore, relationships with relevant suppliers should be discussed in the marketing plan.

Another example of the business relationships audit can be illustrated using a small accountancy firm. Anecdotal evidence from accountants suggests a lot of business is won from referrals. Referrals might come from current customers, or even other accountancy firms which might not have specialist expertise that a client wants – so they might refer them to another firm (for that particular service, while keeping their clients' general business). Also, lawyers may refer their clients to accountants they personally know, and vice versa. Therefore, for an accountancy firm, having a network of other businesses that sometimes refer business to it can be very important.

This section of the marketing plan considers these relationships, not in the narrow sense of how amicably the parties conduct business, but in terms of how important they are to the firm's marketing ability, and its ability to do the things that customers want, as well as the extent to which the firm has been able to cultivate a network of referring parties.

Examples of business relationships that a marketing plan might document and consider for cultivation are:

- *Media/journalists*: Do we have any association with media outlets or writers that allow us to periodically appear in news, current affairs or industry publications?
- *Industry associations*: Do we know, or are we known by, prominent members of a relevant industry association? An example of the importance of this type of relationship is a start-up company developing highly secure, electronic 'last will and testament' technology. A crucial set of stakeholders in getting this concept accepted is the legal fraternity. Accordingly, the business must work very hard to be accepted by the Bar association in that market.

- *Referrers*: Are there entities or people who are likely to act as referrers for us? As an example, certain tradespeople often refer consumers to products and services – plumbers may recommend brands of tapware or bathtubs; medical practitioners may recommend surgeons, physiotherapists, or other allied health professionals. The question for marketers is, how many of these sorts of people can we (a) identify, (b) reach and (c) influence?
- *Installers/repairers*: In many markets, goods or services are installed by professionals – for example, a home security system or a dishwasher. And many goods or services need periodic repairs – from laptops to air-conditioners. The installers or service folk who undertake this work may exert considerable influence on purchases, if their opinion is sought prior to purchase (in which case they are referrers, as above). However, they can also enhance or detract from the brand's reputation by what they say about it during installation or repair. Again, how many of these sorts of people can we (a) identify, (b) reach and (c) influence?
- *Specifiers*: Many goods, particularly in sectors such as building and construction, are specified by professionals for their clients. An example is an office tower or a large hotel, which will have virtually every item required for its construction specified and itemised by an architectural firm, building consultant, hydraulics consultant or electrical engineering consultant. Everything from the brand of windows (imagine how many windows go into an office tower) to the exterior cladding, tiles, lifts, carpets and so on – is specified in advance. So the question for the marketing team is: who are these specifiers and how can we build familiarity, and influence choice among this group of professionals? Many businesses which manufacture building products have specialist teams that endeavour to develop relationships with architectural firms and other specifiers.

The goals of this section are, therefore, to identify the key entities the business needs for its marketing activity to work; to ascertain if there are gaps or shortcomings in its network of business partners; and, moreover, to identify the important external parties that can help it either win business, increase its reach, or act as recommenders.

Relationships Audit: Example

An example of the business relationships audit and its implications comes from the not-for-profit sector. Take the example of a charity that works with domestic violence victims. The key goal of the charity is to help the victim find a safe place for their pet. It is an unfortunate fact that many domestic violence victims stay in an abusive situation because they are afraid they cannot move to other accommodation, because finding rental accommodation with a pet is very difficult. Therefore, this charity helps victims escape by finding a home for their dog or cat – for a time period, at least.

Working with this charity, we learned that its key marketing challenge was not clients (it had plenty of those, sadly) but *funding* to support its good work – all the staff were volunteers. And therefore, what it needed to do was build *relationships* with potential funding organisations. These are essentially any business that could potentially benefit from being associated with a worthy cause, via co-exposure and simply being able to say it was a supporter. But this charity also needed to identify what we might call the 'ecosystem' of related not-for-profit organisations, government departments and agencies that could help it to discern funding opportunities, as well as effectively pitch for that funding. These other players in the charity ecosystem would include: government departments that deal with homelessness and domestic violence, social housing providers, lawyers, social workers, animal welfare organisations, and perhaps politicians with responsibilities for women, animals, justice or family law, or social equity. Therefore, the charity constructed a plan to identify exactly who these entities and the people within them were, to commence a dialogue with them. The mechanisms would range from introduction letters, to following them on social media, to attending events such as fundraisers for other not-for-profits to meet the key players. After a period of time, the charity could take inventory of these business relationships, identify which of them looked like potential partners or channels for funding, and plan for further outreach.

KEY ISSUES

This section identifies if there are key issues that might affect the implementation of the marketing plan. There may also be specific issues that need to be addressed in the plan, but which might not neatly fit into the other sections. For example, suppose there is a business in which some differences in viewpoint exist among the management team. Furthermore, these differences in opinion relate to how the business conducts its marketing activity. This situation is not uncommon. In many businesses, the actual marketing team interfaces with, or has some dependency on, other functions within the firm. For example, a bank has not only a marketing department, but has a retail arm that is responsible for branches, frontline staff, call centres and the customer-facing website. It might also have a sales function, comprising account managers for small, medium and corporate clients. Managers of these other sections are obviously very influential in the firm's overall marketing effort, but they might also have their own ideas and 'advice' they broadcast about marketing.

For example, perhaps the manager of the retail arm of the business thinks more money should be invested in front-line staff development and less on advertising. Or a senior manager in the business has read a *Harvard Business Review* article claiming that the key to growth is deepening customer loyalty, therefore has lobbied for this idea to be part of the next marketing plan. What these sorts of scenarios mean, essentially, is that the marketing manager is facing a bit of political pressure from other leaders in the business to change strategy.

To address this sort of situation, the specific issue raised should be listed out in this section, in an impartial and objective way. Remember the marketing team's critics may read the plan! Next, one canvasses the evidence or logic supporting or negating these issues. Then later, the marketing strategy section will discuss what action will or will not be taken, based on that evidence.

Introduction to the Marketing Plan Case Study: Remedy Physiotherapy Clinic

This is a case study about a small physiotherapy business in the UK. The case presents all the information necessary to write a detailed marketing plan. A slice of the case appears at the end of each chapter from here.

Case Objectives

The objectives of this case are to:

1. Understand how to identify information that is relevant to a marketing plan.
2. Practise how to correctly classify global and market environment factors and their marketing implications.
3. Calculate basic numerical information relevant to a marketing plan.
4. Construct a marketing plan using this prior preparation and analysis.

As you read each section of this case you will find content that could be useful in more than one part of the marketing plan. Indeed, in some instances, you will find material that will reinforce an earlier component of your plan.

An Excel file accompanies the case, available via the supporting online resources at **study.sagepub.com/dawes**. This contains some basic information about patient visits to the clinic over time. Instructions about what to do with it appear shortly.

The case is split into sections. At the end of several sections there are some analysis tasks for you to do. There is also a marketing plan template to use, to enter key inputs for each section of your plan.

Note, names of people and businesses are disguised. Some aspects of the local area and the physiotherapy industry are simplified for teaching purposes.

The case is self-contained, you do not need to obtain wider information about the physiotherapy industry. Nor do you need to undertake further investigation into the town the case is set in. The clinic names are disguised.

Assume the plan is for the 12-month calendar year following whatever year it happens to be at present.

The case starts with information about the business, which forms the basis for conducting the internal analysis. The structure of the case, and where it appears in the book, is as follows:

Internal Analysis	at the end of Chapter 3
Global Environment Analysis	at the end of Chapter 4
Market Environment Analysis	at the end of Chapter 5
SWOT	at the end of Chapter 6
Objectives and Assumptions	at the end of Chapter 7

Marketing Strategy	at the end of Chapter 8
Marketing Programme	at the end of Chapter 9
Marketing Budget	at the end of Chapter 10
Key Metrics and Market Research	at the end of Chapter 11

Once all these components are completed, the executive summary is written and placed at the start of the plan. Details of how to write an executive summary appear earlier in the book.

Marketing Plan Case Study: Internal Analysis

Remedy Physiotherapy Clinic – Background

Joshua and Sarah Brightstone are the proprietors of Remedy Physiotherapy, a small clinic situated in the town of Bournemouth in the English county of Dorset. Both graduated from Southampton University with a BSc (Physiotherapy). After some travel, marriage and some fill-in work with several large clinics in the past couple of years, they have moved to Bournemouth. A practitioner known to Joshua's family, Mr James Bound, is retiring, and has been staying open only to a small number of clients. He has passed the business on to Joshua and Sarah at no cost, they have merely taken over the rent for the premises and the (small) client base of people who have been to the clinic at least once in the previous year. The clinic has always been known as Remedy Physiotherapy.

The Brightstones have high hopes for the clinic, and think it is reasonable to build the clientele in order to provide a good income source for them both, for the foreseeable future. They are considering re-naming the clinic to just Brightstone, which they think sounds inviting and indicates general health and wellbeing and is also catchy, rather than just using the word physiotherapy and the name of the town. Currently the clinic has the original hand-painted sign placed in the front window, which simply says, Remedy Physiotherapy Clinic.

The Local Scene

Bournemouth is a coastal resort town approximately 60 kilometres from Southampton and about 170 kilometres south-west of London. It has a population of 190,000; of those, around 170,000 are aged 10 or over. The Brightstones' clinic is one in a block of four retail shopfronts, with the others being a funeral director, a bridal salon and a solicitor. The shopfronts are all a fairly conventional 3 metres in total height, with door and windows facing the street. The premises are situated around 3 kilometres from the town centre, on a secondary road, to the north of the city centre.

(Continued)

(Continued)

The Bournemouth economy is quite robust. It has many miles of sandy beaches and is a tourist drawcard. Some very large corporations have headquarters or offices in the town. Bournemouth also has a thriving 'digital economy' with numerous (over 100) small e-commerce businesses present in the town, many of which are actually one- or two-person outfits working from a home office. The town has a Chamber of Trade and Commerce which endeavours to support local businesses via engaging with the local council and holding networking events. Many locals are members and participate in the Chamber's activities including the owners of small businesses ranging from retail shops, tradespeople, general practitioners, to some managers of the larger businesses present in the town. Bournemouth has a comparatively old population compared to the rest of Britain and this feature makes it quite an attractive location for a physiotherapy clinic.

Finances

Rental for the clinic premises is £120 per week. A month after taking it over, the Brightstones' clinic is attracting few clients: only one or two per day. Almost all are existing clients who pay £37 for a repeat appointment; the fee for an initial consultation (which involves some background information gathering and assessment) is £47. Repeat-consults tend to be for 40 minutes; initial ones are generally about 50 minutes. People who have not been to the clinic for 12 months or more pay another initial consultation fee because their condition is likely to have changed in the time period between visits (and a 12-month or more lapse suggests a different problem the second time). Historically, for every initial consultation, there are on average 2.5 additional follow-up appointments in the year.

In the past week, only seven appointments have been booked, which is a bit disappointing to the Brightstones. Interestingly, the age of the patients currently coming in is almost all 50+ years. About three-quarters of them reside in a radius of about 4 kilometres from the clinic; another quarter are from all over the town.

Joshua and Sarah take turns to be the 'receptionist' as the level of business is too low to employ a dedicated person. Once the clinic grows, they intend to hire a part-time person for around 20 hours per week. The clinic currently operates Tuesday to Friday 9 a.m. to 5.00 p.m. and Saturday 9 a.m. to midday. Expenses in running the clinic (apart from rent) are principally electricity, which costs about £20 per week, and various other expenses including the internet totalling another £20 per week. The Brightstones take bookings via their mobile phones, with the clinic website listing both numbers. The website was created by a friend of Joshua who had studied IT at university. The site looks quite good, however, it does not have the functionality to accept bookings online, and rather directs site visitors to the Brightstones' phone numbers.

Sarah believes that an appropriate level of income the pair could earn from the clinic over the next 12 months is £100,000. After deducting rent and expenses their net income before tax would be £92,000.

The premises that the Brightstones operate from is an old building but it is very neat and presentable. It features a reception area and two consult rooms, as well as a spare room featuring a sink (where they often sit and have lunch or a coffee). There is also quite a spacious room of about 4 square metres that is currently unused at the rear. It has a pleasant polished wood floor and a reasonable view of the outside. By a stroke of luck, there are modern male and female toilets at the back of the clinic. Patients appear to appreciate the option to attend the 'bathroom' before or after their consult.

Treatments

The Brightstones use a variety of treatments for typical patient problems: lower back and neck pain and stiffness. They also utilise joint mobility work, vertebrae manipulation, deep tissue massage and ultrasound. Recently they have invested in a device to deliver Extracorporeal Radial Shockwave Therapy (ESWT). This new treatment is essentially a powerful pulse of sound to treat painful conditions such as tendonitis or plantar fasciitis. All treatments are charged at the same initial consult price or repeat consult price. They often prescribe certain exercises (such as stretches, leg extensions to tone abdominal muscles and so on) by showing the patient the exercise and drawing a stick figure on a piece of notebook paper for the patient to take home.

Sarah has done some testing to see if their clinic is prominent in internet search results. Typing in a typical combination of keywords, namely the type of service and a location – 'physiotherapy Bournemouth' – she finds that the clinic does not currently feature in the top three or four results – which are ads. Rather, Remedy appears on the second page of clinic listings. She does notice that In Touch (a rival physiotherapy business) tends to appear in the top couple of results. She has also seen that this business runs a small ad in the weekly *Gazette* newspaper, simply showing its name and the range of ailments it can treat. Sarah mulls over this informal competitive intelligence as she checks her phone for messages or missed calls. Both she and Josh have two or three missed calls each evening, but they are both busy people, tired by the end of the day and needing a bit of downtime after 7.00 p.m. She feels if people really want to contact them, they will call back. They both think it would be nice to get back into a bit of sport sometime soon or get more involved in the community. They used to play tennis, and attend a gym, but at present they are a little preoccupied with their business planning for such things.

The Brightstones are an attractive couple. People who meet them often say that Josh reminds them of a young Tom Hardy and Sarah resembles Kate Winslet. Moreover, they are personable, with a pleasant manner which puts acquaintances and clients at their ease. Friends often comment that they are photogenic, exuding an air of warmth but also capability. Both interact well with patients and are skilled professionals. Sarah has a particular interest and ability relating to injuries, while Joshua has an unusual capability for dealing with longer-term debilitating problems such as arthritis and joint stiffness (for example in the neck vertebrae). For a time after her graduation Sarah ran a Pilates class and enjoyed doing it immensely, as did her clientele.

Both Josh and Sarah are curious, intellectual and voracious readers. Both are currently investigating various aspects of running a successful small business and they are looking at the effect of logos, also known as brand identity or distinctive brand assets. They have learned that incorporating a logo along with the name of the brand or business makes advertising more efficient. This works by making the brand name more memorable, by exposing people to multiple pieces of information (brand name and logo for example), compared to name alone. In other words, two bits of visual brand information work better than one. The logo also becomes a visual memory 'hook' that makes it a bit more likely that people will remember seeing previous communication for the brand. This is a good thing, as generally, research has shown that familiarity is reassuring to consumers. Sarah finds this material fascinating, and she feels it would all be useful for their longer-term plans, which are to open and manage several other clinics in the region over the next five years. Sarah feels that one day she would like to spend three-quarters of her time being a manager and might possibly even enrol in an MBA in years

(Continued)

(Continued)

to come. The learning she is undertaking about broader business issues is all good background for that long-term plan. Just the other day she picked up an interesting nugget of knowledge, which was that it is very desirable to spread media spending evenly across time – this is a way to get more reach per dollar of spend and minimise undue frequency of exposure. As well, to spread spending out across media, which likewise enhances reach.

Joshua is also trying to understand more about search engine marketing for the clinic. He finds that the average cost per click for health and medical industry providers is approximately £1 per click in the Google search network. However, that cost is an average, which gets progressively cheaper for more specific terms – for a search term like 'physiotherapy' coupled with a local geography such as Bournemouth, the cost per click is approximately £0.50. The 'conversion rate' from clicks to purchasing or becoming a new customer is, he learns, in turn around 1 per cent (0.01) for a service business such as Joshua and Sarah's.

The pair have also wondered about how much vehicle traffic goes past the clinic. Joshua has counted the number of cars that drive past in a 15-minute period on a couple of mornings. He counted approximately 40 cars per quarter hour on a weekday and 30 on a weekend. He was glad to sit for a bit and rest that morning, having done quite a solid session working on loosening the vertebrae in the upper spine of a client in order to help them gain a fuller range of movement, and thereby recover good posture.

Sarah has an acquaintance, Dr Brian Stern at Bournemouth University, who works in student intern-type placements or short-contract employment tasks. Sarah has become interested in how many patients the other clinics in the town have, and how that information could be obtained. She calls Brian and asks him if there is a student who could do some advice and work experience for the clinic. Brian suggests a very smart Finnish exchange student, Olivia Latvala. Olivia has just completed courses in marketing research and marketing analytics and is keen to apply her skills.

Josh has been wondering if the actual changeover period between Mr Bound retiring from the clinic has caused some sort of dramatic drop in patient numbers for the Brightstones – or whether there has simply been a slow decline over time. He asks Olivia if there might be any useful information about this or other aspects of the business on Mr Bound's old computer. Olivia is surprised it even starts up, it is so old – but she does find two years of patient visit information. The Excel file information is supplied via the online resources at study.sagepub.com/dawes. Olivia also finds some notes and receipts for some advertising that Mr Bound paid for in the four weeks of March in each of the previous two years. Apparently, he paid for a small ad each week in the *Gazette* in those periods, at a cost of £200 each. She manually taps in the patient visit numbers from when the Brightstones took over, which was several weeks ago.

Bournemouth is home to two local newspapers, the *Gazette* and the *Observer*. Both are published weekly. While readership of paper-printed newspapers has dramatically declined in most Western countries, in towns such as Bournemouth readership was still high, with the *Gazette* having around 20 per cent of the adult population reading it in any given week and the same for the Observer. Readership is higher (at about 25 per cent) among people aged 50+. Both newspapers also publish online, with engagement approximately equivalent to their paper readerships. They offer advertising in both the paper and online versions. A small advert (1/8 page, or equivalent on-screen) in either paper cost approximately £200. That is, £200 will buy an ad in the paper newspaper *or* the online one.

Marketing Plan Case Study: Internal Analysis Work Tasks

Past Performance

Task

The Brightstones pay rent, electricity and other consumables each week. The case presents the average price for an initial and repeat appointment paid by each patient. Calculate how much revenue they are currently making per week given the current number of customers in the last week as reported in the case (with all customers currently being repeat customers) before expenses. And then, how much of that money remains after expenses.

How to Do It

Use Table 3.4. Take the number of customers the Remedy clinic had last week and multiply that by the price of a repeat consult. Deduct rent, electricity and the figure for 'various other expenses' mentioned.

TABLE 3.4 *Remedy's Current Financial Situation*

1	Number of patients last week	
2	Cost of repeat consult	$
3	Revenue from patients last week (row 1 multiplied by row 2)	$
4	Rent per week	$
5	Electricity cost per week	$
6	Consumables and internet per week	$
7	Left over after expenses (row 3 minus rows 4, 5 6)	$

Task

Is there evidence that patient numbers for the clinic dropped markedly between the time Mr Bound passed it onto the Brightstones, or was there just a decline over time? Then consider the marketing implications of your finding.

How to Do It

Olivia, the marketing intern, extracted some data from the clinic's old computer. Open the Excel file supplied via the online resources at study.sagepub.com/dawes. First, create a *line chart* of patient visits. Click on the graph series and request a trend line in Excel.

Label the x-axis with the name of each month. Inspect the actual patient numbers relative to the trend line – does it seem like there was a large drop at the end of the

(Continued)

(Continued)

104 weeks of Mr Bound's ownership? Or are the patient numbers that Sarah and Josh are getting now fairly consistent with the long-term trend.

Lastly, consider the marketing implication of your finding.

Advertising Media Audit

Task

What is the cost per 'conversion' from Google search for Remedy Physiotherapy?

What this term means is, how much money does one have to spend to acquire a new customer (on average) from this medium?

How to Do It

Find these figures from the case:

- The cost per click of a Google search term for a physiotherapy clinic in Bournemouth.
- The conversion rate from clicking on a search term to actually purchasing. This figure is a percentage. A percentage of, say, 2 per cent would be expressed as 0.02 in the following calculation.

Enter these figures in Table 3.5.

TABLE 3.5 *Cost Per Click, Conversion, Imputed Reach Cost*

1	Cost per click of Google search for keywords such as 'Bournemouth' and 'physiotherapy'	
2	Conversion rate from clicking (i.e. % of non-client clickers who become a client)	
3	Cost per conversion (row 1 divided by row 2)	
4	Imputed reach cost per 1,000 (all those who see, including those who do/do not click) – as per instructions below	

To calculate row 3 in Table 3.5, divide the conversion rate (row 2) into the cost per click in row 1. Hint: the answer should be somewhere between £40 and £60. If you want to work in pounds sterling use the figure £0.50 for row 1, which means ½ of one pound sterling. Remember you're dividing row 2 into row 1, not multiplying.

Consider, is customer acquisition 'profitable' via this medium, given the price of an initial consult? Does this profitability depend on the average number of repeat consults? Consider that there is a beneficial exposure effect from search as well.

Lastly, calculate row 4, the imputed reach from paid search. What this means is, we work backwards from the number of people who see and click, to work out the number who see and *don't* click as well. If Josh and Sarah pay £0.50 for a click, but only 1 in 100 click, then for their £0.50 they get 100 views. If you multiply that cost by 10, you get the cost per 1,000 views.

This figure is now able to be compared to the figures for news media or other activity that reaches potential buyers. Of course, impressions from search engine results that people do not click on are likely to be fairly fleeting; but the same can be said for news media ads.

Advertising Media Audit

Task

How many people will read one or the other local newspapers (print or online) in a given weekly period?

Assuming all the people who read the newspaper either print or online will see an ad in that paper, what is the cost per thousand for these local newspapers/online newspapers? Cost per thousand is a standard advertising industry measure for assessing media efficiency. Note what we are really calculating here is cost per 1,000 for an opportunity to see or OTS, because not everyone reads every page or every story.

How to Do It

First, go back and ascertain the total population of Bournemouth from early in the case.

Next, we are going to use a bit of information from the external environment part of the case, specifically the market audit. Use Table 3.6.

TABLE 3.6 *Population Splits*

Age	% of Bournemouth Population (Adds to Less than 100% Because Under 10 Omitted)
10 to 19	9
20 to 29	15
30 to 39	13
40 to 49	15
50 to 59	12
60 to 69	13
70 and over	13
Weighted avg.	–

From the total Bournemouth population figure, and the Table 3.6 population splits, calculate rows 1 and 2 in the news readership/viewing table, Table 3.7.

Then enter into Table 3.7 the figures for rows 3 and 4 from the case information. Then calculate rows 5 and 6. Find the cost figure for row 7. Finally calculate the cost per 1,000 people for an ad in one of the papers, row 8, following the instructions.

Task

Is there evidence that news media advertising in the past for the clinic has had a short-term beneficial effect on patient visits?

Is it likely that there is a long-term beneficial effect for the clinic from this advertising?

(Continued)

(Continued)

TABLE 3.7 *News Readership/Viewing*

1	Number of adults aged 20 to 49 in Bournemouth
2	Number of adults aged 50 and over in Bournemouth
3	Proportion of adults aged 20 to 49 in Bournemouth that read one of the weekly newspapers (print or online) in a week – from the case
4	Proportion of adults aged 50 and over in Bournemouth that read one of the weekly newspapers (print or online) in a week – from the case
5	Number of adults aged 20 to 49 that read one of the weekly newspapers (print or online) in a week
6	Number of adults aged 50 and over that read one of the weekly newspapers (print or online) in a week
7	Cost for 1/8 page ad in either print or online news
8	Cost per 1,000 OTS for 1/8 page ad (first, divide the total adults that read the newspaper by 1,000; then divide that figure into the cost of the ad). This figure should be between £5 and £10. Note this cost per thousand is for *one* newspaper, in either print or online.

How to Do It

There are many ways to do this, some of them could use quite complex statistical analysis. We do something fairly simple here. Open the accompanying Excel file that is available via the online resources at study.sagepub.com/dawes.

First, calculate the average number of patient visits in the weeks that Mr Bound had bought advertising space, for last year and the year before last. Then compare them to the weeks just before, and just after advertising. While there is a downward trend in the data, it is not so severe that we cannot compare one month with an adjacent month. The narrative in Table 3.8 will help you complete this task – calculate and insert the required figures for Table 3.8.

TABLE 3.8 *Patient Visits in Periods before, during and after Advertising*

		Year Before Last	Last Year	Average of the Two Years
1	Average patient visits per week Feb (before advertising)			
2	Average patient visits per week Mar (during advertising)			
3	Average patient visits per week Apr (just after advertising)			
	Is there an apparent short-term effect of advertising on patient visits?			

Note, of course this analysis is only ascertaining the possible short-term effects of advertising on patient visits, which are probably mostly initial visits. Research indicates that if one can see short term ad effects, it is more likely there are long-term ones.

Incorporate this analysis and the conclusions from it into your plan.

Resources and Capabilities Audit

Task

How many vehicles drive past the clinic on an average day and in a week?

How to Do It

From the case, take the passing-vehicles figures per quarter-hour and multiply the weekday and weekend figures by 4 to get hourly, then by 8 or 6 (conservative, assuming traffic flow for only 8 hours per weekday, 6 for weekends) for a daily figure. Add up the figures to get a one-week estimate, step out your calculations in Table 3.9.

TABLE 3.9 *Traffic Flow*

1	Vehicles driving past per quarter hour on a weekday	
2	Vehicles driving past per quarter hour on a weekend-day	
3	Vehicles per weekday (row 1 multiplied by 4, then by 8)	
4	Vehicles per weekend-day (row 2 multiplied by 4 then by 6, assuming traffic flow occurs for fewer hours on weekend)	
5	Vehicles per week = row 3 result multiplied by 5, plus row 4 result multiplied by 2	

The answer in row 5 of Table 3.9 is for total vehicles passing by in a week. Arguably, each vehicle has an opportunity to see the Brightstones' clinic; what we could call total exposures. However, total exposures is not the same as *reach* – reach means the total number of unique people exposed to a message. Because many of the vehicles passing by are the same people, reach is considerably less than total exposures. Arguably, in this instance reach in a week might be around 50 per cent of total exposures. Of course, vehicles often have more than one person in them so this could counterbalance the effect of exposure to the same people. For the purposes of the case, let's be conservative and consider that 'passer-by reach' in a week is 50 per cent of total exposures. Over a month, the figure is the weekly figure multiplied by 3 (not 4).

Next, consider the marketing implication of what you have found.

Marketing Plan Case Study: Internal Analysis Template

Use the following template to construct your internal analysis for Remedy Physiotherapy. Note that the suggested content in each section is condensed, refer to the relevant section in the book for full details.

Context Statement

A short summary of the nature of the business and its key challenges.

Resources and Capabilities Audit

Resources

Identify the principal resources the business has, and what they mean for the business.

Include the traffic flow calculations in this section.

Capabilities

Identify the principal capabilities the business has, and what they mean for the business.

Past Performance

Include the table of the current financial situation in this section.

Include the graph of patient visits over time in this section.

Product Audit

Goods/services offered, and their quality or performance, contextualised in terms of what competitors offer.

Channel Audit

The channels by which buyers buy the category, as well as the specific channels the firm uses.

Pricing Audit

Pricing levels, contextualised in terms of what competitors offer.

Advertising Media Audit

The media by which buyers can be reached, whether they are currently used or not.

Include the cost per click, conversion and imputed reach cost in this section.

Include the news readership/viewing calculations in this section.

Include the patient visits in periods before, during and after advertising in this section.

Advertising Content Audit

The ways in which the business currently describes or represents itself.

Business Relationships Audit

Business partners that are important to marketing effort and outcomes.

Key Issues

Identify other relevant points not picked up in the other sections.

CHAPTER

4 The Global Environment Analysis

The external analysis starts with what is called environmental scanning. This involves looking at the wider environment, things that are occurring in the world that have some implication for the business. The word scanning simply means looking and noting. The goal of this activity is to answer the question: what are the most important things going on in the wider world that will affect our market and our business? Will these factors collectively mean our market is going to grow, stay stable or decline? Are there certain parts of the total market that will benefit from or be challenged by these changes?

The term for this level of analysis in most books on planning for the wider environment is the global, or macro, environment (different writers use different terms, but they both mean the same thing). There are six factors to consider in the global environment – demographic, economic, social-cultural trends, technological, environmental/natural resources and lastly political-legal. The key to doing this analysis well is to identify things that are occurring, or trending, or existing in these environment factors that will impact on the business – and we do this by using the logical link 'which means that …'. For example, take a small maker of vitamins in New Zealand. If the NZ$ is forecast to increase, we would say under economic factors, 'the NZ$ is forecast to increase relative to the US$, which means that import prices of competitor products will decrease'. Or perhaps the AU$ is not forecast to increase but is forecast to stay low relative to the US$. In this case the macro environment factor isn't going to change, but the fact that it is at a certain level or has already decreased is significant to our marketing planning. Of course, we still need to derive what the implication is for the business, using 'which means that …'.

One goal of doing this environmental scanning is to understand if the whole industry will grow, and at what rate, in the coming year. If the business can get a good sense that the industry will grow at, say, 3, 5 or 8 per cent it is in a better position to know if it can grow at those rates. A second goal is to understand what specific impacts these changes will have on the business, not just the whole industry. One change might hit certain firms in the same industry much harder than others. Also, it could be that a particular global environment change means that certain of the firm's products, or product-markets, might face increased demand, while others face decreased demand. For example, during the Covid-19 pandemic in 2020–21, a fast-food restaurant chain might find dining-in sales decreased significantly, while take-out sales (including Uber Eats or Deliveroo deliveries) increased. The reason is that many people were reluctant to go into public spaces such as restaurants and preferred to stay home (but still wanted the good taste and appeal of fast food). Adept marketers quickly focused on promoting the qualities of the firm's home delivery and to linking the brand to home consumption.

DEMOGRAPHIC

Demographics are defined as the composition or characteristics of a population. A population (say, the citizens of a country) can be described in terms of the average and distribution of age, gender, income levels, occupations and education levels (among others). Analysing or scanning demographic factors would entail identifying trends or changes in these areas that potentially have an impact on the industry and/or the business itself. An example is the trend to smaller families (i.e. not just fewer children, but more single-parent families or families living in two homes, one parent in one and the other living separately, with children shuttling between). This slow, but important trend has implications for industries such as: home builders/land developers; car makers, as well as employers. We have all heard the story that the population in many countries is ageing – this is true, but what is talked about less is what it might mean for various businesses. In countries like the UK, Australia and New Zealand, as with many other countries, the population is getting older on average, and wealthier on average – due to government policies that mandate a proportion of people's salary goes into superannuation for use later in life; as well as higher wages. This means we will have a steadily larger, older, richer segment of the population. They have a different outlook on life from previous generations – interested in travel, fitness, health and the 'good life'. Demand for products and services that accommodate these desires is growing.

The often-cited point about the population ageing is relevant to highlight the fact that some trends are occurring very slowly and this one has already occurred to a great extent. So not only is the population ageing, it is old already. In the UK, for example, 17 per cent of citizens are aged over 65 as at 2019 (see www.populationpyramid.net/united-kingdom/2019/). This means there is a big market for goods and services that are useful or demanded by older people. But of course, older people don't buy completely different goods and services from younger people – they represent a sizeable chunk of the customer base of most brands or businesses.

Key question: What broad-based demographic trends are occurring that are relevant to our industry or our business, and how are they impacting it?

ECONOMIC

In this section, we assess the potential impact of various economic factors. This suite of factors includes level of GDP growth and forecast growth for the next year: essentially, is the general economy doing well or is it in a downturn? Next, the exchange rate and what it might be expected to do over the coming year. If the country's currency devalues compared to the US$, then imports become more expensive and exports become cheaper and hence more competitive. Of course, a lower local currency is not necessarily all good news for exporters because they may still have to import raw material or services inputs to their business, and these inputs will be more expensive. There are numerous other economic factors to consider, including employment levels and growth, wages growth, disposable income, tax rates and interest rates. If interest rates rise, this lowers household disposable income and makes housing less affordable. As with the other aspects of environmental scanning, the key is to figure out how a trend or aspect of the environment impacts the business, using the logical phrase 'which means that ...' (Corkindale et al., 1996).

An example of the use of this phrase is: 'The number of Indian inbound tourists is growing and projected to grow further, which means that there will be increased demand for accommodation, domestic flights, hospitality and attendance at domestic tourist destinations over the next few years'. Of course, this is a general example that is leaving aside the obvious dent in 2021 figures that would have occurred due to the Covid-19 pandemic.

Key question: What economic trends or events are occurring that are relevant to our industry or our business, and how are they impacting it?

SOCIAL/CULTURAL

Social/cultural trends refers to the way people choose to live their lives, what they consider to be important, their 'outlook' or how they think about things, and their behaviour such as general tastes or preferences.

Examples of social/cultural trends are that there is a higher degree of embracing alternative medicinal therapies, more interest in the source and methods used to produce food, a slowly growing attitude against animals as a food source, massively increased levels of communication with each other via text and social media, and in some cases raised acceptance of multiculturalism but in others the polar opposite. Other such trends include a higher preparedness to exercise by over 50s, and that in general, people eat out a lot more than in the past (aside from the 2020–21 Covid-19 effect). Consumers are generally more informed now than in the past, and this, in addition to increased wealth, makes them more discerning. Another example is the increased ownership of pets such as dogs, and a heightened feeling that the pet is part of the family. This feeling is in contrast to the past where pets were still beloved but considered more of 'an animal' than one of the family. There are considerable implications for pet food makers, as well as producers of pet medicine, toys, clothing and so on – this socio-cultural trend is underpinning growth and premiumisation in the pet industry.

Another very intriguing socio-cultural trend occurring around the world is growing levels of lactose intolerance. In addition to that, more people now believe that non-dairy products are better for their health. This trend is helping to drive growth in non-dairy drinks such as oat and soy milk. Therefore, many food manufacturers are investing in alternatives to traditional dairy products. In turn this is driving a boom in the growing and production of the raw materials for oat milk, soy milk, rice milk and so on. The longer-term growth for the traditional, cow-based dairy sector – and the constellation of suppliers to it – is less optimistic.

Key question: What social-cultural trends are relevant to our industry, or our business, and how are they impacting it?

What if Trends Move in Different Directions? Example: Krispy Kreme

Sometimes one trend seems to move in the opposite direction to another. For example, in many countries there is a growing interest in health and wellbeing, alongside an obesity epidemic. This apparent paradox might be confusing. Suppose you are a retailer considering building a big new store to make and sell donuts. An analysis of social/cultural trends might tell you that consumers are moving to healthier lifestyles and are more informed about the composition and sources of the foods they eat. This means products with health benefits and transparency in production will become more popular. And based on that, you might decide not to build a massive new donut store (with production facility) costing nearly $10 million. Donuts are hardly health food, so investing in a donut store would be going against the 'healthy' trend! But consider that Krispy Kreme has built a new flagship mega-store in New York's Times Square, complete with a donut glaze waterfall and the world's largest 'HOT' light, indicating hot doughnuts are being made at any hour (Abesamis, 2019). And indications are it will be a massive success. Therefore, while marketers need to follow and understand trends, a trend such as consumers moving to healthier lifestyles doesn't mean the market for donuts can't still grow. Or that a donut brand can't markedly expand its sales by making big investments in physical availability. In fact, Krispy Kreme, by building this fantastic store in one of the most prime pieces of real estate on earth, is building mental availability as well since so many people – residents and the hundreds of thousands of visitors to New York as well as those who see the news stories about the store – will see it.

TECHNOLOGICAL

News reports constantly tell us about new advances in technology and what they might mean for business and consumers. Many of these advances relate to the internet. For example, the explosion of social media use, or web-facilitated e-commerce, or the ease of search-and-comparison. But technological changes or trends that are relevant for marketing do not all necessarily relate to the internet. For example, a new printing technology or an improvement in database systems or email marketing software might be relevant for a packaged goods producer or retailer. Another example is that the ability to sell fresh fish was hugely advanced by new technology in vacuum sealing, which meant fresh fish could last for longer in stores or in consumers' refrigerators. This advance had very positive implications for fish product marketers, wholesalers and retailers. While the marketing team aren't likely to be in charge of packaging technology for a firm, they may be the ones to identify how this change could influence buyer behaviour, how it could be capitalised on, and how the benefits could be communicated to channels and end consumers.

There can also be technological changes that themselves do not relate directly to marketing, but they might impact on consumer behaviour, which then does create a potential impact on the marketing activities of a firm. An example is that the advent of smart pay options means that customers rarely need to go to, or talk to, their bank. Or get cash out at an ATM. In the past, many of a bank's customers would go to, or into, one of its branches quite regularly to get cash out and do things like pay in cheques. We hardly do that anymore. This means that organisations such as banks have a completely different level of personal interaction with their customers than in the past. And therefore have less direct knowledge about their opinions or needs.

Another example is the improvements in security for purchasing and paying for goods online. Encryption and smartphone payment systems make it easier for consumers (or businesses) to purchase online. In turn, this ease presents many opportunities for businesses in that if they can reach people with a message or have their product at least looked at by a potential buyer, the task of purchasing by the buyer is very easy.

Key question: What technology trends are relevant to our industry or our business, and how are they impacting it?

ENVIRONMENTAL/NATURAL RESOURCES

In this section we list relevant changes in the natural environment. As an example, suppose an adverse weather event affects certain crops. A poor coffee harvest will mean that coffee prices will rise significantly, which has implications for manufacturers, wholesalers and retailers. Indeed, adverse weather can affect an entire geographic region, depressing general demand. A long drought in a region can have other effects too, such as water restrictions and increased demand for water recycling equipment, rainwater tanks and artificial lawns. Another example is shortages of raw materials (say, a shortage of lithium due to escalating demand), which impacts on costs and prices of various goods that use batteries.

In many cases there are environmental or natural resource changes or trends that require two levels of reaction. One is a reaction at the business or corporate level. The second is a role for marketing to identify consumer sentiment around the issue and formulate communications about it. Here are two examples:

> **Example 1**: It is revealed that tuna fishing is unfortunately killing many dolphins. There is a business-level reaction, namely a producer of canned tuna alters its sourcing policies so that its raw material will be dolphin-friendly, meaning that it only buys from suppliers who can verify they do not kill dolphins in their fish catches. Then there is a role for marketing, namely that the marketing team designs new packaging and advertising content to inform retailers and consumers, and other stakeholders such as the media, that the firm now has dolphin-friendly tuna. It may also be the case that the marketing team has prompted the business-level change, discerning this is a 'hot topic' among consumers and requires action.

> **Example 2**: In many countries around the world, certain regions experience long periods of drought. This can mean water shortages or restrictions, and lowered farm output. Among the many consumer reactions could be heightened demand for low-flow showers, reduced-capacity toilets, and water recycling systems or rainwater harvesting. For many companies directly involved in these industries, these conditions can mean sales growth – for manufacturers of water recycling systems, droughts can mean buoyant business. These expectations would be factored directly into their marketing plans. For retailers, these conditions might mean they expect to sell more of some items, and less of others (fewer lawn sprinklers or lawn seed, for example). These changes have implications for the retailer's purchasing department, but also for which products to feature prominently in the retailer's advertising. More broadly, an event such as a drought means reduced demand for all sorts of agricultural products from seeds, to

farm equipment. And more broadly again, companies in general might discern that an event or circumstance such as a drought is relevant because it is in the consumer psyche at the present time. For example, a bank or a telecommunications provider might use portrayals of the drought (or whatever the circumstance happens to be – floods or unusually icy weather) in its advertising because it is a relevant condition in people's minds at the present time.

Key question: What environmental or natural resource trends are relevant to our industry or our business and how are they impacting it?

POLITICAL/LEGAL

Changes in government policy or legislation can have very significant impacts on entire industries, and on all the players or on specific businesses. An Australian example is that the government wanted to promote household use of solar panel electricity generation, so it offered to purchase the electricity generated by rooftop solar panels for quite high prices. This led to an explosion in demand for solar panels and installation. The scheme was too successful (requiring too much spending by the government), so the government stopped it and the industry crashed for quite some time afterwards. In the period leading up to the cessation of the scheme there was an avalanche of advertising by solar companies saying 'buy now while the rebate still applies'. This is a classic case of marketing activity being shaped by political forces.

Another example is a government enquiry into the Australian banking sector. This enquiry uncovered shocking cases of mismanagement of client funds, even fraud, conducted by bank staff and managers. In response, many of the large banks endeavoured to run recovery advertising campaigns aimed at repairing their public image. For example, one of the four biggest banks in the market, Westpac, ran an expensive TV advertisement emphasising it was 'helpful', highlighting its association with the Westpac rescue helicopter, which is widely known in Australia. This helicopter has been employed by emergency services for many years to rescue people from accidents such as boats overturning or people falling from cliffs in inaccessible terrain. The TV ad featured David Bowie's 'Heroes' in the soundtrack, highlighting the heroism of the helicopter crew and, by implication, the good nature of Westpac, the funder. Of course, this was not the only reaction by businesses in the sector, but it illustrates an attempt at image repair in response to an adverse external change. Westpac wanted to take attention away from the adverse findings against it and other banks – by showing that it supported the community via this and other activity.

Legal changes that are international in scope can also be highly relevant. For instance, the proposal for the UK to leave the EU, or the US to impose tariffs on China, may have ramifications felt by businesses in many countries. An example relating to Brexit (at the time leading up to the UK leaving the EU) is that manufacturers of spirits in the UK had to consider how to cope with potential tariffs being imposed by European countries for the first time in many decades. Tariffs will push the price of their products up against local European brands, so a marketing challenge is how to manage a brand in the face of tariff-induced higher prices.

Key question: What political-legal trends are relevant to our industry or our business, and how are they impacting it?

PULLING THE GLOBAL ENVIRONMENT ANALYSIS TOGETHER

We've now covered the components of the global environment analysis. The next step is to consider how strong or severe the various events or changes are, and how quickly they are moving. Our priorities are then easier to identify: the forces that are going to have a strong effect and are changing quickly. Our lowest priorities are slow moving, weaker trends or circumstances. The stronger and quicker-moving external changes are the ones that will go into the SWOT – the summary of Strengths, Weaknesses, Opportunities and Threats.

Once the global environment analysis is done, we move on to examine the market environment audit.

Global Environment Analysis

A feature of the UK and indeed the Bournemouth population is that the average age of the population is slowly increasing over time, due to longer lifespans and a fairly low birth-rate over the past 20 years. And indeed, in the UK, as is the case across the world, age is related to illnesses, with the common conditions being heart disease and cancer but also stroke and a host of physical ailments consequently occurring as a result of the debilitating effects of the illness itself, as well as age-related impairments such as reduced mobility, joint pain and so on. For some older people these impairments (as well as poorer eyesight for some) mean they no longer drive and find public transport more difficult to use.

Self-test Question

Take these three industries: fast food (quick service restaurants), smartphones and up-market clothing retail. Identify a relevant trend, change or circumstance in three of the global environment factors for these industries (and by implication for the firms in those industries). Note these trends do not have to be relevant *only* to these industries, they could potentially have widespread effects.

TABLE 4.1 *Global Environment Trends Relevant to*

	Fast Food	Smartphones	Clothing Retail
Economic			
Demographic			
Social-cultural			
Technological			
Environmental/natural resources			
Political/legal			

An apparent paradox in UK population health is that while levels of obesity are increasing, overall interest in health and fitness had increased over the past two decades. Moreover, older people (arbitrarily, people aged 50+) exhibit a heightened interest in maintaining their health and fitness, with higher incidence of participation in organised sports, jogging, countryside walking and attendance at gyms or fitness clubs.

Physiotherapy is available at no cost to patients through the National Health Service, but according to the Chartered Society of Physiotherapists, over the past two years the average waiting time for an NHS physiotherapist has grown from 10 to 13 weeks. Use of private physiotherapy is linked to household income, with wealthier households having a somewhat higher incidence of attending; and periods of economic expansion tend to be favourable for private health practitioners including physiotherapists. By contrast, in periods of economic downturn there tends to be a reduction in the proportion of the population with private health insurance (having private health insurance means that a proportion of the cost of treatments such as physiotherapy is paid for by the insurance company).

The near universal use of smartphones in the population, coupled with the fact that many people seemed almost addicted to their use, is leading to upper spine and neck problems. Apparently, the practice of looking at a small screen with the head craned forward greatly exacerbates the weight of one's head, leading to spinal stress and sore muscles. Even many teenagers in the 2020s have upper spinal curvature and a forward-leaning neck that used to be only associated with people aged over 65.

It is well known that the digital economy has been transformative. However, one downside of the digital economy, particularly for those working in it, such as e-commerce providers and especially small ones who spend their entire days almost glued to a computer screen, is the danger of inadequate ergonomics (poorly planned chair/desk/screen setups) causing RSI injuries (repetitive strain syndrome). A recent UK government study found that RSI complaints were highest among process workers (i.e. people packing goods in a warehouse or processing foodstuffs in a factory) but were also very high among small and owner-operator digital-oriented businesses (such as digital ad agencies, SEO businesses, web designers and so on), with around 10 per cent saying they incurred such problems in any given year.

Technological advances have certainly changed business and buyer behaviour in many ways. One interesting new piece of technology is software that plugs into a firm's website and allows online bookings, showing available times and sending a confirmation text or email to the person booking. Apparently, this software often facilitates sending reminders about bookings, events or other communication about which the business wishes to remind clients. There are at least a dozen brands of such software, priced at about £15 per month for a business with two employees who could log into the system.

While searching for information to inform their plan, Joshua happens to come across the extensive documentation from the UK government rules for advertisements. He is aware that the clinic is not in an area of 'special control of advertisements'. One thing that catches his eye is what is referred to as 'Class 5' signs.

Class 5 gives consent for a wide variety of notices, signs and advertisements to draw attention to any commercial services, goods for sale or any other services available at the premises where the advertisement is being displayed. 'Business premises' means any building in which a professional, commercial or industrial undertaking is being carried out, or where any commercial services are being provided for the public. This term includes: office buildings, banks and building societies, shops and shopping arcades, supermarkets and hypermarkets, theatres, cinemas and dance halls, bingo halls and amusement arcades, vehicle showrooms and garages, privately owned factories and works, restaurants and cafes.

Class 5 is not intended to permit all forms of outdoor advertising on any business premises; it only permits advertisements for the goods or services available at the particular premises. This means advertisements which refer to:

- the business or other activity at the premises
- the goods for sale or the services available
- the name and qualifications of the firm or person providing the service in the premises.

An advertisement permitted by Class 5 must not:

- have any letters, figures, symbols or similar features in the design over 0.75 of a metre in height, or 0.3 of a metre in height if they are in any Area of Special Control of Advertisements
- have its highest part at more than 4.6 metres above ground-level, or 3.6 metres in any Area of Special Control of Advertisements
- have its highest part above the level of the bottom of the first-floor window in the wall where the advertisement is
- be illuminated, unless the illumination is intended to indicate that medical or similar services or supplies are available at the premises
- if the premises are in any Area of Special Control of Advertisements [note, the Remedy clinic was not in one of these], exceed in area 10 per cent of the external face of the building, measured up to a height of 3.6 metres above ground-level.
- if the business premises is a shop, an advertisement may be displayed only on an external wall which has a shop window in it. (Department for Communities and Local Government, 2007)

The Covid-19 crisis in 2020–21 caused widespread sickness and death and dramatic drops in economic activity around the world. One longer-lasting consequence of the pandemic is a heightened sensitivity by people to the apparent cleanliness and health safety of premises and people. To a greater extent than before, consumers expect service providers to be very attentive to concerns such as cleaning of equipment, clean personal appearances of service personnel and tidy premises (which they take as a cue for sanitisation).

Task

List out trends, changes or occurrences in each aspect of the global environment, and for each, state what they mean for Remedy using the logical phrase ‘which means that …’ or something similar.

Marketing Plan Case Study: Global Environment Analysis Template

Use the following template to construct your global environment analysis for Remedy Physiotherapy. Note that the suggested content in each section is condensed; refer to the relevant section in the book for full detail.

Demographic Audit

Demographic trends and what they mean for the business.

Economic Audit

Economic trends and what they mean for the business.

Socio-cultural Audit

Socio-cultural trends and what they mean for the business.

Technological Audit

Technological trends and what they mean for the business.

Environmental/Natural Resources Audit

Environmental trends and what they mean for the business.

Political/Legal Audit

Political/legal trends and what they mean for the business.

Once these audits are complete it will be useful to identify which of them pose the most significant consequences, or which are the fastest moving. These will then be the priorities to address in the plan.

CHAPTER 5 The Market Environment Analysis

After doing the global environment analysis, we turn closer to home. We examine our specific market (in some other books this could be called industry), then our customers and competitors. Again, we are looking for trends, occurrences or events that are relevant for the business, which might make it easier or harder to reach its goals.

MARKET AUDIT

Before auditing our market, we need to be clear on what market we are in!

Market Definition

Many firms will have a very clear idea about what they consider their market to be. However, for others a question that can immediately arise is, what market are we actually in? Take the example of a maker of organic orange juice, which sells to retail stores. Is it in the organic orange juice market? That certainly seems likely, but of course it is defining its market in terms of the product it makes. The problem of defining a market in this way was written about long ago in a classic article called 'Marketing myopia' by Levitt (1960). Levitt argued that firms in many industries defined their market in terms of the products they offered (while ignoring the *need* they were satisfying) and when those products became obsolete, they went out of business. Examples were buggy-whip makers and the US railroads (the latter still exist but the industry was overtaken by the advent of the motor car and airplane). Returning to the juice maker, it could define its market more broadly – orange juice, recognising that its organic juice probably is a close substitute for regular juice; but what about the market for (any sort of) juice? Or cold drinks in general, or beverages? This example shows it is not necessarily clear how widely to specify one's market or category.

A way to overcome this quandary is to use a simple framework as shown in Table 5.1. The examples are based on what the organic orange juice maker might answer, and for contrast, a bank or credit union. The end result from using this framework is that the business has a clearer definition of its market: for instance, it offers organic orange juice to refresh thirst, its customers are general consumers, in city X, and it sells to those consumers via retail stores. And it decides that relevant substitutes for its particular product are orange juice and fruit juice more broadly (not say, carbonated juice drinks or carbonated soft drinks in general). Of course, these can be revised over time if, for instance, the business chooses to broaden its product range, or expand its geographic scope.

TABLE 5.1 *Market Definition Framework*

Need being satisfied	State the customer need here, for example 'refreshment, thirst relief' or 'managing money'
Technology or product used to satisfy the need	Identify the technology or way in which the customer need is being satisfied, for example 'organic orange juice' or 'retail branch network, internet account management'
Buyer type	Identify the broad buyer class, for example 'consumers' or 'businesses'
Geography served	The local geographic area served, such as a city, region, country or worldwide
Channels	Direct to buyers or via specified intermediaries (retail stores, brokers)
Relevant substitutes for our product	Bottled orange juice, fruit juice. For a bank, these could be: credit unions, mortgage brokers, tech financiers such as Afterpay

In the market audit, we consider factors such as the size of the market, price levels, growth rate and major changes or events that have occurred recently. Put simply: how big is it, how fast is it growing, are there parts of it growing more quickly than others? What sort of prices are typically charged, are prices buoyant or under pressure to drop – if so, why? And so on.

Many books and indeed university courses in business or marketing planning prescribe the use of a famous tool called the 'Five forces industry analysis' (Porter, 1979). This book does not endorse that tool or encourage its use. In the author's experience, the use of this tool rarely leads to any particular insight that could not be gained by just assembling information on the industry and thinking about what it means. But we can consider the industry using some of the concepts that Porter used, which came from a branch of economics called IO, short for Industrial Organisation (Bain, 1968). The focus of this area of economics is the performance of businesses in an industry, which is believed to be the outcome of their conduct, which in turn is driven by the structure of the industry – barriers to entry and industry concentration. In short, the IO 'school of thought' will look at industries with few players and higher barriers to entry and will deduce that the structure leads to the entry barriers. In turn these high barriers mean there will be only a few incumbent firms. This can lead to collusion or at least some implicit co-operation among the incumbents to drive prices higher, or to refrain from robust competition. The end result is high levels of profitability for firms in the industry.

For example, the home mortgage market in Australia is dominated by what are called the 'Big 4' banks – they collectively have approximately 80 per cent of the lucrative home mortgage market (note, no suggestion is being made of improper conduct in this industry, it is used merely as an example of high entry barriers). This situation has persisted over decades despite the concerted efforts of smaller players to get more of a slice of this market.

The reason for the dominance of the Big 4 in Australia is their overwhelming mental and physical availability. First, almost all Australians already have a bank account with one of these players, so when they come into the market for a home loan or mortgage, that bank has quite a good chance of being at least considered by that consumer for purchase. In addition, they have a huge branch network, as well as having relationships with many of the leading home loan brokers that exist. In other words, it actually takes some effort to avoid at least talking to or evaluating one of the Big 4 banks for this type of product. The point of this example is to illustrate the idea of analysing market structure in one's marketing plan. It could be argued that a small player in mortgages considers two markets – the 80 per cent that is entrenched with the Big 4, and the remaining 20 per cent, which is more contested among smaller competitors.

A similar situation is in the UK, where the Big 6 banks – namely Barclays, HSBC, Lloyds, RBS, Nationwide and Santander – account for 70 per cent of mortgages. While there is certainly very active competition in this sector in the UK, the massive size and spending power of these institutions makes it difficult for new players to enter, which in turn means the incumbents can be very profitable. Note, Santander is a comparatively new brand in the UK, but it was formed from well-established building societies and other financial services players. The Big 6 preserve their profitability by spending on advertising and physical availability to make it difficult for smaller competitors to grow. As we saw at the start of the book, a spectre for these big banks is new technology that could sidestep their physical availability advantage.

Another key question to ask in the market audit is whether there are clearly defined factors that the market derives its demand from. For example, the pet food market is growing well in many countries because pet ownership is growing (and incomes are rising, so people can afford to buy high-quality pet food). Or, take the example of car tyres: demand for car tyres is clearly derived from the number of cars and people's travel habits. More cars on the road means more demand for tyres, both in the original equipment market and replacements. If we know that market demand for our product is derived from some other long-term factor – and we have a good idea that *that* factor is expected to keep growing reasonably well, then we know demand for our market is healthy in the medium term.

Key question: What aspects of our market or industry have most impact on our firm's ability to compete and grow?

CUSTOMER AUDIT

There are five key questions for this section.

Who Buys?

Who Buys This Product Category?

Or put another way, what are the distinguishing characteristics of category buyers? In many cases the answer might be, 'everyone over 10 years old'. In other cases, category buyers might be a sharply defined subset of the population (say, women over 30, men over 50). Indeed, in many cases buyers might be defined by their occupation and employer, for example if one sells surgical equipment the buyers are surgeons or hospital purchasing officers; or in the case of selling market research the buyers are marketing professionals, or market research/insights managers.

Who Buys Our Brand?

Next, we want to check who buys our brand – are they any different from the general category buyer, and in what ways? Understanding these differences can yield some insights into why or how the brand performs as it does. Note that we generally do not expect a brand's buyer base to be very different from the rest of the category (i.e. competitors!) – well, direct competitors anyway (Uncles et al., 2012). But sometimes there can be some differences, for example a research project the author undertook for a financial services provider showed its client base tended to be a bit more 'blue collar' (working class) and a bit lower-income than the population generally. This insight helped the business to understand why it underperformed in home loans – the types of people that were its clients were also a bit less likely to get/have a home loan.

Some marketers get enthusiastic about the idea of analysing who buys their brand to the point of creating what are called 'personas'. A persona is an idealised profile of a person, with specified characteristics. A fantastic example of this is shown in the PBS documentary *The Persuaders*. A marketing team tasked with the job of creating a new airline, Song, as a subsidiary of Delta, created a persona for what they believed was the idealised Song customer. They even gave the persona a name: Carrie. The marketing director described Carrie's characteristics:

> [Carrie and her husband] have an SUV and a sports car … She has a Nieman Marcus credit card but shops at Target. She has a propensity to read high end literature but finds guilty pleasure in reading *People* magazine … and she doesn't have an airline. (PBS, 2004)

As well, the Song team labelled Carrie with market research indices, such as scoring highly on 'downhill skiing … kickboxing … yoga … museums … first to try new products' (PBS, 2004).

The problem with this kind of misguided analysis is that only a small fraction of potential buyers could ever be like the persona. And carrying this belief system through the marketing planning process means the business is intentionally ignoring almost everyone who buys the category! As a postscript, Song went broke very quickly.

Why Do They Buy

Why Do They Buy This Category?

Here we try to identify the reasons people buy the product, in other words what uses do they have for it. In many cases the reasons are obvious, for example people buy sliced loaf bread to eat it. But arguably there is scope for further understanding: for example, in which eating situations is sliced bread used most often, and perhaps in what form or for which meals? It used to be extremely popular for breakfast as toast, but breakfast cereal has slowly overtaken it over a period of decades. Sliced bread can be used for sandwiches, toast and many other consumption modes. How much is purchased and used within a day or two, and how much is frozen? How much is used in school lunchboxes, and what are the most common fillings? What other products are bought with bread? Romaniuk and Sharp (2016) refer to the concept of identifying purchasing or consumption situations as 'Category Entry Points' or CEPs.

Another example is personal loans from a bank or credit union – what are the most common purposes? Some people take out loans to go on a holiday – how many? If there were an appreciable number this might be a good message to include in communications about personal loans. Another example is postgraduate university education. What are the principal reasons people undertake graduate diplomas or master's degrees? If one surveyed a sample of people who were intending to do such study the most prominent answers might pertain to a change in career direction, and as a step towards getting a more senior position.

Understanding the most common purchasing/consumption scenarios can help with product planning and communications. And knowing if there are some situations or needs that are becoming more prevalent or less prevalent can also help. Note that asking 'why do they buy the category?' isn't the same thing as asking 'what is important to people?'. Far too much market research and marketing strategy is predicated on the idea that the key piece of information marketers need is 'what is important?'. It is this idea that drives so much of what we call evaluation research – asking buyers to evaluate brands on supposedly important factors. In many cases people can tell us what they think is important, but they may not necessarily understand what influences their behaviour.

Why Do They Buy Our Brand?

Here we try to identify if there is anything in particular about our brand that leads people (or businesses) to buy it. A trap to avoid is to simply think of anything that's specific about the business or brand and say: that's why people buy it. For example, we could be the managers of a high price, organic, local, ecologically responsible skincare brand and pose this question, and echo back the answer: people buy our brand because they want an organic, local, ecologically responsible skincare product and are prepared to pay a high price for it. This could indeed be the case sometimes, but in general buyers pay less attention to the nuances of product features than marketers think. It is dangerously simplistic to think in this way, and it ignores the fact that the principal reason that so many people do not buy a certain brand isn't because it's not what they're looking for, instead it is because they haven't heard of it or haven't noticed it.

The reasons why buyers buy your brand may be extremely simple. Take the example of a suburban hotel on a busy main road. The reason it gets drive-through or bar or dining room clients is: it is located on a busy road and is therefore very visible to a large number of passers-by. Indeed, its location makes it a convenient destination for workers who have finished for the day and want to have a drink before going home. Similarly, it is convenient for passers-by and locals to use the drive-through alcohol store. The pub is very busy on nights in which a nearby entertainment centre has performances (rock bands, musicals), again mostly due to its favourable location. Another example is the case of a party hire company. The reason clients buy from it is that some of them have bought before and they are familiar with it, they know the staff and have learned it offers good service and pricing; new clients buy because the company has enough presence on the internet to come up in some digital search returns, and the brand is passingly familiar enough so that they will peruse its website (as well as looking at one or two others) and decide that the range, prices and service promises are good enough to warrant a purchase.

What Do They Buy?

The answer to 'what is a person buying?' when someone buys, say, a laptop at a retail store is obviously, a laptop. But more broadly the word 'what' pertains to the number of items bought, whether they are bought one at a time or as part of a series of purchases, or whether there are ancillary goods or services purchased at the same time. For example, a laptop purchase might also involve a new case, extended warranty, software and so on. Understanding what other products are bought around the same time as a focal product can give insight into how to promote bundles, and what to say in advertising.

A person 'buys' a doctor's appointment which is a one-off consult, but a person 'buys' a hospital stay, including the bed, personal care, medication and so on – not all necessarily directly decided on by the patient.

A related 'what' question pertains to how many people buy occasion to occasion, versus buying for the next month in advance. For example, some people 'buy' a one-off visit to a swimming pool, others buy a season membership. Suppose we find that 95 per cent of people who come to *our* public pool buy tickets on the day and only 5 per cent buy season tickets. Is there a way we can sell more tickets that are not just for one day? Perhaps people find the season tickets poor value, and we could create a new product – family tickets, or a one-month ticket instead of a season ticket, which better suit customer's needs.

Answering the 'what' question might mean examining what other products people buy when they purchase the product in question. Examples are, airline travel and car hire and travel insurance, or a home insurance policy and content for the same residence.

The reason to investigate what people buy is that it can give insights into what other products your business could easily sell (i.e. a retailer's inventory or a brand adding products to its range). It might also give you an indication of how to frame advertising for your product – showing that product A is ideal for people who have product B.

Understanding the 'what' question can also give insights into better product offerings. An example is that when people buy new bedding, they have heavy, bulky mattresses to dispose of, which is expensive. An insightful solution is for a bedding retailer to offer home delivery of the new mattresses and a free or small-fee disposal of the old ones. This adds attractiveness to the retailer's offer as it solves a problem for the customer.

Products come in various forms and so 'what' is bought can be dissected by product form. For example, dog food is sold (and bought) in small to large cans of wet dog food, which can be sold individually or in 6- and 12-packs, as well as dry dog food, which is generally sold in medium to large bags. Assessing the relative popularity and growth rates by each type of product or product form is essential knowledge, to understand the principal sources of volume, and where the market is growing. Doing this sort of analysis may also give an indication of market gaps – indicating an avenue for a new type of product to tap into a need. For instance, suppose we noted that a large number of people who shop for dog food each week bought two cans of food each time. This might suggest a '2-pack' could find acceptance in the market.

When Do They Buy?

Here one would investigate if there are important factors in buying behaviour such as: seasonality or other time-based purchase triggers. For example, are there peak times of the year when people look for or purchase motor vehicles, or homes. Or perhaps peak days of the week, or time of day. The value of examining this issue is that it can provide insight into when to schedule marketing communications, as well as whether physical availability can be adjusted to correspond with lower or higher demand. For example, if one is in the suit hire business, knowing when the peak demand time for suits occurs (perhaps coinciding with marriage seasonality) would help with timing of marketing communications as well as planning for longer opening hours, more stock, additional staff.

Moreover, the question about *when* do they buy can also include life stages or life events – for example there are life events that put people into the market for insurance (buying a house or car), there are events that put people in the market for legal services (marriage, divorce, bereavement).

How Do They Buy?

Here we examine how the purchase takes place. The sorts of questions to ask here are: is the purchase planned or unplanned? Do buyers take lots of time to consider their choices, and if so? What factors do they consider and from which information sources do they consult? How much pre-purchase information search goes on, and if it does, what form does it take? Knowing the extent of 'shopping around' helps the marketing team get a sense of the value of an enquiry. If on average potential buyers consult or actively evaluate two brands before purchasing, this means that on average, every two active enquiries will result in a sale!

Summarise the Outcomes of This Analysis as Insights

The answers to these customer analysis questions form insights, which in turn can be used or capitalised on in the marketing strategy. For example, we might uncover the *insight* that intending users of allied health services such as physiotherapy often have a preference for the gender of their practitioner, and so a practice run by a male and a female practitioner has an advantage in appeal. This feature could then be emphasised in its communications.

Customer Insights

Key Customer insight 1: ________________________________

Key Customer insight 2: ________________________________

Key Customer insight 3: ________________________________

Are There Distinct Segments in the Market?

After conducting the analysis of who, why, what, when and how, the marketer then writes a section that explains if the firm considers there are specific market segments. In other words, are there groups of people or businesses that have marked enough differences in buying behaviour that make them worth thinking about as separate segments. Note that segmentation is not the same as targeting. Segmenting is merely recognising that there are differences in behaviour across buyers. It recognises that certain groups exist that have commonality in buying behaviour, and those groups are different from other groups. Targeting is deciding what to do about the segmentation. It might be that you identify segments, but choose to do nothing about it, and do not create a different marketing mix for each group. These choices are explained in the following section.

The Concept of Segmentation Explained

The term segmentation confuses many marketers and students. This confusion arises because of two apparently conflicting facts:

- There is overwhelming evidence that competing brands do *not* appeal to different segments, or that there is little difference in the buyer bases of competing brands (Dawes, 2009; Uncles et al., 2012).
- Consumers/buyers *are* different in terms of their needs, wants, preferences and perhaps what influences them. The evidence for this is apparent from everyday observation.

The first point suggests brands do not appeal to different segments, but the second one says there *is* market segmentation. To understand this apparent paradox let's take a step back and consider what the term segmentation means. Segmentation means that there are groups of people (or other entities – organisations, perhaps) in the buying population that have some managerially relevant *difference* in their buying behaviour compared to other groups. If there are some people with very high incomes who can afford cars priced over $100,000, then arguably people on this or higher incomes could represent a segment for motor vehicles. Or some people are car enthusiasts who prize high-performance or vintage cars, and many of them own multiple cars, or are members of car clubs. They are different from the general population, in this regard at least (they might be undistinguishable in any characteristic). Arguably, car enthusiasts then represent a segment for car makers, car sellers, and perhaps insurance companies. The question then turns to whether they can be selectively reached, without incurring the cost of hitting those not in the segment with the message.

Next, take the example of a company that makes built-in wardrobes. It could sell these items to general consumers. But there are other buyers of wardrobes – for example, home builders, who contract out to joinery companies to make these items. The needs and wants, buying behaviour and price sensitivity of home builders is arguably quite different from general consumers. A home builder, particularly a budget-end builder, might be constructing up to 20 homes each month, based on a limited set of plans or designs. It therefore wants its suppliers to make fairly standard wardrobes, at high volume and at low prices (far lower than what consumers would pay). It would negotiate an annual contract with one or two suppliers with little variation in prices from home to home. By contrast, consumers will want to come to a showroom, see the product, get a 'measure and quote', and the final product for each consumer might be somewhat different from others. Here, there are plainly two market segments, consumers and home builders. Both buy broadly the same product, but the needs and wants, and buying behaviour are different or at least manifest in different ways (e.g. both would like a lower price for what they get compared to a higher price, but the price levels the business would charge a builder are very much lower than a consumer would pay). A wardrobe company could readily identify these segments, and choose to target one of them, or both perhaps. Success in the home builder segment might require having sales representatives who build long-term relations with their builder clients; whereas in the consumer segment, while salespeople would be needed they would focus on only one home at a time and would rarely cultivate a relationship with a client. The point is the firm would employ different strategies for the two segments.

Let's now reconcile the apparent paradox from the two points outlined at the start of this section. How can it be that competing brands don't appeal to different segments, when there are segments of buyers in the population?

The answer is, first, when studies talk about a lack of brand segmentation, they are talking about competing brands. Which means we're generally talking about brands that are in roughly similar price and quality levels. So, perhaps the profile of Toyota buyers is actually different from that of Lamborghini car buyers, but they're not really what we'd call competing brands, they are in completely different price and quality levels. It's doubtful a potential buyer would say 'I'm tossing up between a Toyota and a Lamborghini'. And remember for the wardrobe company, there would be other wardrobe companies – some of whom sell to consumers, some to builders, some to both. The user profile of builders who use wardrobe company A isn't likely to be very different from those who use B or C.

Second, buyers in various categories – take cars for example – differ in terms of the specifications they're looking for (small versus large), the price range they want or can afford (probably reflecting income levels) and the specific features and options they like (sports wheels, sunroofs). In other words – segments exist. Those segments might not map onto other identifying characteristics such as age, occupation type, or geographical location, although perhaps income might link to price range and family size probably links with size of car desired. But even then, some people who are on fairly modest incomes spend big on cars!

To accommodate these buyer differences, each car maker makes many versions of cars, or what are called variants. For example, for buyers who want a mid-sized family sedan, Toyota make the Camry, Honda has the Accord, Nissan has the Altima, Mazda has the Mazda 6 and Ford makes the Fusion. For buyers who want a smaller car, all the major car makers produce smaller versions (the Toyota Corolla, the Mazda 3 and so on). Therefore, while there might be car buyer segments (groups of people who want different things) the big car makers produce variants to suit them and those variants are quite similar across brands – so the buyer of a Corolla is hardly likely to be different from the buyer of a Mazda 3.

The next point is that in repeat-purchase markets, like grocery products or fast food or retailing, people buy multiple brands over a period of time. For example, the buyers of Crest toothpaste also buy Colgate. And while someone might survey people about their needs and wants in relation to tooth-care, and develop some potential segments (some people might say fresh breath is their number one concern, others tooth whiteness or decay prevention), if people buy across multiple brands then the users of brand A can't be much different from the users of brand B because many of them are the same people. It could be that some people who really want fresh breath or have sensitive gums represent a segment.

However, they can satisfy that particular need with multiple brands. And while they could be a segment, they can't be selectively reached with marketing communication. You cannot target people who unduly desire fresh breath or have sensitive gums – the only way you could is if they share some media habit like they all watch similar TV shows or go to the same websites, but of course they don't.

This cross-brand purchasing pattern occurs not only in packaged goods – we see the same thing in retail banking (Dawes, 2014) or motor vehicles (Colombo & Sabavala, 2013).

Therefore: segments do exist. But competing brands generally don't appeal to different segments for the reasons above.

Why Then Do We Do Segmentation Analysis?

Despite the fact that directly competing brands do not tend to appeal to markedly different types of buyers, there is still a very good reason to undertake segmentation analysis. This reason is true particularly at the broadest, industry level. In simple terms, we segment an industry to determine which sorts of buyers we are best suited to pursue.

Take the simple example of a firm in the business of transporting goods. It owns a fleet of trucks and, at present, delivers general freight in a Western country from a port city to several other cities in a geographic state such as one the states of the United States; or a country such as France. The goods it delivers are things such as: machinery, timber, steel. It has a general-purpose warehouse, a large loading and unloading yard, forklift trucks, as well as small and large trucks so that it can deliver to various sorts of clients with different payload requirements and premises sizes.

This transportation company is a player in one specific type or sub-category of goods transportation: general freight. It could be quite competitive and do well financially in this business because it has the resources and capabilities to offer clients good service, reliable delivery times, a very low rate of in-transit damage, proper documentation and so on. Its clients include manufacturers, fabricators, primary producers, timber product producers and so on. These clients have quite general, non-specific needs – mostly, they simply need their bulky, heavy goods transported to them in good order without damage.

Perhaps the trucking company now wishes to expand its business. As part of this planning it is considering how it could broaden its operations into other related transportation fields. Therefore, it conducts a segmentation analysis of the transportation of goods industry in its country or geographic state. It quickly finds that this is a very diverse industry, and that there are client types with completely different needs. For example, there are:

- *Fuel companies* – that need liquids such as petrol/gasoline hauled.
- *Food companies* – these companies often have quite time-sensitive requirements so that the produce being transported does not spoil. A subset is food companies that need haulage in refrigerated vehicles. These clients are also highly time sensitive as refrigerated foodstuffs can spoil quickly.
- *Livestock* – these companies need live animals transported from one place to another. The animals require special trailer construction to keep them safe once they are loaded onto a large vehicle.
- *Vehicle companies* – car manufacturers or car dealers need motor vehicles transported from car plants or ports to dealerships. The vehicles need special trailers to keep them immobile and undamaged.

- *Parcel companies* – producers who need small items delivered to businesses and homes. This often involves small vehicles to collect and deliver items to a depot, large vehicles to transport to other depots, and small vehicles from depot to end-destination.

In many cases, the key to being able to offer a competitive solution to the client's requirements is the type of vehicle. But it's more than that – a general freight company that merely bought some particular vehicles to suit a client's requirements would be extremely unlikely to win any business from, say, a food producer because they would also need to show that their drivers had experience and an understanding of food product transport, that their depots were suitable for the storage of foodstuffs and so on. But by understanding the different requirements of these diverse clients – in others words, by segmenting the market – it might be possible for the trucking firm to identify a client type that it could offer a competitive product, perhaps clients who need vehicles hauled are the types of clients that the trucking company is in the best position to be able to satisfy. Once it has *segmented* the market this way it could choose to *target* the companies that need vehicles hauled (car dealers, car manufacturers). At face value it would appear to be feasible to treat these as a distinct client group.

Key question: Are there segments that are important enough for us to consider separately in the marketing plan? *Remember, targeting segments means you have to be able to selectively reach them.* If all category buyers are exposed to your advertising, including segment A, that is not really targeting a segment!

Self-test Question

1. A colleague at work says to you: How can it be that there are segments, yet competing brands don't have quite different buyer types? Explain in your own words.
2. Explain the difference between segmentation and targeting.

COMPETITOR AUDIT

Why do we examine and analyse competitors? There are several reasons. First and most simply is that we can learn from them. Maybe they are doing some things better than us, and by inspecting them closely we can learn from what they do. It can sometimes be the case that small businesses get used to their own limitations to some extent and just accept them. But examining how competitors operate can be extremely enlightening in the sense we could discover: their telephone service is really good compared to ours, or their website functionality is a lot more user-friendly than ours. In turn these open our eyes up to areas for improvement. We might not have considered them if we are not for looking at how competitors do the same sorts of functions. For example, it used to be reported that Japanese car makers would, as soon as an American company launched a new model, immediately order one and dis-assemble it to learn what components embodied desirable new technology or were marked improvements – and if there were any, they would copy them.

Of course, perhaps there are some aspects of our competitors' business that aren't as well done or accomplished as ours. But we can learn from that as well – it's good to know what things we might be better at, and we can reflect on how we came to be better in those areas.

The second main reason to take a close look at competitors is that if we are to grow, it's likely it will be at their expense! A sound knowledge of factors such as our competitors' products, prices, marketing approach and key strengths will hopefully make it easier to figure out how we can win some business from them. Getting some sense of what one's competitors are planning to do in the future, and when, would be very useful for us. It could help us to understand if their future actions will hurt us unduly, and if so, what we might do to minimise that impact.

Example of a Clever Use of Competitor Analysis to Save One's Own Business

B-tiles is a large importer and reseller of ceramic tiles. The business supplies a wide range of large homebuilders. The way this arrangement works is that the builder sends its customers (people who are building a new home with the builder) to the tile company's showroom to select their tiles for bathrooms, kitchens and laundry. The tile company then assembles the order and sends it out on a truck to the building site when the tiles are needed. B-tiles is the largest importer of tiles in the country. Its large volume means it has a busy showroom and employs a big, well-trained team of salespeople to help these builders' clients as well as general public customers. In turn this makes it easier for B-tiles to win new builder customers and retain existing ones, on the basis that it offers a really professional and pleasant tile selection experience for the builders' clients.

All is well, until one day B-tiles learns that a new competitor (I-tiles) is visiting its key builder accounts promising what appears to be ridiculously cheap prices for tiles in an effort to win business. The competitor also imports tiles from Europe and Asia and has its own showroom too, albeit not as nicely designed as B-tiles. This price-cutting poses a serious risk to B-tiles, because if it loses some of its large customers, it will obviously lose revenue and might have to cut back on sales staff.

Fortunately, the general manager of B-tiles is very familiar with the international pricing of tiles and how the tile manufacturers in Europe and Asia deal with companies like his own, and competitors like I-tiles. Prices are linked to annual volume of tiles ordered. And he knows that B-tiles' costs of importation for tiles are considerably lower than they would be for I-tiles. So, he arranges meetings with the principals of B-tiles' three biggest clients. He explains that while I-tiles are indeed offering lower prices than B-tiles, it will be impossible for I-tiles to maintain those prices for longer than six months, even if they win that builder's business. The reason is that I-tiles' prices are so low that they will make no money on the business at all. This will likely drive them close to bankruptcy within six months, forcing them to either close, forsake their newly won business, or increase their prices. And that would be a disaster for the builder because the tiles their clients have chosen might be unavailable or unable to be delivered by an insolvent supplier. The only way that I-tiles' strategy can work is if it wins all three of the largest builders in the region together. In which case each builder is placing a risky bet on a new, untried supplier. The builders accept B-tiles' line of reasoning and keep their business with it.

This example illustrates that knowing about competitors and being able to intelligently exploit their weaknesses can be very valuable.

Another Example – Higher Education

A higher education institution finds that it has started to lose significant numbers of student in its home market to rivals from other geographic locations. When it examines what the largest (new) competitor is doing, it finds:

- this provider dominates keyword searches – its name leads the list for several commonly used search terms
- it has formed a partnership with a large job-seeking website provider whereby it has prominent banner ads exposed to people perusing the site.

This competitor is not doing much else, so it seems reasonable to conclude these activities are working very well.

The institution decides to increase its investment in keywords and also make an agreement with the same jobs website.

This example shows the potential benefits of understanding competitors' strategies.

Key Question to Ask about Competitors

Who Are Our Competitors?

For a small business primarily facing competition from other small businesses, the starting point is simply to identify competitor businesses. Keyword searches for the product category will reveal competitors and their location. A small business may wish to prioritise competitors who are geographically close (especially for retail or premises-focused businesses). To keep the task manageable, restrict competitor analysis to five or six that are either the closest or the most similar to one's own business.

The idea is to identify key competitors, then learn about what they do, so that we have a good point of comparison to our own offerings, service levels, communications.

What Do They Offer?

We want to know the product/service offers of our competitors so that we can determine if they have particular areas of strength or weakness compared to ours. The reason is that we need to ensure our offerings look competitive for those buyers who are perusing or explicitly comparing across different providers. A simple example might be personal loans offered by banks: what is their 'headline' interest rate, and do competitors offer any inducements to potential clients such as honeymoon rates (low rates for first three or six months), loyalty programme points or other bundled offers?

It would be very revealing to find out that our brand suffers from some deficiencies compared to certain competitors. Perhaps we are not as prompt or courteous, we are priced a little high, or we don't offer extended warranties like some competitors. These all offer scope for improvement.

Are Competitors Very Different from Us?

It can also be very instructive to learn that we aren't that different from competitors on key marketing aspects. One example is customer service or satisfaction. Many marketers, or managers more generally, believe good service or high satisfaction are key to success and growth. And indeed, it is hard to imagine a business being successful if it markedly underperforms on customer service. But that belief can be taken too far in that the business fixates too much on customer satisfaction scores, believing that this metric is the holy grail for future growth. In fact, publicly available data such as from the American Customer Satisfaction Index shows that often, competing businesses have very similar levels of satisfaction – yet one could be much bigger than the other. Table 5.2 shows an example from the banking industry in the US (www.acsi.org). PNC has very similar scores to Citibank and better than Bank of America, yet it is much smaller.

TABLE 5.2 *Comparing Competing Firms on Satisfaction Metrics*

		Satisfaction Score/100			
	Revenue 2019	**2016**	**2017**	**2018**	**2019**
PNC Bank	$21 bn	78	78	78	79
Citibank	$103 bn	82	81	79	81
Bank of America	$113 bn	75	77	76	77

Sources: www.acsi.org, www.macrotrends.com

Another example of satisfaction and market share is for cars. Table 5.3 shows 12 years of customer satisfaction and market share data for Ford and Toyota in the US. We see Toyota at the start has higher satisfaction than Ford but lower market share; its satisfaction score changes a couple of points up and down over the period but its market share trends consistently upward. Ford improves its satisfaction over time, but its market share goes down.

TABLE 5.3 *Satisfaction and Market Share over Time*

USA	**2008**	**2009**	**2010**	**2011**	**2012**	**2013**	**2014**	**2015**	**2016**	**2017**	**2018**	**2019**
Toyota												
Satisfaction	83	85	84	87	87	84	86	86	84	87	85	86
Market share	10.3	11.0	11.9	13.0	15.0	16.0	16.5	16.7	15.0	12.6	14.1	14.1
Ford												
Satisfaction	78	80	76	75	77	80	80	83	82	84	83	83
Market share	19.9	19.2	18.0	17.0	16.0	14.6	14.2	15.3	16.5	16.5	15.1	15.7

Sources: www.acsi.org, www.goodcarbadcar.net

What these tables tell us is that customer satisfaction – while undoubtedly important – is not what distinguishes big from small competitors or growing versus declining ones. And therefore, if the business wants to grow, but has always strongly believed the primary way to do so is via customer satisfaction – it needs to rethink its strategy priorities. Of course, this does not mean letting satisfaction go down the drain! But other factors that drive growth need to be identified.

How Big Are Competitors?

We should ideally identify how big each of the principal competitors are. Large firms can either purchase this information from syndicated providers like Nielsen or Kantar who run consumer panels or have deals with retail businesses to buy their raw data to extract from it the sales levels of all the manufacturer brands they buy – such as how many jars of Kenco coffee are sold in Tesco and Sainsbury each month. Smaller firms, and firms in fragmented markets, would find it much more difficult to identify how big their competitors are. Take the example of a small chain of fitness studios – how many members does its five closest competitors have? A determined marketer might decide to join some of the competitors' gyms, attend and get a sense of customer numbers. Or perhaps observational methods (counting foot traffic coming in and out) could be another way. Knowing how big competitors are is not merely for self-satisfaction, it can help the marketer know how much potential business it can possibly gain. It can also help to get a sense of how much their own business could grow if it built the same level of mental and physical availability as these competitors, together with comparable or better offerings.

What Are the Competitive Strategies Employed by Principal Competitors?

Are there some competitors that have distinct competitive strategies? For example, do some competitors place more emphasis on low prices while others try to position as more 'premium'? Do some competitors use quite different distribution channels – some might sell direct, others through retailers or via agents. It could be that some competitors emphasise personal selling more so than direct to consumer advertising, for example. By undertaking this audit we might be able to learn about how some approaches work better than others, or how competitors might react to our new strategies.

In this section we may also note the themes and messages our competitors use to represent their brand. In other words, the sorts of attributes they project in their various communications. Another communications aspect is whether competitors have brand elements that are striking, unique and widely recognised. The reason we should know these facts is to help us decide how we can make our own brand distinctive in the market.

Can We Learn from Competitor Websites/Social Media Use?

Small businesses may learn a lot from examining their competitors websites. A firm can obtain considerable insight from comparing the visual appearance and functionality of competitor websites compared to its own. Given that many enquiries and purchases are made via a website, it can be important to ensure one's own website is comparable to or better than competitors. This is not necessarily a matter of spending more money on graphic design. Some key things to look for are: is the website visually appealing, does it instantly convey what the business is or does, is it easy to navigate to find information like product ranges, prices, opening hours, booking times and personnel available? An important consideration is to assess a competitor's website from the viewpoint of an intending buyer (rather than an expert, such as the business owner or the person managing or undertaking this review of competitors). A good way to do this, without incurring much expense, is to ask new employees, or possibly acquaintances, to look at competitor websites, ask them to put themselves in the position of an intending buyer and briefly report what they see. These insights can lead to practical improvements in the firm's website. This activity can be very worthwhile: a study by Sinarski et al. (2020) found that a website re-design markedly improved the conversion rate to purchase from website visitors.

Social media can be an important communications tool in some industries. Moreover, its content can reveal a lot about the competitor. Some questions to ask here are:

- How many followers do they have?
- How many likes do they achieve in a week or month?
- How often do they post?

Of course, we need to be discerning in doing this analysis, as with all the others. Because social media is the subject of so much hype in the marketing industry, it is often what might be called 'low-hanging fruit' in terms of looking for quick things to examine and focus on. But in some cases, it is hardly relevant to a business. Consumer-oriented social media like Facebook, Snapchat or Instagram might be irrelevant to, say, a company that replaces tyres on your car. Or to a business that makes electronic components that go inside phones or refrigerators. But it could be highly relevant to a personal trainer or a clothing boutique.

What Is the Visual Appearance of Competitors' Premises?

Many businesses have retail premises as an integral part of their marketing – from law firms, to dentists, to clothing retailers. The question arises, how do our competitors premises compare to ours, are they superior in any way? Once we start taking a look at them we might realise they have some aspects that we can learn from. For example, we might notice their shopfronts look more appealing than ours, they have more prominent signage, or they are simply in better locations. Or perhaps their merchandising is far superior, or they have appealing store layouts. Understanding these facts help us to understand our overall competitive situation, and areas in which we are comparatively strong or weak.

How Much Money Do Competitors Spend on Marketing – and on What?

Many authors and commentators write about how marketing is meant to be more accountable. And that means how marketing needs to learn the language of finance to be taken seriously by CEOs or general managers. But before getting too carried away trying to explain how marketing might fit in with finance concepts, such as 'make future cash flow less vulnerable', there are some more basic facts that marketing can assemble to make the case that investment in marketing is necessary, and that the team actually do invest prudently. One question to ask is simply, how much do our competitors spend, and what do they spend it on? For example, we have a competitor who is growing, seemingly at our expense – we estimate they have spent £50,000 in the last 12 months on advertising, have employed two additional sales reps and a part-time social media person. That is twice as much as what we are currently doing! This scenario illustrates that competitor analysis can help us to understand if we are investing enough to grow, let alone just maintain our current level of business. Senior management presumably would not be content to think their business had second-rate IT systems, or was under-investing in staff training, so it should not be comfortable with the idea that it spends comparatively less on marketing than rivals.

In the next section we outline some approaches for exploring the nature of competition in the market, and some ways to summarise competitive information.

Key Competitor Analysis Approaches

Duplication of Purchase

Duplication of purchase, which can also be called cross-brand purchasing, means the proportion of any brand's buyers who also bought other brands A, B, C, D and so on. Hence a buyer can appear in the buyer base of multiple brands, as if the buyer is 'duplicated'.

Table 5.4 shows an example of a duplication table. Note that the key to interpretation is ordering the brands by size (penetration, which is the proportion of households that buy the brand in a period such as a year) in rows and columns. We see the overall pattern is that brands share their buyers with each other approximately in line with their size, which is measured as penetration.

TABLE 5.4 *Cat Food Purchasing, UK*

	% Buying (12 months)	Who Also Bought ...									
		Fe	Wh	Te P	KeK	Go	As	Go	Mo	Sa	Sh
Felix	26		77	46	38	54	29	23		23	27
Whiskas	25	73		42	35	52	28	22	22	27	20
Tesco Premium	9	71	68		39	52	35	19	26	29	17
Kit-e-Kat	5	83	81	55		62	42	21	31	30	20
Go-Cat	4	73	74	45	38		30	22	23	28	20
Asda	4	66	67	52	44	51		16	34	29	15
Gourmet	4	83	85	43	34	58	25		25	35	54
Morrisons	3	69	69	50	42	52	43	21		28	22
Sainsbury	3	72	75	49	37	55	33	26	25		23
Sheba	3	82	83	43	36	58	24	59	28	34	
Average Duplication		75	75	47	38	55	32	25	26	30	24
Penetration		26	25	9	5	4	4	4	3	3	3

If a much larger than average proportion of one brand's buyers also buy some other particular brand, this generally indicates the two brands are highly substitutable, and are therefore close or intense competitors (for further reading see Lam, 2006; Lynn, 2013b; Mansfield, 2004).

Key question: Are there some brands in this market that compete (i.e. share buyers) intensely, given their penetration level?

This method often 'opens up the eyes' of marketing people in that they are shocked to see how open and direct competition is between brands. It is common for managers to carry beliefs about which brands are serious competition and which are not. For example, a manager in a cat food manufacturer of a brand like Felix might think that their brand does not compete against store brands like Asda because 'Felix is more premium than that' or 'it has a different brand image'. Seeing how buyers actually buy across brands would be a way of dispelling this faulty thinking. We plainly see in the duplication table that Felix buyers are about as likely to buy Asda as the buyers of any other brand are.

2-purchase Data

This is similar to a duplication of purchase table, but it looks at the last brand purchased and the brand currently used. For example, we could ask people in a survey, what is your brand of car – and what was your previous car? Or, what was your last brand of mobile phone and which is your current one? This can tell us what brands our buyers tend to switch to, and what brands our buyers tend to switch from. In other words, it can inform us which are our closest competitors. Table 5.5 shows an example derived from Dag Bennet's (2008) work on brand switching, in this case the product is television brands in China.

TABLE 5.5 *Brand Switching: TV Brands in China*

Buyers of ...	% Buying Brand at All	% Who Switched to ...								
		TCL	**Konka**	**Chang**	**Sky**	**Global**	**Other**	**Hisense**	**Sony**	**Toshiba**
TCL	20	29	17	17	11	6	6	11	0	3
Konka	16	17	9	14	17	14	3	9	11	6
Changhong	14	18	32	12	12	9	6	6	3	3
Skyworth	11	28	19	19	6	13	6	6	3	0
Global	11	15	12	6	9	21	9	3	15	9
Other	11	19	10	17	14	10	15	5	5	5
Hisense	6	25	20	15	20	5	5	0	5	5
Sony	6	8	23	8	0	8	15	8	34	0
Toshiba	3	17	17	25	0	25	0	8	0	8
Avg. Switching		18	19	15	10	11	6	7	5	4

Source: Bennett, 2008 with permission from Elsevier.

We interpret a 2-purchase table such as Table 5.5 this way: of those who bought TCL, 29 per cent bought it again next time they bought a TV; 17 per cent of TCL buyers switched to Konka; 17 per cent to Changhong and so on.

If we were the marketing director for Konka, for example, this simple analysis would tell us (a) the brands our buyers switch to the most are TCL, Sky, Changhong and Global and (b) we gain the most buyers from consumers switching from Changhong. Of course, the sample size in this analysis was only several hundred consumers so there is bound to be some 'random fluctuation' or inexactness in the table. A commercial study would use a larger sample size and ideally repeat the exercise every year to discern trends in acquisition and switching.

Brand Image Similarity/Perceptual Mapping

Brand image is derived from asking people questions like this in an online survey: here are some brands – A, B, C, D – which ones would you say are good for a snack? Which ones would you say are a good low-calorie option (and so on)? If there are some brands that have a lot of overlap in what people say about them, this suggests they have similar brand images, or similar 'positioning' in people's minds. In turn, that suggests when a need or usage situation comes to someone's mind, the brands that are similar are more likely to be evoked together and considered for purchase – hence are closer competitors.

Buyer Preference in Certain Purchase Situations

Arguably, methods such as brand image similarity as discussed above tap consumer memory. It may also be useful to understand buyer preference. Of course, preference may also be influenced by memory, in the sense we prefer what we are familiar with. But here we focus more on understanding which brands or providers buyers say they would prefer in certain situations, after taking a little time to consider the options. This method is used widely in fields such as transportation research, such as whether people prefer toll roads or free roads that take longer to travel on (e.g. Richardson, 2004). As an example, if we were a bank marketer we might ask potential buyers which provider they would prefer if they had need of a credit card, or a mortgage, or perhaps investment advice.

Research findings from this method will help managers understand which are their key competitors according to the situation.

Direct or Indirect Competitors

A direct competitor is one that accommodates the same sort of needs, and its physical product or service is also similar to the focal brand. So, a direct competitor to Hyatt Hotels is Hilton or Sheraton – the need they satisfy is accommodation, and the physical product is a room, usually in an inner-city location, with full services such as porters, room service, restaurants and so on, which the client pays for by the day. Arguably there are now alternatives to hotels, such as Airbnb, which fulfils the same sort of need but the physical product (or the way in which it is delivered) differs. Likewise, there are now express hotels that offer much lower levels of facilities (smaller rooms, less choice) and service (no in-room meals, a very basic eatery, concierge desk staffed only part of the day). Therefore, the marketing director for Sheraton would certainly want to know not only about direct competitors, but also the features, benefits, size and growth of express hotels, because they will be a source of sales loss. If Sheraton could identify the key perceived weakness of the express hotels and show how its accommodation offers are superior on that attribute, it would be in a better position to compete against those indirect competitors.

As another example, take the beer brand Heineken. Its direct competitors are other beer brands, so in the UK this would include Carlsberg, Carling, Bass, Fosters and so on. Therefore, Heineken would take a lot of notice of the strategies and tactics of these direct competitors. But it would also pay attention to indirect competitors – other alcohol products that provide the same sort of need (alcoholic refreshment, an aide to conviviality, intoxication) – such as spirits, wine and cider. Arguably, Heineken as a leading beer brand still competes for alcohol purchase and consumption occasions against not only other beers, but these indirect competitors as well. And if indirect competitors such as wine or cider grow quickly it may be at the expense of beer – which would be at Heineken's loss. Therefore, managers should be cognisant of their direct and indirect competitors, and the extent to which they gain and lose sales to them. The key question for the marketing plan writer to ask is: do we have significant indirect competition that we could gain sales from, or that we lose sales to – and if so, is there anything we could or should try to do about it?

Market Gaps and Competitor Features Analysis

So far we have considered competitors in terms of brands or products. Tools such as duplication of purchase or 2-purchase analysis use the brand or product as the object of interest. But we can also consider our competition in some simple summary ways. One is a market gaps analysis, and the other is competitor features analysis.

The market gaps analysis simply endeavours to see if there are some parts of the market that are comparatively underserviced in terms of some marketing mix attribute. An example is shown in Table 5.6 using price as the key attribute. We make this simple by saying the market has four price tiers; then simply look at how many competitors are active in each tier. This example is purely to illustrate the idea. It appears the budget sub-market is comparatively underserviced. The market gaps matrix is based on price, but it could be based on quality level or product type.

TABLE 5.6 *Market Gaps Matrix – Example*

	Sub-market According to Price Level			
Criteria	**Budget**	**Value**	**Medium**	**Premium**
Our brand		✓	✓	
Seismer (competitor brand)		✓	✓	✓
Portrat (competitor brand)	✓			
Odilo (competitor brand)			✓	✓

Another approach is to summarise competitors on some key features, as in Table 5.7. This example shows a firm that appears to underperform in account service (although no competitor does particularly well on it) and has an advantage in supply reliability at least, over two other competitors.

TABLE 5.7 *Competitor Features Matrix – Example*

Criteria	Performance (Score/10 – Higher Is Better)			
	Our Brand	**Competitor 1**	**Competitor 2**	**Competitor 3**
Pricing	7	9	7	6
Account Service	5	6	6	6
Supply (in full, on time)	8	6	4	9
Product Range	7	6	6	9
Advertising Support	6	6	5	9

Summarise the Outcomes of This Analysis as Insights

The answers to these competitor analyses form insights, which in turn can be used or capitalised on in the marketing strategy.

Competitor Insights

Key competitor insight 1: ______________________

Key competitor insight 2: ______________________

Key competitor insight 3: ______________________

Self-test Question

1. How can it be that customer satisfaction is important, but it doesn't distinguish bigger brands from smaller ones?
2. What is meant by an indirect competitor? Give an example.
3. Why might a duplication of purchase analysis be eye-opening to many managers?

Marketing Plan Case Study: Market Environment Analysis

Market Audit

The Bournemouth population is somewhat more affluent than the broader UK. Indeed, economic growth and income in the Bournemouth area have grown by a reasonable 2 per cent over the past two years, outstripping the rate of growth in the UK generally.

Bournemouth is also home to three chiropractic clinics, which some people tended to use as substitutes for physiotherapy when they had back or neck problems. Joshua has heard these are growing quite quickly, many people seem to like the appeal of their vertebrae 'cracking' during a chiro appointment. A dozen medical practices are also in the town. The town also features a hospital that services the town itself and the surrounding county, with 300 beds.

Bournemouth boasts a wide variety of sporting clubs. There are three tennis clubs, and a cricket club with approximately 400 players. The club had a good reputation, and even once featured an ex-England player in the twilight of his career. The club hosts 20 games per year at its home ground. There are four bowls clubs (which, while being predominantly made up of hundreds of members aged 60+, does have dozens of younger players), two squash centres and two health and fitness clubs that offer weight training as well as the usual array of fitness machines. All are quite socially oriented and pleased to lend support to local businesses where they can, more so if the proprietors of those businesses are members or supporters of the club. A local community 'pinboard' seems to be present in all of them, with local tradespeople among others taking the opportunity to pin cards or small notices about the services they offer. For example, when Sarah visits one of the health clubs she notices a local business called Yorkie's Plumbing offering pensioner discount, and a signwriting firm offering to create a professional-looking outdoor sign for approximately £200. While waiting to chat to the club proprietor she takes the time to read the news, which is reporting economists' rather pessimistic predictions that over next couple of years the national economy will experience slow growth or even a mild recession. The proprietor, on hearing Sarah mention her clinic, says 'Oh, is old Mr Bound not running that anymore? – huh, I must tell the wife'. The club owner, who is a keen amateur cricketer, mentions that he is looking forward to playing the following day and that recent games have drawn quite good crowds of over 1,000 people. He jokingly mentions to Sarah that the club is always looking for sponsors, and for as little as £200 per year her clinic could become one. Apparently sponsors receive some exposure on the club's website, can place a sign on the oval fence, and of course are welcome to engage in the club's social activities such as BBQs, quiz nights, awards presentations and so on.

A recent study examined the incidence rate of attending private physiotherapy in the UK population. Results are shown in Table 5.8, along with related figures for Bournemouth. The average number of private physiotherapist appointments was 3.5 visits in the year.

Price levels for private physiotherapy tend to rise at slightly above the overall rate of inflation. This is partly because of the nature of the industry – demand has steadily risen over the past ten years, and while there are many more practitioners than in the past, demand still to some extent outpaces supply. And there is little incentive for clinics to engage in price cutting.

A trend that has occurred in the industry is the use of ESWT, which stands for Extracorporeal Radial Shockwave Therapy. Use of this treatment in the UK has grown quite sharply over the past five years, as patients as well as practitioners learn of its benefits. The therapy uses a device (a good one costing around £1,000) that emits a 'shockwave' of sound energy into the patient's body where there is an injury present. In general, a treatment involving ESWT is charged at an extra £5. Another trend is Pilates, a total body exercise that was developed to help injured soldiers back in World War I. The general idea of Pilates is to build strength, but using the weight of the body rather than 'weights'. The regime is meant to increase flexibility and possibly reduce back pain. Because it assists in strength and flexibility it is often used as

(Continued)

(Continued)

TABLE 5.8 *Attending Private Physiotherapy*

Age	% of National Population (Adds to Less than 100% because under 10s Omitted)	% of Bournemouth Population (Adds to Less than 100% because under 10s Omitted)	Incidence of Visiting a Physiotherapist in Last 12 Months (National %)	Incidence of Visiting a Physiotherapist in Last 12 Months: Towns with Population 100,000–200,000 (%)
10 to 19	10	9	3	3
20 to 29	15	16	4	4
30 to 39	13	13	6	6
40 to 49	15	15	7	7.5
50 to 59	12	12	8	8.5
60 to 69	11	13	9	10
70 and over	12	13	10	11
Weighted avg.	–	–	5	6

an adjunct to physiotherapy. Pilates has grown in popularity to a great extent in the past 20 years. It is often done by a group of about five to ten people (generally, females account for about 65 per cent of participants), in a studio or exercise room, using simple floor mats under the guidance of an instructor. Some providers also use equipment such as pulleys to assist with strength exercises. Instructors are usually a qualified physiotherapist or someone with a degree in exercise science. Participants usually pay around £5-20 each per 45-minute session.

Interestingly, as part of her general perusal of facts and figures, Sarah learns that Bournemouth residents are unusually likely to be participants in what is called a 'research panel'. What this means is that a large information services provider (selling to the marketing industry) offers incentives such as direct payments or retailer loyalty points to do market research surveys periodically. There are apparently nearly 700 Bournemouth residents who are members of this panel. Interested marketing firms can commission an entire survey, which typically takes 10 minutes for people to complete costing around £6 per person, or buy three or four questions in what is called an 'omnibus' survey (the cost being shared across many businesses) for around £200.

As everyone knows, Google search is a commonplace practice for pre-purchase information gathering. Aside from Google search, there are other information sources about physiotherapy, such as www.csp.org.uk. One that Sarah has noticed is an internet business directory, www.yell.com. It provides a 'first page' visibility for searched brands and also shows reviewer scores for clinics. It apparently charges approximately 50p per click and businesses can select the weekly budget they wish to spend, with no lower bound.

Industry sources suggest approximately 80 per cent of new business to allied health practices involves at least some internet search. But, as Sarah had read recently, familiarity increases the likelihood of clicking on a search ad or link, from an average of about 0.5 per cent for brands that are unfamiliar to a consumer, to 2 per cent for brands that are quite familiar to a consumer (these would be brands with very high awareness levels in their market). Also, presence in the top 5 or so 'easily visible' search returns yields far higher click rates than those on the second page of search results. Of course, the extent to which a business appears in the top 5 results is a function of its spending – more spending means the business is more likely to feature in the top results.

Perusal of information from industry sources reveals that approximately 20 per cent of new physiotherapy patients result from recommendations by another provider. In most cases, this recommendation includes a specific provider, for example a GP referring a patient to a specialist the GP is familiar with, or one specialist referring a patient to another (a physiotherapist making a recommendation to a patient that they get treatment from a podiatrist, for example). While obtaining recommendations from GPs (general practitioners, colloquially 'doctors') or other specialists is highly prized, it is very difficult to achieve. Allied health professionals, and particularly GPs, dislike being pestered with 'marketing' – a large amount of effort is directed at them from pharmaceutical companies and they shield themselves from it using their administrative staff who deter would-be salespeople and requests from other businesses to engage. Recommendation is something that comes more from personal familiarity developed over time.

Customer Audit

The principal ailments of people attending physiotherapy are: lower back pain, neck soreness/stiffness, and arthritic pain in the knee, ankle, shoulder or elbow. These are generally linked to age and/or physical inactivity. However, approximately 20 per cent of visits are sparked *by* physical activity, with problems such as lower back or knee pain from people suddenly taking up a new sport like tennis, squash or jogging. Cricket is certainly one that prompts some back or shoulder problems from participants, especially among players aged over 30. And tennis seems to spark tendonitis among a fair proportion of players, especially ones who have recently taken it up or returned to the sport.

While the obvious benefit sought from physiotherapy treatment is relief from pain or discomfort, an important consideration for people is to reduce the uncertainty about when their ailment will subside so they can 'get back to normal'.

One interesting feature about buyer (or patient) behaviour in relation to physiotherapy is that the therapist will often prescribe certain exercises for the patient to do, in the weeks following the appointment. For example, someone with neck pain could have their muscles and vertebrae treated, as well as being given stretching exercises. However, the incidence of people actually doing these exercises is quite low, only around 30 per cent of people do them more than once or twice. This low rate could be because the condition eases, or could be due to the patient simply forgetting, or being too busy to take the time to self-work on the condition over time. Interestingly, people who fail to do the follow-up exercise are also less likely to continue treatment from their physiotherapist.

Approximately 30 per cent of people have no real preference for the gender of their physiotherapist. Some people, around 20 per cent, prefer either that their physiotherapist be the same gender as themselves (somewhat more common among women) or that physiotherapist is the other gender to themselves (somewhat more common among men). While

(Continued)

(Continued)

physiotherapy patients are just like everyone else, and don't wish to pay more than needed, they are not especially price-sensitive to a difference of a couple of pounds (£) from one possible provider to another in the cost of a treatment.

In large cities, there is a definite location effect, with the majority of people forming a small consideration set of two or three clinics (often one, rarely more than three) within about 5 kilometres of their residence and choosing one of them after what is often a fairly cursory search. In towns with under 200,000 people, there is still a location effect but not as strong as for cities, as distance or travel time from home is less of an issue. That said, older people tend to want to travel smaller distances to appointments.

Pre-booking information search by new clients will often include a quick perusal of the website and a 'check out' of the practitioner – many people just want to ensure the person they will see (for the first time) is a gender they prefer to treat them, and to gain some subjective sense that the practitioner seems 'nice' as well as 'capable'. Video testimonials are apparently quite valued by intending clients. If they can see a person who was in a similar situation to their own explaining how their treatment helped, they feel much more confident in the purchase decision.

Consumer demand for physiotherapy is fairly constant all year round. Over the recent past, patients have used website information about treatment times to select a day or evening appointment, with the more popular preferred times being Monday to Thursday late in the day or Saturday mornings for working people; daytimes for retired people.

Internet search is commonly used by people who have not been to a physiotherapist for two years or more. People who have been more recently than that invariably return to one of the clinics they have used before (around 25 per cent of physiotherapy users will use more than one clinic in the course of a year). The most common search term combination is simply 'physiotherapist' or 'physiotherapy' plus the desired location, be it a town or a suburb in a city. Most actual bookings for physiotherapy are made directly via an online booking system embedded in a clinic's website, but around 30 per cent are made via telephone.

An interesting fact is that patients of physiotherapists are quite loyal. Of the patients that consult a physiotherapist, over 90 per cent will have subsequent appointments with the same practitioner, only 10 per cent will seek an alternative. Over a longer period, however, patients tend to visit more than one clinic – the average patient will use 1.5 clinics over a two-year period. Those who need more physiotherapy tend to use more clinics, their average patronage is around 2.2 clinics over a two-year period.

Competitor Audit

At school Sarah was quite good at maths and she has been digging into the question of how much money to spend on marketing for the clinic. She has read about several different methods: one is the objective and task method, but she has difficulty translating this into a feasible spending figure because there is no available algorithm to compute the association between outcomes like 'awareness' or 'mental availability' let alone enquiries and sales, from spending or reach. That is, while she might be able to calculate how much reach the clinic could engender from spending, say, £100, how much reach over what timeframe does one need to get, say, 10 per cent awareness? This seems a thorny problem. But what does catch her eye is the deceptively simple idea that a firm's *market share* is strongly associated with its *share of voice*[1] (in other words, the proportion of a firm's spending on marketing activity as a proportion of the total marketing spend by all businesses in the market). Given that each of the clinics in Bournemouth have one location, and they are all roughly comparable in terms of location, this notion seems to be a reasonable heuristic with which to work. Therefore, she thinks excitedly, 'if we can work out what market share we want to get in the town, and what the total marketing spending is in the town, this will tell us approximately how much we should spend to get that market share'.

Sarah decides to first try to calculate the size of the market in Bournemouth in terms of total annual visits. For this she uses information on the incidence of visiting a private physiotherapist in towns like Bournemouth.

Sarah then goes to the library and examines some back issues of newspapers to look for clinic advertisements; she also does this for the online versions of the papers. In addition, she finds a terrific source on the internet that allows her to calculate what adwords competitors use, and an approximation of their adwords budget. There are no indications of other media being used. After several mornings working on this, she calculates the total 'voice' or advertising spend in the town in a year by all physiotherapy clinics is £26,500. Moreover, Sarah thinks out loud, 'if our business could spend advertising money more efficiently than the other clinics, we could perhaps do even better than expected'. A key part of efficiency is apparently to avoid hitting the same people multiple times with advertising (in any time period, like a week, month or quarter) if there are other potential buyers of the product category who have not yet been hit with advertising. Of course, she thinks, there is no getting around some parts of advertising, like their signage which is necessarily seen often by regular passers-by and is near invisible to people on the other side of the town.

Bournemouth has seven physiotherapy clinics in addition to the Brightstones' Remedy clinic. They are shown in Table 5.9.

The largest clinic in terms of staff and patient numbers is In Touch Physio. A friend of Sarah mentions that on a typical weekday this clinic has around 30 patients come through. In Touch also runs a Pilates class most mornings of the week. It is unclear if the Pilates class helps the physio business, but it certainly adds to the vibe around the premises in the mornings.

TABLE 5.9 *Remedy and Its Competitors*

	Number of Physiotherapists in Clinic	Number of Years in Operation	Cost for Initial Consult	Cost for Follow-up Consult
Remedy	2	10	£47	£37
Back to Movement	3	7	£47	£37
In Touch Physio	5	6	£48	£38
Spinal Tap Physio	2	9	£48	£37
Reiwoldt Physiotherapy	1	5	£47	£37
My Choice Physiotherapy	2	6	£46	£36
Moderne Physio Clinic	2	5	£47	£36
Patricia Heikkinen	1	6	£49	£38

(Continued)

(Continued)

TABLE 5.10 *Reviews*

	# Google Reviews	Stars Rating/5
Remedy	1	3.0
Back to Movement	37	4.9
In Touch Physio	49	5.0
Spinal Tap Physio	27	4.8
Reiwoldt Physiotherapy	7	4.7
My Choice Physiotherapy	26	4.7
Moderne Physio Clinic	24	4.6
Patricia Heikkinen	9	4.5

Josh and Sarah drive around the town one Saturday afternoon and take a look at all the other physiotherapy clinics. They are all quite presentable, with neat and tidy exteriors and reasonably prominent, modern signage. The pair also take a look at each of the competitor clinic's internet reviews. They assemble them together as per Table 5.10.

Josh asks Olivia, the marketing student, to think of a way to estimate competitors' market shares. After some thought, she comes up with an ingenious solution, albeit one that will take around 20 hours of fairly boring work. Olivia's idea is to simply observe how many customers enter and leave each clinic over two 1-hour periods over three different days. While this information is based on only a sample of times and will give an imprecise estimate of total patient visits, it is better than nothing. The idea is to obtain the patient traffic numbers, then check or validate them against the number of physiotherapists at each clinic – the clinics with more staff should attract more patients. Olivia consults with Sarah as to the times of day and week in which most clinics would be expected to be busy, to make these observations. Sarah says, great, go ahead!

Olivia summarised her patient visit observations as per Table 5.11.

TABLE 5.11 *Clinic Visits*

	# Patients in 1 hour, Monday 9.00 am	# Patients in 1 hour, Tues 4.00 pm	# Patients in 1 hour, Fri 9.00 am	Average Patients per hour
Remedy	NA	NA	NA	NA
Back to Movement	4	5	3	4.0
In Touch Physio	7	6	6	6.0
Spinal Tap Physio	2	3	2	2.3
Reiwoldt Physiotherapy	1	2	2	1.7
My Choice Physiotherapy	2	3	3	2.7
Moderne Physio Clinic	3	2	3	2.7
Patricia Heikkinen	1	1	2	1.3

While Sarah and Josh recognise it is somewhat optimistic to be able to extrapolate from three sets of one-hour observations, Olivia then calculates the likely annual number of visits to each competitor clinic based on a conservative seven-hour day for each clinic, and 5.5 opening days each week, for 50 weeks per year. Adding in the very small number of current Remedy physiotherapy clinic clients at the present time (7 in the last week x 50 weeks per year) gives an estimate of the total annual private physiotherapy market in Bournemouth in terms of patient visits.

Josh has also come up with a task for Olivia. He asks her to look at the websites of the other clinics to see if anything useful can be learned in terms of their appearance, functionality or features offered. She hasn't finished the task but has determined that all use an online booking system and that Back to Movement mentions on its website that it offers ESWT. In Touch says it is getting ESWT in a couple of months.

Olivia also mentions that another possible method to ascertain client numbers for all the other clinics is to go to each one's website and attempt to book a session and see how many appointment times are booked. She has taken a look and they all offer various times from morning to 6.00 p.m. at the latest during the week, plus Saturday mornings. Over a period of time this would likely reveal total bookings per day. Josh and Sarah are impressed with her thinking but feel this additional work can wait.

Olivia has also discerned that In Touch goes a bit further than the other clinics in terms of offering treatment types with a specific 'name'. For example, it offers a specific post-surgery rehabilitation treatment and a 45-minute sports massage treatment. The post-surgery treatment is charged at a premium price of \$55 for initial consult and \$40 for a repeat. Sports massage is charged at \$50.

Marketing Plan Case Study: Market Environment Audit Work Tasks

Market Audit

Task

From the information in the case, work out how many residents (aged 10+) of Bournemouth will visit a physiotherapist at least once in a year. Then use other case information to calculate the total number of patient *visits* to physiotherapists in Bournemouth in a year.

How to Do It

The case mentions the total Bournemouth population, and has tables showing the percentages of the total population of Bournemouth according to age group, as well as the incidence of going to a physiotherapist, for all age groups from 10 years and over. Enter the total population figure in row 1 of Table 5.12. Then calculate the number of residents

(Continued)

(Continued)

in the town for each age group. For example, for age group 10 to 19 this is the Bournemouth population multiplied by 9 per cent.

Then calculate the proportion of each age group that will go to a physio in a year. This is the number of people in each age group multiplied by the incidence of visiting a physio. Convert that to the total number who will visit, and sum these to make a total for Table 5.12.

Then look at the people who attend physiotherapy: how many annual visits do they make on average? Multiply the total people attending, that you just calculated, by average number of visits. This will give you the market size in terms of total patient visits. Enter the figures in Table 5.13.

Task

If every initial consultation leads to 2.5 follow-ups, what is the percentage of all physiotherapy consultations that are initial and follow-up?

TABLE 5.12 *Incidence of Physiotherapy Visiting*

1	**Total Bournemouth Population:**		**Enter Population Figure in Here:**		
	Age	**% of Bournemouth Population**	**Number of People in This Age Group**	**% Incidence of Visiting a Physiotherapist in last 12 months Bournemouth**	**Number Who Will Visit a Physio in a Year in Bournemouth**
2	10 to 19	9		3.0	
3	20 to 29	15		3.0	
4	30 to 39	13		5.0	
5	40 to 49	15		6.0	
6	50 to 59	12		8.5	
7	60 to 69	13		10.0	
8	70 and over	13		11.0	
9	Total				

TABLE 5.13 *Calculating Total Visits*

1	Total number of people visiting a physio in a year in Bournemouth	
2	Average number of visits people make to a physiotherapist in a year	
3	Total number of patient visits in a year (row 1 x row 2)	

How to Do It

Hint: what is 1 divided by (1+2.5)? That gives you the proportion that are initial consultations, the rest are follow-up appointments. Check your answer: the initial proportion multiplied by 2.5 should equal repeats.

Task

How big is the private physiotherapy market in Bournemouth in terms of *revenue*?

How to Do It

You previously calculated the total number of patient visits made in the market, in a 12-month period. And you also calculated the percentage of visits that are initial and repeat consults, and you know that the average price for an initial consult is £47.50 and a repeat is £37.50. Enter the required information into Table 5.14.

TABLE 5.14 *Market Size in Revenue*

1	Total visits to physiotherapists in Bournemouth in 12 months	
2	Percentage of total visits that are initial	
3	Percentage of total visits that are repeat	
4	Number of total visits that are initial (row 1 multiplied by row 2)	
5	Number of total visits that are repeat (row 1 multiplied by row 3)	
6	Price for initial consult (from the case)	
7	Price for repeat consult (from the case)	
8	Total revenue from initial visits (row 4 multiplied by row 6)	
9	Total revenue from repeat visits (row 5 multiplied by row 7)	
10	Total revenue for the market (sum of row 8 and row 9)	

Then, still using Table 5.14 calculate total number of initial visits x average price, and total repeat visits multiplied by average price – rows 8 and 9. Add these together for row 10.

Task

Is there any evidence that there is seasonality in patient visits? In other words, that at certain times of year patient visits are a bit higher or lower?

How to Do It

The data that came from the former proprietor can be used for this task. While it pertains to only the Remedy physiotherapy clinic, if we notice a seasonal trend in its data it would be reasonable to think it occurs more generally. Locate the accompanying Excel file from the supporting online resources at study.sagepub.com/dawes.

(Continued)

(Continued)

The patient visits data trends down over time, so we need to be careful not to confound the time of year with the downward trend. If patient numbers have trended down over time, then the end of any year will show fewer patients than the start of any year (so it will look like December attracts fewer patients than January, for example).

Open the accompanying Excel spreadsheet, available from the book website. There are columns for week (1 to 106, including two weeks of the Brightstones' occupancy), month, year and patients.

First, simply graph the data in Excel with a line chart. The x-axis will be time, the y-axis will be total patient visits in the week. What do you notice about patient visits over time? Click in the data series in the chart and ask for a trendline, and the equation for it. This will appear along the lines of 'y = 20 – 0.09x'. What this means is, customer numbers started at about 20, and are declining by about 0.1 patients per week, in other words by 1 patient every 10 weeks.

Next, look at the chart and see if you can discern if there are some months in which patient visits tend to sit above the trendline.

Alternatively, type in the months of the year starting with January in cell J2, February in J3 and so on. Then in cell K2, put in the average weekly visits for January for both years, this will be =AVERAGE(D2:D6,D54:D57). Repeat for the other months. Now, are there some months when the average number of patient visits is higher?

Customer Audit

Task

The case gives some indications of what buyers are thinking about when they buy or consume physiotherapy. What are these themes or Category Entry Points? (Note, strictly speaking one would need to commission a consumer survey to properly establish these, but we use the case facts here.)

Category Entry Points:

1 ______________________________

2 ______________________________

3 ______________________________

Competitor Audit

Task

Calculate estimates of annual patient visits to each clinic, and then each clinic's market share.

How to Do It

Follow the instructions in Table 5.15, which includes the headings from Olivia's observations. Start with the average number of patients per hour, then calculate the figures for day, week and year. Add up the per year figures to get an overall total number of patient visits for the whole town for a year. Then calculate each clinic's market share by dividing the clinic's per year figure by the overall total. For Remedy, start with the current weekly visits figure.

Check the estimated total number of patient visits per year you calculated in Table 5.15, with the figure derived from the Bournemouth population and the percentages of each age

TABLE 5.15 *Annual Patient Visits and Market Shares*

	Average Patients per Hour	Average Patients per Day (per Hour x 7 Hours)	Average Patients per Week (Day Figure x 5.5 Days)	Total Patient Visits per Year (Week Figure x 50 Weeks)	Market Share of Patient Visits
Remedy	–	–	7		
Back to Movement	4.0				
In Touch Physio	6.0				
Spinal Tap Physio	2.3				
Reiwoldt Physiotherapy	1.7				
My Choice Physiotherapy	2.7				
Moderne Physio Clinic	2.7				
Patricia Heikkinen	1.3				
Total					100

group that attend private physiotherapy. They should be within about 2,000 total visits of each other. Bear in mind these are *estimates* so if they are close, that's a very good result!

Marketing Plan Case Study: Market Environment Analysis Template

Complete the market audit, customer audit and competitor audit for Remedy Physiotherapy using the following template. If certain sections are not relevant, simply note that as you work through the task.

Market Audit

Market Definition

Use the framework in this chapter to define the market.

Market Size

The size of the market in terms of revenue and annual buyers.

(Continued)

(Continued)

Market Growth Rate

How fast is the market growing (or declining)?

Price Levels and Changes

What do the principal products sold in the market sell for?

Other Key Facts

Other relevant facts about the market not picked up in the other sections.

Customer Audit

Who Are the Category Buyers?

Identify in terms of demographics or any other useful descriptor.

Why Do They Buy the Category?

Main purposes, needs, situations.

Who Buys Our Brand?

Are they any different from category buyers generally?

Why Do They Buy Our Brand?

Any reasons for brand buying that are different from category buying?

What Do They Buy?

Typical purchase amounts, series of purchases, other products co-bought.

When Do They Buy?

Seasonality or other triggers than prompt purchase.

How Do They Buy?

Extent of information search, comparison, time taken.

Key Insights

Summary of up to three key findings or insights about buyers that we can use.

Competitor Audit

Who Are Our Competitors?

Identify the principal competitors in the market.

What Do They Offer?

Highlight how competitors offerings compare to our business, and to each other.

Are Competitors Very Different from Us?

How much variation is there among competitors on key marketing aspects?

How Big Are Competitors?

What are the sales levels and market share of significant competitors?

How Do Competitors Represent Their Brand/Business?

What are the principal themes or messages that competitors employ? Are there certain attributes that they emphasise, or that buyers associate with them?

Can We Learn from Competitor Websites or Use of Social Media?

Do competitors have superior website appearance/functionality, or more widespread social media use?

How Much Do They Spend On Marketing?

Is it possible to identify or calculate how much money or human investment competitors are putting into marketing activity?

What Is Their Competitive Strategy?

What aspects do these competitors emphasise in the way they compete? For example, are there some that advertise heavily, use different distribution channels or selling methods, or try to focus on particular parts of the market?

Key Insights

Summary of up to three key findings or insights about competitors that we can use.

NOTES

1. This is a bit simplified but conveys the general idea. In practice, larger brands can spend under the level of their market share (i.e. in a market with fairly low levels of advertising, a large brand's share of voice can be, say, 0.8 x its market share and a smaller brand's share of voice needs to be a bit higher than its market share, say 1.2 x its market share). For the purposes of this case we can assume that if a brand has an objective to grow to a certain level of market share, it should plan to spend in-line with the market share level it wants to achieve.

CHAPTER

6 Bringing the Analyses Together: SWOT

The term SWOT stands for Strengths, Weaknesses, Opportunities, Threats. A SWOT summarises the principal outcomes of the internal and environmental analyses.

THE BASIC SWOT

To construct the SWOT we now take the top three (or so) internal factors that we deem to be good, and another two or three we deem to be poor or lacking, and classify them as strengths and weaknesses respectively. Note that good or poor should ideally be relative – relative to other businesses in the industry. There is no point in saying one's own customer service is good – therefore a strength – if it is no better than the average firm in the industry. Or saying that your broad range of products is a strength when every competitor has that. For example, a bank that sells transaction accounts, personal loans, home loans, credit cards and high-interest saver accounts would not necessarily list 'broad range' as a strength because every bank has this sort of range.

Following the internal factors, we take the most important two or three favourable and unfavourable external factors and classify them as opportunities and threats respectively.

Remember:

Strengths are internal factors that will help us reach our objectives.

Weaknesses are internal factors that we might underperform on, or that may be hindering our ability to reach our objectives.

Opportunities are external factors that we may be able to harness or capitalise on. Do not confuse opportunities with strategy choices.

Threats are external factors that are unfavourable to us.

The basic SWOT will be presented like Table 6.1 below. It uses the example of a small brewery that has a cellar door sales outlet and is trying to gain distribution in several retail chains.

TABLE 6.1 *Example SWOT for a Small Brewery*

Strengths	**Weaknesses**
Good location, situated close to nearby tourist attractions. Good range of beers and ales – seven different types that accommodate diverse tastes. Good relationships with several tourist bus operators.	Brand has almost zero recognition outside local area. Feedback suggests packaging labels don't give best impression. Peak periods at tasting room result in very slow service. Poor system of handling delivery orders.
Opportunities	**Threats**
Projections are that tourist numbers to Hills will increase in coming year. Heightened market interest in two particular beer types that we produce.	Influx of new entrants/brands into the boutique beer market. General lowering of beer sales sector-wide (consumers switching to other drinks).

A MORE ELABORATE VERSION OF SWOT

There is a more complex version of the basic SWOT, that classifies environmental changes in terms of the speed with which they are occurring, and the impact they are likely to have on the industry and the business. It is certainly sensible to not treat all environmental changes equally. They vary in their speed and impact, and therefore some must be allocated higher priority than others. This version can readily be used depending on one's particular situation. Alternatively, it is quite easy to just make a note in the SWOT if there are some factors of markedly greater importance or happening more quickly than others.

Self-test Question

Elaborate on the points in the example SWOT for the brewery by writing a 'which means that ...' statement for each one.

Marketing Plan Case Study: SWOT

Using the SWOT template in Table 6.2, complete the SWOT for Remedy Physiotherapy clinic.

(Continued)

(Continued)

TABLE 6.2 *SWOT Template*

Strengths	**Weaknesses**
Resources, capabilities, aspects of the product offering that help the business be competitive and will help the business reach its objectives	Resources, capabilities, aspects of the product offering that may be hindering the business's ability to be competitive or might hinder the business reaching its objectives
Opportunities	**Threats**
External events, trends that are potentially positive to the business	External events, trends that are potentially unfavourable to the business

CHAPTER 7 Objectives and Assumptions

OBJECTIVES

The marketing objectives are laid out in this section of the marketing plan. The senior management of the business will probably have already set revenue and profit targets. Hopefully, the marketing team has had a say or participated in formulating these objectives. Given that the scope of a marketing department is to be knowledgeable about the market – factors such as its size and growth and current trends in the market – it should have had input into the businesses' objectives, so that they are realistic.

If the business has an objective to grow from, for example, \$1.2 million revenue in a calendar year to \$1.4 million the next, then the marketing objectives need to show how this revenue objective will be met. Marketing will break the revenue objective down to the required unit sales and pricing objectives (X units sold at an average price of \$Y). It will then calculate how many new customers, buyers or clients are needed to reach the unit sales figures. From that information, it will calculate how those clients or customers will be acquired – principally by making improvements or increases in mental and physical availability (see Romaniuk & Sharp, 2016). It will usually also work out the required sales mix of products. A simple example is a business that provides baked goods to retail outlets – how many pies, pasties, sausage rolls, cakes and so on will be sold in the next 12 months. Or, for a university – how many Bachelor's degree students it needs to enrol, how many Master's degree students it needs to enrol, and within those, the mix of local and international students.

The question might arise, why does the section on marketing objectives appear here, instead of right at the start? One could argue the plan should start with the objectives, not formulate them halfway through. The answer is that once the internal and external analyses have been done the marketing team is in a better position to know which sorts of marketing objectives will best help achieve the overall business objectives. For example, if marketing knows that one part or segment of the market will grow more than another in the next year, then it can set appropriate growth objectives and strategies for each segment.

Four Types of Objectives

There are four types of objectives. First, those that reflect the end result of current and past marketing activity, namely sales. Second, the interim effects of marketing activity – that can be thought of as sitting between or occurring between what the marketing team do, and the sales result (and that also underpin long-term sales) – we call these market-based asset objectives. Third are direct precursors to sales such as website hits, phone or email enquiries. Fourth are activity objectives – things the marketing team do. The reason that it is desirable to have multiple types of objectives is that in order to achieve the end-result objective – namely sales – one has to achieve or improve one's performance on the others. For example, if we want to achieve an extra $300,000 in sales revenue this year, it can't just happen from wishful thinking, we need to implement more efficient or more effective marketing activity, and probably apply more resources than before. And we need to ensure that those changes in marketing actions actually occur, otherwise we won't hit our target! So, we say in order to make our extra $300,000 in revenue we need: (a) to increase market-based assets like awareness or physical availability, and (b) to build on our relationships with key clients – and to achieve these, we need to reach more potential and existing clients, with more or better communications. So, we need to set targets for those key factors; and also monitor things like enquiries or website hits, which could be leading indicators of sales.

Objectives should have a direct link to metrics. This means that once objectives are set, appropriate metrics-gathering and reporting systems are needed to help the marketing team know the extent to which they are being achieved.

Below we list out the four types of objectives with several examples of each.

End-result Objectives

An end-result objective is, as the name suggests, a desired final result of marketing activity.

Examples

Unit sales: such as, room nights sold for a hotel, number of personal loans sold by a bank, number of motor vehicles sold for a car retailer or manufacturer.

Sales revenue: in dollars, euros, yen, etc. Simply, sales revenue, which is number of units sold multiplied by the price they are sold at.

Market share: our sales as a proportion of total sales of the category. Sometimes it is easy to calculate market share – many large consumer goods companies subscribe to information providers like Nielsen and Kantar who supply the information from their network of co-operating stores or from panels of consumers. Some companies can obtain market share information from doing surveys of category buyers asking which brands they have bought, and how much they bought from each of them. But market share calculation sometimes presents challenges which relate to the definition of the category. Suppose we are the European brand manager for Volvo. We want to know Volvo's market share – but share of what market? To make things a bit simpler, let us consider only cars, not trucks. Volvo sells a variety of car models but is certainly not an 'everyday' car brand, it sells at a far higher price point than a typical Hyundai, Kia, Ford, Toyota and so on. Therefore, should its market share be of 'luxury' cars, and how is this subset of the market defined – what price bracket should be used? This simple example shows market definition, and therefore market share, is not necessarily a simple exercise.

Customers: number of new customers acquired. This would be an essential metric for any services business that can identify individual customers, for example a bank, insurance company, broadband provider, subscription entertainment provider like Netflix or Stan. An alternative metric for businesses which do not necessarily identify specific customers is the number of customers who purchase in a time period. For example, a fast food chain like Shake Shack, or a bricks-and-mortar retailer like H&M. These businesses would tally up the total transactions made by clients in the course of days or weeks.

Same-store sales: in some cases, businesses set objectives for what are called *same-store sales*. What this means is that the business wants an increase in sales across its existing stores. For example, McDonalds enjoyed a 7.2 per cent increase in same-store sales globally in January and February 2020. This metric allows the business to see if its existing outlets are improving, distinguished from any sales increases or decreases from opening new stores or shutting old ones (Chung, 2020).

Market-based Asset Objectives

A market-based asset is an asset for the firm that exists out in the marketplace.

Examples

Brand awareness: many businesses use brand awareness as their key mental availability measure. Brand awareness has the virtue of simplicity – it is easily used in a survey, and easily understood by managers. It can be measured as prompted (are you aware of this brand …) or unprompted (name four brands of car tyres). And brand awareness has the advantage of assessing the brand's link to the category name or the name of the product ('credit cards'), and that could be important when the category name is something that many people actively use or think about as a precursor to buying. Brand awareness is a narrow measure of the broader concept of mental availability, simply being the link between the brand and the category name (car tyres? – Goodyear). The limitations of brand awareness are discussed in the chapter on metrics.

Mental availability: such as, 'mental market share'. In short this metric taps the extent to which the brand is easily thought of or easily comes to mind, across the buying population and across the spectrum of relevant buying cues. This metric is discussed further in the metrics section.

Brand image: many brands or businesses set objectives for being known for certain things or being thought of in a positive way. For example, a bank might want to be thought of as trustworthy and sets the objective that a percentage of the population think that way about it. Ikea is a good example of a brand that desires a certain image, related to sustainability.

Building a Good Brand Image: Ikea

Ikea is the world's biggest furniture chain. It is obviously interested in sales and profits, like all corporations. But it is also firmly committed to what it calls a circular business model, in which raw materials and end-products are recycled or re-used; and more broadly, that it contributes to a sustainable world. In part, this strategy is because Ikea's senior management wants to make it an environmentally friendly player. But in addition, all this good work needs to pay off in terms of influencing buyers.

Ikea knows that consumers – and other stakeholders such as governments – desire to see positive action on sustainability. Therefore, it works to communicate what it does. Ikea endeavours to build its brand image in several ways. First and most simply is the way it sources its materials. It is fairly obvious from perusing its products that sustainability is embedded within the business. For example, we read that the timber is ethically sourced, and the packaging is recyclable. Ikea also does not permit the use of PVC plastic on its products, and tells people this (Ikea Group, 2014).

The second plank of image building is the reinforcement via in-store messaging. Visitors to an Ikea store see ample evidence and information about the company's enlightened approach. The third component is that Ikea launches big-idea strategies that link to sustainability, rather than just talking about it in ads. For example, it has launched a scheme to buy back unwanted furniture at about half its original price in countries such as the UK and Ireland (Butler, 2020).

More recently, Ikea has launched an alternative Black Friday campaign to highlight sustainability concepts, offering products designed to save water, energy and waste (IKEA Canada, 2020).

These strategies help to create a link in people's minds that Ikea is a business that cares about sustainability. There is some evidence this approach has helped create a positive image for the company. Each year there is a large survey of UK consumers asking them a series of attitude and image questions about brands. Retailers tend to score well in this brand health index, but Ikea does particularly well, coming in second overall out of hundreds of brands (Hammett, 2019).

Physical availability: setting a physical availability objective pertains to being present in a certain proportion of all the 'places' the category is or can be learned about and purchased. 'Places' can be physical, or virtual, such as presence and prominence on websites or the ability of people to access the brand via phone apps. Another example of physical availability relates to referrers. Take this unusual example: a small business that places elderly people in nursing homes. This business relies heavily on a network of referrers (social workers, discharge officers at hospitals, senior nurses). If it knows who all these referrers are, it can calculate how many of them at least are familiar enough with it to potentially refer clients to it as a measure of physical availability.

Relationships: the marketing (or, perhaps the sales team) of a business may cultivate relationships with business clients, and the quantity and quality of these relationships forms a potentially strong market-based asset. But we probably need to know more detail to manage this asset. For example, an accountancy firm might have several hundred clients, but how many of them would be considered to be 'actively engaging' with the staff or management of the business? Moreover, does the accountancy provider deal with and know multiple people inside its client businesses? For example, it might have 200 businesses as clients, but having some familiarity with 420 individual people inside those businesses is a better market-based asset than only one client contact within each of those 200 businesses.

Precursors to Sales Objectives

Precursors to sales: Some things occur as a direct precursor to sales. Indeed, they can reflect the extent to which potential buyers have actually started the buying or at least enquiring process.

Examples

Examples are website visits, or telephone, email or website enquiries. If a small party hire equipment business gets a 25 per cent increase in phone enquiries about hiring tables, chairs, lights and crockery it would seem like this is a good leading indicator that sales in anywhere between a week and a month's time will also lift. Therefore, it seems appropriate to set objectives for various precursor or leading-indicator type factors such as these. Setting precursors as objectives helps the business figure out which marketing aspects are working or not. For example, suppose we find precursors to sales are very responsive to our advertising efforts, but actual sales are not responding. This could indicate that there is some shortcoming in the process of dealing with or responding to enquiries, that is, the 'conversion rate' from enquiries to sales is lacking. If we didn't explicitly set precursor objectives – and monitor them – we might not identify this problem.

Activity Objectives

Activity objectives relate primarily to what the marketing team does, but also certain outcomes it accomplishes. It is quite common to set targets for marketing activity. Many of these targets revolve around the concept of reach, and also building a knowledge base about one's buyers.

Examples

Reach: reach is simply how many target customers will have an 'opportunity to see' a message in a time period, such as the last three months, or last year. In other words, how many people did we put a message in front of? There are two parts of the objective: the activities to get reach, and the actual reach achieved. Reach can take various forms and can be paid and earned. Examples of earned reach include

- a senior person from a business consultancy speaking at industry events. Ideally the firm would set objectives for how many events, and how many attendees, recognising that not all events have equal potential for reach.
- holding one's own events, such as a private school holding principal's tours, or a luxury car retailer holding a champagne and caviar dinner event for wealthy prospects.
- writing content for relevant publications. An accountancy firm might set objectives to have been featured in six newspaper or magazine features in a year; or make four appearances on talkback radio.
- a business to business (B2B) firm might set objectives for its salespeople to meet or present to a certain number of prospects each month. In aggregate this would amount to a certain amount of reach, but of what we could call 'high impact' or 'high touch' reach.
- many marketing teams set objectives for activity on social media activity such as Twitter and LinkedIn, such as number of posts and the reach of those posts.

Knowledge base about customers: this activity objective pertains to the size and quality of the firm's customer database. If a firm has learned many details about its key clients, this can give it a competitive edge. Take the example of a B2B marketing situation in which account managers service large and important clients for a firm. Within any particular account, there are multiple people that suppliers need to liaise with, service and sell to. In one instance, the supplier business has carefully collated numerous facts and feedback from the key individuals within each of its clients, over years. This allows it to provide its account managers with a lot of information about the people inside their client businesses that would help them tailor any proposals, approaches to working or communicating with these individuals. In this sort of situation, the marketing department could rightfully say it is accomplishing a very important activity objective relating to client knowledge.

ASSUMPTIONS

The assumptions section pertains to factors such as that the market will keep growing at a certain rate, or that there will be no unexpected changes in product costs, staffing or resources. An example of an assumption: take a university in Australia that attracts international students from Malaysia, China and India. It has an objective to increase recruitment from India by 10 per cent in a year. The assumption is that the overall market in Australia for Indian students will be approximately stable over the next year (no unexpected collapse in demand, no changes to student visa requirements, etc.).

Listing out assumptions makes it possible to then consider how robust the plan is to any departures from them. Testing this robustness is called sensitivity analysis. For argument's sake, if a marketing plan is projected to earn a modest net profit for the year, what if product costs increased 4 per cent, 5 per cent, 6 per cent? Or the category grew less than expected by 1 per cent, or 2 per cent, or 3 per cent? A sensitivity analysis would work out how much the (forecast) net profit would change under each of these scenarios. If the projected outcome were completely blown apart by even a small change in these scenarios, we would conclude the marketing plan is highly sensitive to changes in its assumptions. The sensitivity analysis is conducted after constructing the marketing budget.

Self-test Questions

1. Why do we need multiple types of objectives? Surely if we just set sales as our prime objective, everything else will fall into place?
2. Is there a potential problem with setting *activity* objectives for a marketing team?

Marketing Plan Case Study: Objectives and Assumptions Work Tasks

To complete these tasks, refer back to the marketing plan case study: internal analysis section in Chapter 3.

Task

Calculate Remedy's marketing objectives in terms of customer visits.

How to Do It

Step 1: The case mentions that Josh and Sarah have a desired income objective for next year. We use the 'gross' income figure, which does not include costs of running the clinic. The case mentions this, specifically that Sarah believed an appropriate level of income was £100,000 next year. Enter this figure into Table 7.1. It is arguable whether this is a business objective or a marketing objective, but for the sake of the exercise let us treat this as a business objective, while the primary marketing objectives relate to the number of customer visits to the clinic.

Then we need to calculate how many customers and visits the clinic will need to achieve next year to reach the income objective. We assume that prices stay the same next year, or certainly do not decrease. If they decreased, the Brightstones would need more customers than what is planned for here to reach their income target.

Step 2: Enter the Remedy clinic current prices for initial and follow up visits in Table 7.1.

Step 3: Calculate the percentage of visits (or consults) that will be initial visits and the percentage that will be follow-up visits. Hint: if there are 2.5 repeat visits on average for every 1 initial visit then initial visits as a percentage of total visits is 1 divided by (2.5 +1). And of course, follow up visits are 100 per cent minus the per cent of initial visits.

Step 4: Calculate the weighted average price per visit. The term weighted means that we take into account the fact that a large proportion of all visits are repeat visits, which earn less money than initial ones. Calculate it this way:

> Weighted average price per visit = (cost of initial visit x percentage of visits that are initial) + (cost of follow-up visit x percentage of visits that are follow-up)

Use the pricing figures provided for the Remedy clinic. Your answer should be between 37 and 47 (and closer to 37 than 47).

Step 5: Now that we know what the average price per visit is, we can calculate the total visits to the clinic needed in the year. Divide the income objective by the weighted average price per visit. The answer represents your total clinic visits needed per year.

Now we are really making progress!

(Continued)

(Continued)

TABLE 7.1 *Customers and Visits Needed to Meet Remedy's Objectives*

Income objective for next year in £	£
Cost of initial visit/consult	£
Cost for follow-up visit/consult	£
Percentage of visits that are initial	
Percentage of visits that are follow-up	
Weighted average price per visit	£
Marketing objective 1 Total clinic visits needed next year	
Marketing objective 2 Total initial visits needed next year	
Marketing objective 3 Total follow-up visits needed next year	

Step 6: Using the information we have already produced, we now calculate the total initial visits per year and total follow-up visits per year. You already calculated the percentage of visits that are initial, so multiply total clinic visits per year by that percentage. And then multiply total clinic visits per year by the percentage of visits that are follow-up. Check the two add up to the total clinic visits needed next year.

Task

If the Brightstones' clinic can attain its next-year revenue goal what share of the Bournemouth physiotherapy market will it have (i.e. what will its market share be)?

How to Do It

We know, from completing earlier tasks from the case, what Remedy's revenue objective is for next year. And we previously worked out the total market size in terms of revenue from the previous task. Enter these figures into Table 7.2. Then calculate the answer, as per row 3.

Task

The case also mentions a calculation of the total amount of marketing expenditure by all the physiotherapy providers in Bournemouth. If the Brightstones' spend on marketing in

TABLE 7.2 *Remedy Clinic: From Revenue Objective to Market Share*

1	Total revenue for the market	
2	Remedy's revenue objective	
3	Remedy's revenue market share will be ... (row 2 as percentage of 1) Sense-check your answer, it should be between 0.02 and 0.08, or 2% to 8%	

the next year is going to be in-line with the market share they want to attain, how much will they spend?

How to Do It

Identify from the case the total amount of marketing spend by all providers in Bournemouth. Enter this in Table 7.3. And then use the Remedy physiotherapy clinic market share goal as the other input to this task. Follow the instruction in row 3 of the table.

TABLE 7.3 *Remedy Clinic: Total Marketing Budget If Spend in Line with Market Share*

1	Total market spend on marketing by all providers	
2	Remedy's market share objective	
3	Remedy's spending if it spent in line with its market share (row 2 multiplied by row 1, divided by 100)*	

*If you have row 2 written as a number, like '6' for example, you need to divide by 100. If you have it written as a decimal like 0.06 then you don't need to divide by 100.

Hint: your answer in row 3 should be between ₤1,500 and ₤2,000.

Marketing Plan Case Study: Objectives and Assumptions Template

Write appropriate objectives for the Remedy clinic using the template below.

Objectives

End-result Objectives

What are our end-result objectives (e.g. revenue, market share, customers, usage, average price)?

Market-based Asset Objectives

What are our market-based asset objectives, such as brand awareness, mental availability, brand image?

Precursors to Sales Objectives

What are our objectives in terms of precursors to sales?

(Continued)

(Continued)

Activity Objectives

What activity objectives will we set for the coming year (e.g. reach, customer knowledge)?

Assumptions: Marketing Plan Construction

List out any important assumptions that have been made – i.e. factors that if they change, might markedly affect the plan outcomes.

CHAPTER 8

Marketing Strategy

The marketing strategy sets out how the marketing objectives will be reached. After briefly restating what the overall marketing objective is, the marketing strategy describes in what markets the business will compete in; it identifies the characteristics of the buyers that it will sell to; then explains how the business will compete (i.e. how will it obtain sales). The strategy will describe how strengths will be used and built on, how weaknesses will be either remedied or improved, what opportunities will be pursued and the mechanisms by which threats can be dealt with or mitigated. The marketing strategy will also identify how the firm will 'present' or portray itself to its buyers – what impressions does it want to impart to buyers, the anticipated number of buyers, and how it will make the brand available to buy. The way in which the strategy capitalises on customer insights would also be spelt out. The strategy doesn't have to be written in this exact order, but these are the necessary components.

A NOTE ON WEAKNESSES

One thing to bear in mind about weaknesses is that sometimes they can't be fixed. They could be structural features of the business that are not possible to change, or are extremely expensive to change, or just come about because the business has some other feature that is a strength. An example is the international bank HSBC. HSBC is one of the biggest banks in the world by capital size (Ali, 2020). It is a truly international bank, being present in virtually every country in the world, and extremely proficient in dealing with the needs of global businesses – that need banking and financing products across the globe. But in countries like the US, HSBC has a fairly small branch network, which means it cannot realistically compete (put a competitive offer together) for US businesses which are primarily domestically focused: the big four US banks are far stronger in terms of business account managers and branch access compared to HSBC. Therefore, this is a weakness for HSBC, but it can hardly fix it without a mammoth investment in physical availability. And so, it doesn't aim to – it is selective about the clients it pursues. It selectively pursues businesses in the US which really have a need for what it can offer, which is global presence and capabilities.

To illustrate writing a marketing strategy, here is an example for a small builder of 'specification' homes (which are homes built to a predesigned plan the builder has a series of these plans and clients pick one). Note that this is a small business scenario, so formalised metrics such as brand awareness and so on could not be feasibly gathered. The name is fictitious. A complete marketing strategy would probably be longer than shown here (by simply adding in a bit more detail for the principal initiatives) but this succinct version shows the way in which a marketing strategy should be written.

EXAMPLE MARKETING STRATEGY: ASKREN HOMES

Askren Homes will accomplish a sales objective of selling 18 new homes in the next 12 months by utilising our presence in key locations, modest advertising spending, good sales staff and our quality product. Askren will continue to operate in the entry-level new home market in greater metropolitan Adelaide. We will offer new homes as build-only (not house and land packages) from a range of 12 designs. These 12 designs are attractive and affordable, starting from $137,000 to $327,000. The price per square metre of our homes is comparable or slightly better than the three major home builders in the state. We see the buyers of our homes as not limited to any particular type of person other than they want a home built in wider Adelaide. Our small size precludes a large-scale advertising budget, but in order to ensure exposure to potential buyers, we will continue to have one display home (see note) in each of two developing areas, in the Southern Suburbs and Northern Suburbs, in addition to our office which is situated close to the central business district. Approximately 2,200 homes will be built within five kilometres of the location of our two display homes in the next 12 months, and each week approximately 200 prospective (single or pair of) buyers travel to these suburbs to look at display homes. This means that large numbers of potential buyers will have an opportunity to see our product. We will continue to employ two very competent salespeople to engage with prospective clients and explain the benefits of building with Askren. Over time we have built a portfolio of past work as an audio-visual showcase, together with a dozen testimonials from satisfied customers. This content will provide reassurance among prospects to build with us, based on an insight gained from our informal consumer research. We will endeavour to present Askren as a friendlier, more flexible alternative to the large builders. This presentation matches reality, as our smaller size allows us to more easily make modifications to designs pre- and post-commencement than larger builders can deal with. We will capitalise on the present low-interest rates environment and first homeowner grants that are making the local industry reasonably buoyant. We will conduct minor refurbishments of our two display homes for furnishings and kitchen appliances to keep up with recent design trends. To maintain and build familiarity with our brand we will spend a modest amount on advertising, emphasising quality construction, a modern look, friendliness and flexibility. We will employ a distinctive logo that will aid prospective buyers link our advertising to our brand. We anticipate at least 1,000 prospective homebuyers will have an opportunity to see our advertising in the next 12 months. This exposure, along with our physical presence, will drive an adequate number of enquiries (anticipate five per week) from which we can realistically sign contracts for 18 homes in the next 12 months.

Note: A display home is a home built by a builder to allow prospective buyers to walk inside and see to a fair degree of accuracy what their home would look like if they chose that particular design. Display homes are often built in new suburbs or 'subdivisions' in which the government releases land for sale, builders or property developers buy large chunks of it, break it into house-lot sizes (usually between 300 and 600 square meters in Australia) and sell the land in a 'package' with a built house. Alternatively, they build a house on land the client has bought themselves.

Note that in this example strategy statement, the business identifies it has a strength in relation to small size, giving flexibility; and having competent salespeople. It is likely to be the case that these strengths are not necessarily better than many competitors. This seems like a violation of the prescription that strengths should be only classified as such if they are comparatively better than competitors (and match the resource-based theory tests discussed elsewhere in the book). However, the description of Askren Homes is quite realistic, showing that innumerable businesses may not have strengths that are markedly better than competitors – they just have to operate with what they possess.

The marketing plan should set out *why* the chosen strategy should work – in other words, what logic underlies it. We can see this approach used in the Askren case.

This prescription sounds obvious but is not always followed. For example, the author recently sat in on a briefing session on the plan for a new educational service. Many sorts of improvements to the service itself were outlined, and a very ambitious goal of tripling sales in two years was unveiled. The market was very competitive, with large competitor players spending considerable sums on advertising. The author asked the presenter about the marketing investment to reach this target. The answer was that there was no provision for advertising investment, because the managers involved thought the improvements to the product would be enough for it to become far more popular. A year later, sales had not markedly improved. The product may have improved, but potential buyers didn't know it had improved, therefore the improvements had little effect on sales. By contrast, in the Askren Homes example there is an explanation of how the strategy is feasible – the combined marketing activity will generate enough enquiries for the salespeople to convert to sales.

Let's now look at the components of the marketing strategy in more detail.

Self-test Questions

Refer to the Askren Homes marketing strategy:

1. What key strengths is Askren basing its strategy on?
2. What opportunity or opportunities are being pursued?
3. What weakness has been identified and potentially mitigated?
4. What threat has been identified and how has it been handled?
5. Identify the text in the marketing strategy that outlines 'what markets the firm competes in'.
6. Identify the text in the Askren marketing strategy that identifies the firm's buyers.

COMPONENTS OF THE MARKETING STRATEGY

What Markets Will the Business Compete in?

In some cases, the resources or capabilities of a business lend themselves to accommodate a particular part of a broader market. For example, there is a huge market for dentistry, but some practitioners (who have done additional training) choose to specialise in paediatric dentistry. Or another way of looking at it is that the skills, resources or capabilities of the business particularly suit the paediatric market. A marketing plan for a paediatric dentist would, therefore, say something along the lines that the business will choose to have children from five to 12 years old as patients (and, therefore the parents of children around five to 12 are the 'target market'). It's useful to specify which markets the business will choose to compete in because (a) simply, everyone internally knows the choice, and (b) it makes it more apparent that additional markets or a change of markets will need support – we can't just say we're now competing in an additional part of the market without stipulating the resources that would then be needed.

The term 'markets' can mean geographic market (a local city, region, country) or multiple geographies; it can be used in the context of the type of client as well. For example, Askren Homes chooses to build new homes for consumers. There are other types of builder clients such as property developers, or commercial businesses that might want shops or office buildings constructed, as well as consumers who want alterations and additions. The strategy statement for Askren doesn't mention these. It may be that Askren simply sees its capabilities as best suited for new-home consumers, therefore its market is by default the consumer market. But another builder, to continue the example, might decide it could build homes for consumers and for property developers, and do alterations and additions also. So, it would be in the consumer (new homes) market, the 'small construction for property development market' and the home alterations and additions market.

In this case, the logical follow-on is that the business now needs to consider how it will communicate to the different types of buyers in these markets (note, consumers are the same in new homes and alterations) and how it will accommodate the presumably different requirements of those different types of buyers.

What Buyers Will the Business Sell to?

Once we identify the market or markets we will operate in, the strategy would then outline some relevant characteristics of the buyers. Now if we said the market is 'consumers', then it might seem redundant to have another section talking about consumers. But here we want to add some more detail about our buyers or intended buyers.

In this section, we summarise key findings from our earlier customer analysis (who, what, where and so on). The strategy statement should explain how we will capitalise on what has been found about buyer behaviour. Suppose we are writing a marketing plan for a party hire equipment company. We have learned that most of the sales in the (consumer) part of the market are to homeowners who are throwing a party, inviting between 10 and 20 guests, usually on either a Friday or Saturday evening, typically they have a maximum budget of $1,000 for equipment, have searched for information about providers using search terms such as 'party hire' or 'hire tables', will want the products delivered on the Friday and picked up on Sunday, and often want some additional 'party vibe' decorations (objects d'art, curios, ceiling decorations, lanterns, etc.), but have little idea how to actually create a 'good look' by themselves. In the 'How we will portray our business', we would use this information to align what we say with what buyers want or are thinking of when they are searching the category. We will accommodate or capitalise on their needs, based on the key insights we gained from our customer audit. For instance, based on the insights we gained, we will offer package deals for bundles of chairs/tables to suit between 10 and 20 guests priced at just under $1,000, ensure our keywords are appropriate, emphasise reliable delivery on Friday and pickup midday Sunday, and show pictures of the additional bits and pieces we can hire out to add to the 'party vibe', as well as perhaps offering a small-cost 'party look design service'.

How Will the Business Compete (How Will We Obtain Sales)?

We know that the size (measured as sales, penetration, market share) of a business correlates with mental and physical availability, as well as the business or brand's competitiveness in terms of product quality and price. The marketing strategy statement should spell out how the firm will build or maintain a level of mental and physical availability that is adequate to achieve its sales objectives. How does it know what is adequate? It could arrive at a conclusion from either market research or some reasonable test of logic. In the Askren Homes example, we have a very small business that could not really afford to do market research. But it has two display homes in new subdivisions that it knows around 200 prospective clients will be in the vicinity of each week (mainly weekends). If we assume that even one in ten passers-by stop and look at a Askren display, that's 20 prospective clients and perhaps one in three could be converted to a sale. That leaves another dozen clients to obtain either from enquiries prompted by advertising, publicity and the exposure effect from actually building new homes – one per month. This figure also seems feasible. On top of that, since the product appears quite good financial value and the price is competitive there is little reason to doubt the strategy will work.

How Will the Business/Brand Be Presented?

The way in which we present our business or our brand to buyers is often called 'positioning' (e.g. Blankson et al., 2008). But positioning is usually defined as what buyers actually think about a brand, and often interpreted as the attribute people most associate with a particular brand. For example, many people have said things like: Qantas is positioned on safety; or that McDonalds is positioned on family and value; or Nike is positioned as rebellious. And these statements imply that the main attribute people attach to Qantas is safety, or for Nike it is overwhelmingly that it is rebellious. But when researchers actually investigate the extent to which brands like these are attached to various brand attributes they find two patterns: first, the larger brands get mentioned for almost all attributes, and second, while some brands are indeed 'known' for certain attributes, brands share a lot in common with each other in terms of the attributes they are linked to.

To illustrate this point, Table 8.1 shows an example of brand image data taken from a study conducted by the author. A large number of consumers were surveyed and given a list of financial services brands – the names are disguised in Table 8.1 for commercial confidence reasons. They were then administered a series of brand image statements, or brand attributes – such as 'If I needed to get a loan quickly', 'Good mortgages' and so on. For each attribute, the respondents were then asked which brands, if any, possess that attribute. The responses were converted to percentages, that is, the percentage of all responses for that attribute that were attached to the brand.

For example, brand C got 27 per cent of all the responses for 'If I needed to get a loan quickly'. Looking across the row, we see that brand C gets a higher response, on average, for all the attributes – 25 per cent on average. In comparison, brand A2 gets a lower rate of response: about 16 per cent for every attribute. And in fact, this difference in responses is in line with the brand's market shares: C is the biggest and A2 is the smallest in this market.

Brand B scores a bit higher for 'good mortgages' compared to what it scores for the other attributes, but not that much higher. Brand S scores comparatively highly for 'If I needed to get a loan quickly' – 22 per cent compared to its average of 18 per cent. However, overall we see that there is not a lot of difference in the positioning or brand image of these brands. This sort of finding has been revealed in many other studies, for example Romaniuk & Ehrenberg (2012), who found little difference in consumer perceptions of brand's 'personality'.

Therefore, it is one thing for the marketing strategy statement to stipulate what it will say, or how it will present the brand; but quite another to assume buyers will actually believe it or think it. Looking again at Table 8.1, we can pose a question, which is, if we were the manager of brand A2 and we had a desire to grow to the size of a bigger brand like A or B – what would our performance on these attributes look like if we succeeded? Does

TABLE 8.1 *Brand Performance on 'Positioning' Attributes*

Bank Brand (in Descending Size Order)	Percent of Responses Given to Each Bank Brand for These Positioning Attributes							
	If I Need to Get a Loan Quickly	Good Mortgages	Trust-Worthy	Ongoing Financial Advice	Safe and Secure	Professional	Financial Planning	Average
C	27	24	25	27	26	25	25	25
B	20	24	20	20	20	19	20	20
A	18	19	18	21	20	21	20	20
S	22	17	21	16	17	19	18	18
A2	13	16	16	16	17	18	17	17
Total	100	100	100	100	100	100	100	

Source: Author data.

this imply we need to build a unique position on one attribute, or build our overall association with a range of attributes?

There is other evidence that consumers/buyers tend not to think brands are as unequivocally positioned as marketers think they are. For example, Romaniuk et al., (2007) reported on surveys in which consumers were asked if brands in product categories like soft drinks and banking were 'different' or 'unique'. Only around 10 per cent of people did think so. So, having a strong 'position' doesn't seem to be needed for a brand to be bought.

That said, we do want to make decisions about how we represent the brand. It's important to set out these decisions to ensure consistency across communication vehicles, as well as across time. Since buyers don't often pay much attention to what we say, being consistent at least increases the chance what we're saying makes some impression and makes it easier for our communications to be attributed to our brand. By the word 'say', we mean using words or visuals or other mechanisms to communicate about the brand. And if there are some aspects of the business, or memory cues, that we particularly want to attach our brand to, this is where in the plan those ideas are made plain. Note that coming up later in the plan is the communications strategy that sets out in detail the choices about how we reach people with messages, and what sorts of things those messages are going to convey. In this section the emphasis is broad – what overriding theme do we want to portray our business or brand as to the world? To a large extent this choice will link to internal considerations such as vision and mission that relate to what sort of business do we want to be.

Let's expand this idea using an example. Suppose there is an accountancy firm that predominantly has a small business and consumer customer base. It does a lot of tax returns for consumers and book-keeping/auditing for its small businesses. The principal brand or firm attributes it wants to convey are: obliging, honest, smart. It would endeavour to project these attributes via its website (imagery and words), written information, proposals or tenders, advertising, even the office décor, and the way that staff personally interact with clients. But it should not necessarily think these attributes alone will persuade or convince intending buyers to enquire and become clients. They are mostly requirements to be seen as a credible provider in the category. If the firm had a particular expertise in, say, accounting for farm owners it could also convey this as an additional attribute that conveys a benefit to those sorts of clients.

How Does the Strategy Relate to the SWOT?

The last part of the marketing strategy section ties the strategy to the SWOT. If we've taken the trouble to identify strengths, weaknesses, opportunities and threats, then we should identify how the strategy will use this information. The idea is we utilise the firm's strengths, as well as identifying how our activities in the following year will build on them; we consider how we can work around weaknesses or address them – fix them or improve them where feasible; if we have identified opportunities we show how the strategy is going to capitalise on them. And lastly, if we have identified threats, we discuss what we are going to do to minimise their impact. We can't stop them from happening, because by definition they are uncontrollable external events or circumstances, but we need to think and decide how we can mitigate their effect.

UNDERSTANDING STRATEGY CONCEPTS

Businesses undertake many sorts of activities. We read about them launching new products, making new deals with distributors, forming alliances with other businesses, putting prices up or down and so on. We can observe these activities, but we can also infer that they are conducted as part of a broader strategy. That is, the business intends to achieve some additional favourable outcome, which is sometimes obvious, but sometimes we can't discern it immediately.

In this section, we go through a list of strategy concepts. First, being aware of these concepts help us to understand why firms make certain decisions. They provide a framework against which we can compare a firm's (perhaps a competitor's) actions in order to develop a better understanding of their strategic plans. This then provides a basis for better response, and perhaps anticipation of future actions. It could be that we look at our own decisions, think 'why did we do that?' and realise that our decision was implicitly based on assumption of an outcome of one of these strategy concepts – rightly or wrongly.

Second, we can derive a checklist of these concepts for our marketing plan. The idea is to see if we are using any of them, if we are making assumptions based on any of them, or if we have ignored them. The strategy concepts fit into three different classifications, which approximately – not completely – correspond to either features of the business itself, or features of the market, or features of decisions the business makes. The concepts can overlap across the features. For example, the concept of economies of scale is a feature of a business, and indeed a business seeks to achieve scale economies, but we can also consider this as a feature of a market or an industry too. For example, the passenger aircraft industry, commercial shipbuilding and pharmaceutical industry have high barriers to entry. And, of course, businesses may make decisions with an eye to building scale economies too, to continue the example. Despite this overlap, it is still useful to classify the concepts into three groups:

1. strategy concepts which principally relate to features of the *business* itself: efficiency, effectiveness, leverage, economies of scale, economies of scope and complementarity.
2. strategy concepts which principally relate to features of the *market*: barriers to entry, threshold effects, network effects, switching costs and information imperfections.
3. strategy concepts which principally relate to features of *decisions* the business may make: opportunity cost, pre-emption, irreversibility, control, risk reduction, information value and signalling.

Once we have discussed these concepts, there is a checklist with key questions about each of them for the marketing team to complete. This checklist can be used to review the marketing strategy. Then, a summary of the checklist results can be inserted into the marketing plan. This identifies if there are strategy concepts relating to either the business, the market or specific decisions to be made, and what they are. For example, that the marketing strategy implicitly recognises the existence of threshold effects, or that it assumes that switching costs for buyers are reasonably high.

Strategy Concepts that Principally Relate to Features of the Business

Efficiency

Efficiency is the ratio of outputs that are produced from a certain amount of inputs. A writer who writes for two hours a day and completes an entire novel in a month would be said to be very efficient. Another way of thinking about efficiency is 'doing things right'.

It can be quite difficult to distinguish between efficiency and effectiveness, perhaps in some cases doing one accomplishes the other, but in other cases doing one doesn't achieve the other. For example, the efficient book author might not sell many books.

Efficiency can be applied to marketing, for example the concept of return on marketing investment is an efficiency measure (sales, divided by spending to stimulate the sales). But while it is efficient, it might not be effective. Suppose a highly efficient marketing campaign only brings in two customers per week – this figure could be trivial and not materially useful for a larger business. Another example is that a firm might have a very lean cost structure but is not capitalising on opportunities to grow in its sector, in which case it is not operating effectively.

The idea of adding products to a range is to some extent based on hoped-for efficiency. For example, P&G, which makes many food and personal care products, has ventured into pest control products launching the Zevo brand in 2018. It may have thought that adding this product would not incur a lot of extra costs because it has existing distribution strengths, including an army of account managers, sales representatives and merchandisers that already call on retailers to sell-in this brand. Therefore, from this viewpoint the new brand is an 'efficiency' strategy. Arguably, Zevo might also be viewed as an effectiveness strategy – if P&G discerned there might be significant growth to be had in organic pest control, then it could appear to be making the most of the opportunities available in its environment. We now discuss effectiveness.

Effectiveness

Effectiveness is about 'doing the right thing' – making the correct or insightful decision about what should be done. Actions or strategies can be effective, but not necessarily efficient. A firm might run a campaign that results in significant sales growth or customer acquisition – and so was effective. But perhaps it was wasteful to a certain extent, in that the same result might have been achieved with less money spent – and so it was also inefficient. A generally accepted measure of effectiveness is growth – in sales or earnings (Mouzas, 2006).

There is a logical argument that a business needs to balance these two factors. Overemphasising effectiveness (going for growth) could send the firm broke if margins or acquisition costs are neglected; while overemphasising efficiency would result in what is referred to as 'ephemeral profitability' – temporary profit gains from cost cutting, which reduce the firm's competitiveness in the long term. As an example, suppose a firm instigates severe cost-cutting to preserve margins and profit. Included in the cost cuts is advertising, product development and market research. The only way to grow sales, then, is to cut prices and run promotions with resellers. But competitors follow, squeezing margins even more. So, the firm resorts to more cost cutting, in a vicious cycle. Mouzas (2006) calls this cycle the efficiency trap.

The overall managerial take-out is to consider if the firm has too much of a focus on efficiency, and is neglecting long-term effectiveness – i.e. strategies for revenue growth. Consider discussions at management meetings: are these mostly to do with coping with what the business already does, but in a more efficient way – reducing wastage, financial reports pertaining to margins, refining current processes – and not enough discussion about pursuing growth opportunities?

Self-test Question

A company can examine its growth in terms of sales revenue, units or volume sold. It can also examine growth in terms of margin as a percentage of sales revenue, total net profit. Growth can also be considered in terms of market share, and perhaps also market share in particular sectors of the total market. Which of these tend to be indicators of efficiency and which tend to be indicators of effectiveness?

Leverage

This term is often used in finance to mean the use of borrowed capital. We use it differently in this discussion. Leverage is a concept from physics, whereby force is applied to an object via a lever (a rigid bar). Using the lever gives the user a mechanical advantage, enabling objects to be lifted or moved that could not be moved otherwise. Force is concentrated on the object via the lever. The simplest example is using a lever to lift a car off the ground. No one could lift a car off the ground without aid, but with some bricks and a long iron bar it could be done. As Archimedes said 'give me a lever long enough and a place to stand and I will move the world'.

While leverage is a concept from physics, it has applications in business and marketing more specifically. The idea is to use what you currently have to get something more (say, an accommodation from a client or distribution channel or media partner). If you have something of value to another party, you can potentially leverage a favourable outcome from them. For example, suppose you are a self-employed marketing consultant. You happen to have done a recent project on the food and wine industry. You see there is an upcoming industry conference on marketing and business development for food and wine, so you contact the organisers. They think you would be great as a speaker for this conference because of the work you've just done. The conference organisers agree for you to come and do a presentation at the conference (not a headline act, but on the list). You've used your past work to leverage yourself into a position of more prominence. Then your talk leads you to another project in the industry and this gives you more potential leverage to find another industry conference where you can say you have more expertise and past speaking experience. So now you're really leveraging your small amount of fame into more!

Self-test Question

Suppose you work for a producer of fragrances that sells through retail stores such as pharmacies, department stores and gift shops. Your company makes a range of six different perfume brands, and one of them is about to be re-launched with a massive media and social media campaign. The re-launch will be supported with an extravaganza of prizes to be won by people entering in-store or online. You are working with a team to plan the selling-in of the brand to retail chains. The launch is confidently expected to give the entire fragrance category a sales boost from all the publicity and prizes. It will be obviously an attractive promotion for retailers to participate in. How can you *leverage* this sequence of events to maximise the benefits to your firm from these retailers?

Economies of Scale

As the magnitude or size of something done by a business gets larger, the unit cost of producing that good or performing that service gets smaller. A classic example is car manufacturing. If you have a car plant that produces 500 cars per day the cost per car will be much lower than another plant that makes only 100 cars per day. Doing things at a large scale can make them more efficient and therefore cheaper. Scale economies apply to services or retailing too. A large services firm or retailer with many premises could enjoy lower rental costs, for example. Firms like this could achieve efficiencies in hiring and purchasing inputs as well. In general, bigger firms have more negotiating power with their suppliers, which is a type of scale economy.

Thinking more broadly than just costs, it can be the case that a business can simply do things better if it is bigger. For example, a tiny brewery that makes beer might not be able to afford very expensive production technology, whereas a larger one could. This might give the bigger player a slight edge in either per-unit cost or product quality. Or, a small business could not afford a full-time accountant or website person, but a bigger one could – this sort of problem is called the indivisible assets problem. Given there are benefits from getting bigger, the desire to achieve size or scale, and the benefits this brings, could be a consideration in at least some marketing strategy decisions. At the business or corporate level, mergers are often undertaken with a key consideration being to achieve scale economies.

Self-test Question

Can you think of an economy of scale that can occur in marketing activity? In other words, a marketing activity in which there is a cost or efficiency reward from doing more of it.

Economies of Scope

Superficially this sounds the same as economies of scale, but it relates to the breadth of a firm's operations or product line helping to lower costs or create efficiency.

A simple example of economies of scope is a business that is in the building products industry and makes and sells bricks as well as lightweight concrete wall construction material.It could have an economy of scope in that it can produce and deliver both types of products to a construction project more cheaply than other companies could who only make one type or the other. It could also be the case that clients like dealing with suppliers who can accommodate a wide variety of requirements – dealing with a multi-product firm might be more attractive than dealing with two single-product suppliers. In this case it could be easier to win or retain customers based on having a broad product line.

Another example might be a media company involved in TV and radio, it could use one premises and share people across both types of media production, thereby saving costs and introducing efficiencies in hiring, training, retention and skill development.

Another example of economies of scope in marketing relates to having products sold under the same brand name across multiple categories. For example, the Japanese brand Suzuki sells cars, small trucks and motorcycles. It seems reasonable that its advertising for any one product helps the others as well – especially since they all relate to personal transportation.

Self-test Question

You mention the concept of economies of scope to a colleague, and they ask, how is that different from economies of scale? Explain the difference.

Complementarity

Complementarity is closely related to economies of scope. The idea of complementarity is that having (or doing) A and B helps you sell both A and B. A simple example might be a medical practice that offers both general medical services and X-ray and ultrasound in the one place; or perhaps general medical and day surgery. The idea is that it will attract some clients because it offers both, in other words each product helps the other. The idea of complementarity is closely related to the concept of synergy, where an outcome is greater or better than the sum of the parts. The idea of complementarity is easily understood in the context of what's offered, in other words the range of products or services offered by a firm. A beautiful winery chalet offering high-quality wines, pretty views, accommodation and fine dining could benefit from the complementarity of all these factors – it gets dining guests in part because of the fine wine, and gets wine tasters and buyers attracted by the reputation of the food and the view.

What this concept means more generally is that when planning out the future of a business, we could consider new products or activities that do not just work in an additive way. Rather, we try to assemble things that could work in a complementary way, helping us sell more of what we already offer. It also means that in some cases ceasing a product or an activity might have more consequences than first thought – deleting product A from our range might mean product B suffers.

Self-test Question

A global bank like HSBC operates in the general consumer banking market, the small business market, the large corporate banking and finance market as well as having special banking services for wealthy consumers. Can you think how this might result in economies of scope, or complementarity effects?

Strategy Concepts that Principally Relate to Features of the Market

Barriers to Entry

Barriers to entry are a classic strategy concept from industrial organisation economics. Barriers to entry are factors that make it difficult for potential new entrants to enter a market. They help the existing players in an industry to be profitable. The usual factors that are classified as entry barriers are economies of scale, and what economists call product differentiation (e.g. Bain, 1968). For example, suppose you were an international airline that wants to enter the Australian market, and has virtually no brand recognition in Australia. There would be formidable barriers to entry – not only would you need a fleet of planes and a workforce (pilots, crew, airport staff, plane maintenance, customer service), but you would also need to negotiate and pay for airport terminal access, and build brand recognition even before your first flight took off. When you need a certain amount of scale to even commence operations, as in this airline example, entry is particularly hard because there is so much up-front investment required – which is highly risky. In some other cases a business might be able to 'start small' in a market and build experience and scale over time. Therefore, a rationale for advertising (and doing things like building a distribution network and maintaining good relationships with distribution channel partners) is to create barriers to new entrants – as well as obviously battling for market share among the existing competitors.

Marketing strategy, especially for a new entrant, may have a central focus of trying to overcome or sidestep barriers to entry. And preferably without huge investments! We saw in the Starling case in Chapter 1 that technology enabled Starling to sidestep a formidable barrier in the form of physical branch networks. Later, it formed a strategic alliance with the UK Post Office to remove this barrier to its operations even further.

Loyalty is often talked about as a barrier to entry, and commentators sometimes say things like 'build customer loyalty as a barrier to entry'. An example of a loyalty tactic is a rewards programme – firms from airlines to supermarkets offer these sorts of programmes.

While such moves can make things a little more difficult for new entrants, they are unlikely to stop them altogether.

In some markets there may not necessarily be barriers to entry, but rather barriers that stop many players from growing to more than, say, 1 per cent market share. For example, it is not impossible to enter the beer brewing market. In recent years there has been an explosion of small brewers and brands. But almost all of them will not grow beyond a tiny market share, because there are barriers to growth, such as the necessity of securing national distribution in retail networks.

Self-test Questions

1. Think of a market with high barriers to entry. What are the barriers?
2. Do these stop new entrants completely, or just make it difficult for them to grow at all.
3. What might be an approach to side stepping these barriers?

Threshold Effects

A threshold effect is when there is a change in the rate at which an output occurs, in response to the amount of input. Threshold effects are usually talked about in terms of when some activity or asset becomes more efficient. Sometimes people use the term 'critical mass'. An interesting example an agricultural economist told the author about is that in rural India there are many poor farmers who own one cow. Now it is obviously difficult to try to commercially gather and sell the milk of one cow – 'not economic' is a phrase used. The commercial challenge for these farmers therefore is either to pool their resources to form something like a co-operative, to which they could sell their milk to, and/or to own some more cows so it is financially viable to warrant the trouble of travelling for the cow(s) to be milked. In industrial economics this is called the Minimum Efficient Scale problem. In simple terms, if a farmer could go from having say, one cow to two, three, four, five, ten then perhaps at ten it would become commercially viable to sell the milk they produced. In other words, the threshold here is ten cows. This sort of effect can occur for retailers operating in physical stores, in that they may need to have a minimum number of outlets in a city before it is feasible to use mass media advertising.

Threshold effects can appear in all sorts of marketing phenomena, including buyer's response to prices. There is a concept called a reference price (Jacobson & Obermiller, 1990), which means people judge prices not in isolation, but in comparison to previous prices they paid, to the prices of competitors, and in some cases where prices pass a significant point such as \$10, \$100 or \$1,000. The threshold effect is where a price change that doesn't pass the reference price has less impact than one that just does. For example, an item priced at \$9.45 is increased by 50 cents to \$9.95. The impact on demand for it is smaller than if it was originally say, \$9.55 and it was increased 50 cents to \$10.05. In this case the threshold is the $10 mark. Crossing the price threshold might mean the price increase really hurts sales for the item.

It used to be believed that there were threshold effects in advertising. The belief was that one needed to expose people to an advertisement three times, at which point it would suddenly 'work'. This belief has been shown to be false, in fact advertising response exhibits what we call diminishing, not increasing, returns.

Diminishing Returns: A Kind of Threshold Effect

Diminishing returns is a kind of threshold effect, but it can be considered the negative version of threshold effects. It means that the efficiency of some output gets lower as the inputs increase. The idea is simple to imagine – for example, packing more and more activity into a shorter time period doesn't result in the same incremental gains. Doing a workout for an hour, three times a week can help with building fitness. Going to four, five, six times per week, or two workouts per day, means that the incremental benefits get much smaller. Another example is salesperson contact in B2B contexts. Seeing a client once a month might be about right, popping in every week won't result in more sales. An extremely important facet of diminishing returns is exposure to advertising: the biggest increase in propensity occurs when buyers go from zero exposure to one in a time period, a diminishing returns effect then sets in from each additional exposure (Taylor et al., 2009).

Self-test Question

Can you think of an aspect of marketing that has a threshold effect: either positive or negative (apart from the examples given)? A positive one would be where there is a gain in efficiency or effect at a certain point, a negative one would be where there is a loss in efficiency or effect at a certain point.

Network Effects

This is where the value of being a member of a network increases in-line with the size of the network. There are many examples. One is to imagine the idea of the telephone soon after it was invented. If there were only three telephones, the usefulness of them would be limited, as a user could only talk to two other households – a small network! Obviously as the network size grew to millions, its worth to all users increased.

Network effects take many forms. Some famous business schools, for example, have a very wide network of graduates, many of whom have become senior managers. And it is the case that sometimes this wide alumni network benefits new graduates from those same schools. One can see how being an old, famous business school has a potential payoff in terms of attracting new students and being able to charge high fees.

Another example of a network effect is seen in professional or trade associations. The CPA (Certified Public Accountant), for example, is a widely accepted qualification, but it is also an entry ticket into a large professional clique which offers benefits to members of the network.

Network effects can potentially be capitalised on by firms that intentionally target a particular industry to win clients. For example, suppose a legal firm decides to specifically target property developers and commercial builders. Choosing to specialise like this might mean the firm develops particular expertise in dealing with the unique legal requirements of such clients. However, if the firm has discerned that people involved in property development comprise what is referred to as a 'cliquish network' (Choi et al., 2010) – i.e. participants in it talk a lot to each other – then it could *also* unduly benefit from word of mouth recommendation.

Self-test Question

How might an airline's frequent flyer programme, for example, benefit from network effects? Think about people who frequently travel internationally.

Switching Costs

A switching cost means there is some cost, either monetary or time/effort involved in switching from one provider to another. The strategic implication of switching costs is that for existing, larger players in an industry switching costs are good – they help keep the firm's large current customer base. By contrast, new or smaller entrants have an interest in reducing switching costs. Arguably, all players are to some extent nervous about any lowering of switching costs in their industry because high switching costs add some degree of certainty about the size and composition of their short- to medium-term client base. The ideal situation for a business is that it has low start-up costs for new customers (easy to become a customer), but high switching costs (hard to leave) for existing ones. Of course, ideally the high switching costs for existing customers relate to them not wanting to leave, rather than them wanting to leave and not being easily able to. Investing in good physical availability and service levels for, say, an accounting firm creates a switching cost (it's convenient to keep going to that business and inconvenient to go to a new one).

Some switching costs relate to learning effects. If people learn to use or interface with a certain provider over time this impedes their desire to switch. The reason is they (a) feel their past learning may have been wasted, and (b) they may not want to invest in re-learning how to use the new provider. Some suppliers in sectors such as software like to get users to learn a lot about their product, because it can create a switching cost.

The extent to which people can compare prices and features of providers is a switching cost. For example, if it is very difficult to compare prices for similar goods or services, it is difficult to decide if switching to a certain provider is worthwhile. And this uncertainty itself increases the switching costs! This is why many larger established players use tactics such as bundling multiple products together. The bundling makes their packages more difficult to directly compare to competitors.

In some cases, businesses may be operating or making plans on the assumption that switching costs are high, or that they can make them high. For example, a firm selling consumer goods via retail channels might think it could set up a direct-to-consumer model, which consumers would 'learn to like'. The upshot would be, it would create a large client base, together with a purchasing model with switching costs, and therefore keep customers for a long time. In cases like this, the firm in question should carefully examine past attempts by other firms to do similar things. Invariably such outcomes don't occur because consumers generally don't like to concentrate their requirements with one provider as much as marketers think they do.

More generally, firms should not focus too heavily on building switching costs. An undue focus on them very likely means the business is taking its attention away from acquiring new customers – the essential pre-requisite to growth (Romaniuk & Sharp, 2016; Sharp, 2010) and focusing too much on trying to keep existing ones.

Self-test Questions

1. Governments often dislike the idea of switching costs for consumers and try to reduce or dismantle them – why do you think this is the case?
2. Sometimes it may be the case that businesses incur a considerable cost-per-customer acquired. Why might they endure this? Answer with reference to the switching cost strategy concept.

Information Imperfections (among Buyers)

The concept of information imperfections is extremely important for marketing strategy, because it is a basis for advertising. By advertising, we create information about our brand among current and potential buyers, stored in their memory. And so, some people know more about brand A and little about brand B, others know about brand B but little about brand A. In other words, there are variations, or imperfection, in consumers' knowledge about brands. Moreover, buyers often don't have the time or inclination to think hard about things such as which brand to choose. Therefore, if they have a memory about a brand, linked to the purchase situation they are facing, their chance of considering and buying that brand becomes much higher. If we can create memories about our brand in people's minds, we are building a 'market-based asset' (Sharp, 1995) for our business – an asset that is valuable, that exists out in the marketplace, in people's heads. That's why long-term investments in advertising create brands, which can generate income for their owners for decades! Advertising can create information about the brand in some people's memory; that means the people who are exposed to the advertising know more about the brand than those who are not. Furthermore, memory is a 'competitive process' in that if one brand creates more prominence in our memory, it detracts or degrades the memory traces we have for competing brands (Vieceli & Sharp, 2001; 2002).

One should not underestimate the importance of the information imperfections concept. Many businesspeople simply do not understand the idea that they don't have to offer the best product in the market to win sales. Rather, they need to just get better at telling the market about their product or brand. If people know about the brand, that massively up-weights the probability of its purchase among those people, because they don't necessarily want to go to the time and bother of finding out about many other brands. In fact, in many cases the thought of even searching for alternatives doesn't come up.

The extent of information imperfections can vary market by market. It is not difficult to figure out that many brands of orange juice, motor oil or scissors offer fairly comparable quality. In some other markets, perhaps health-care providers, expensive professional services and in some business to business markets, it can be difficult to discern these differences. We know the overarching rule is that familiarity with a brand (even one not tried before) by an individual helps to underpin trust in it. However, firms in markets with higher levels of information imperfection, and in which it is harder to judge quality, need to place a somewhat higher priority on identifying and communicating quality cues.

Self-test Questions

1. You work for a services business which has a heavy focus on product and service excellence. In a planning meeting, there is a considerable amount of discussion on how the features of your various offerings can be improved even more. One of your colleagues says to you, 'I think we should hold back on all this advertising your team is planning to do, until we're sure we can offer the best suite of products in the market'. What is your response?
2. What is the marketing implication for the strategy concept of information imperfections? Does marketing activity always have the goal of either reducing or increasing information imperfections, or both? Explain.
3. How might marketing priorities differ in markets where buyers find it difficult to judge the quality of competing brands or products (and also think these differences are important)?

Strategy Concepts that Principally Relate to Business Decisions

Opportunity Cost

The concept of an opportunity cost in this context is that all strategy decisions have a cost in that some other decision could have been made, perhaps with a better outcome. In other words, the cost of any decision is foregoing the outcome of some other decision you might have made instead.

Let's consider some examples. A small manufacturer of high-quality gin decides that the best way to grow is to sell direct to consumers via its own website and at its distillery premises. It expends a lot of effort and money to set this up professionally. Perhaps this strategy works and perhaps it does not. The opportunity cost is the possible outcome from a different strategy – for example, deciding to find retail partners to sell through, rather than selling direct. And likewise, if it had gone down the retail partners route, the opportunity cost is the potential outcome from selling direct or finding some completely different strategy, perhaps supplying a supermarket chain with private label gin, for example.

Another example is a small business based in a medium-sized town (population around 200,000), which wishes to grow its clientele. After some research, it decides that sponsoring various sporting teams is its chosen strategy to publicise the business. It pays a fee to several sporting clubs, in exchange for signage at their venues, some mentions in their monthly newsletters ('support our sponsors') and logos on the players' jerseys or uniforms (imagine a cricket club or bowls club, and the players have a small logo on a sleeve, chest or back of the uniform). The opportunity cost is that the money, and time, taken by management of the business to develop this association with the sports clubs could have been expended doing something different. For example, if the various sponsorships cost $500, could that money have generated a better outcome if it had just been spent on advertising? We don't know one way or the other, but the point is that the concept of opportunity cost induces us to at least consider the potential outcomes of an alternative course of action.

It is likely to be the case that managers have an implicit idea about the opportunity costs for actions that involve spending money. For example, a marketing manager will usually intuitively consider the trade-off between media in terms of costs, reach and impact. But it may also be the case that managers do not adequately consider the opportunity cost of people's time. For example, suppose a particular strategy involves creating partnerships with many small businesses, in a kind of 'mutual referral' arrangement. The idea is the focal business will get a lot of client referrals from being a central player in a network of businesses that all refer people to each other. This idea doesn't cost a lot, but it takes up a lot of management and staff time and the question arises, what other option could there have been, that could have better used all that people-time? Indeed, if we added up that staff time in total hours and dollars, it could be that the strategy incurred a huge opportunity cost in foregone sales from implementing a different strategy.

The managerial take-out is that many strategy options seem attractive, but we need to consider opportunity costs. We can read about how direct-to-consumer advertising worked particularly well for a business, or how a firm employed clever social media over a period of time to develop a market presence, or how a business targeted a niche market and succeeded. All these things sound good (of course we tend not to hear about the failures) but we always need to ask: what was the opportunity cost? Maybe the business could have even done better if it had done things differently!

Self-test Question

Does opportunity cost relate only to money?

Pre-emption

Pre-emption means that a strategy or tactic is designed to prevent a rival from starting some particular activity; or to prevent some other stakeholder pursuing a line of action. In some case a pre-emptive move may simply be an announcement of some intent (a business says it is going to invest considerable funds into a particular market) that might discourage rivals from doing the same. The idea of pre-emption implies that timing is sometimes very important – a decision or an action at one point in time might be much more rewarding than doing it at a different time point.

A classic example is a retailer in a city that becomes aware that a rival from another region or country is planning to enter its market. The key resource this new rival will need is real estate to build a store. The retailer might purchase land to pre-empt the rival's entry. Or, perhaps the incumbent retailer would seek an exclusive deal with local suppliers of staples such as milk, bread and meat to make it more difficult for a new entrant (Lee & Ng, 2007).

Grocery retailing provides another example of pre-emption. Retailers around the world have watched so-called hard discounters such as Aldi and Lidl enter their markets and steadily take market share. In Australia, the big two grocery chains nervously awaited the arrival of Aldi and were worried they might have a perception of being expensive compared to Aldi. Therefore, they tried to pre-empt its arrival. They doubled down on efforts to slash prices before Aldi launched in the Australian market, partly to try to project a stronger low-price image to avoid a disadvantage once Aldi launched.

Pre-emption may involve up-weighting advertising for a period before and during when a new entrant launches into a market. The intent is to make it more difficult for the new entrant's advertising to make an impression on potential buyers.

Lastly, product proliferation is a potential pre-emption strategy. The general idea is to launch a large variety of product variants so that there is very little in the way of consumer needs or wants that is not accommodated. Arguably, if a market is highly proliferated it is more difficult for competitors to find untapped pockets of market demand.

Self-test Question

Why would an airline launch another brand of low-priced air-travel, when doing so would seem to undercut its own prices?

Irreversibility

As the name suggests, this means something that once done, is very difficult or impossible to undo. A good strategy principle is that where there is greater uncertainty, the less desirable it is to make an irreversible decision. A wonderful example is from an incident at a US hospital. A man in a deep coma was brought to the hospital and doctors discovered he had a tattoo on his chest saying 'do not resuscitate'. However, the doctors did decide to resuscitate him, because they said the decision not to was irreversible – and fatal. In the end the man, once conscious again, said the tattoo was a joke. It may be that decisions are not just either reversible or irreversible, but on a spectrum – some are much harder to reverse than others. In which case we will want to reduce the uncertainty associated with making a decision that is more difficult to reverse.

Irreversibility can occur to different extents. And so another aspect of irreversibility is that we should expect a bigger reward for making choices that are less reversible. For example, suppose we export food products from the EU to Asia. We have two choices. One is to sign an exclusive distributor – we could only sell to that distributor for the next three years. The other is signing that distributor, while also having a right to sell to others in the near future if we choose to. The first choice is irreversible in the sense that if things do not work well with that distributor, we have limited ability to do anything else in that market. Therefore, we would want a higher projected payoff from the exclusive distributor arrangement.

In general, marketing investments can be thought of as irreversible in the sense that if we have spent the money, we cannot get it back. But some decisions are irreversible to a greater extent than others. Signing a contract for a 12-month media plan is less reversible than a six-month purchase, simply in the sense that the duration of the commitment is longer. Another example is signing an agreement to sponsor a nationally known sports club. This is a very irreversible decision. Aside from the fact that such agreements tend to be for multiple years, the initial decision is likely to prompt subsequent actions such as co-branded merchandising, corporate hospitality and the use of club players in advertising. These actions will have their own lifespan and link the business to the sporting team for a long period. It would be difficult to extricate one's business from this arrangement. Therefore, the firm would want to be sure it would get a much better payoff from the money spent on this sponsorship deal, compared to simply spending on other marketing activities that would give it more flexibility. A business needs to think through the consequences of a particular action – if we make this decision, what will be the 'knock-on' decisions that follow from it? If a whole host of knock-on or consequential actions start occurring as a result of one particular decision, then that decision is highly irreversible.

In some cases, not making a decision is also irreversible. Take the example of a retailer trying to pre-empt the arrival of a competitor. Buying a piece of land to deny the competitor a premises could be reversed later – the land could be sold eventually. But *not* buying it is a decision that is irreversible – if the land is available, the competitor buys it, and once that happens the incumbent retailer now faces that competitor.

Self-test Question

Why would a marketer want a better payoff from making decisions that are less reversible/less flexible?

Control and Flexibility

We all know the general meaning of the word control: having the power to influence or direct some behaviour or course of events. Control is a strategy concept because many marketing decisions are based on a desire to control aspects of the marketing mix. Furthermore, control is a useful concept because firms desire to exert control over their marketing mix, but also to retain flexibility in their ability to respond to marketplace changes. Often, control comes at the cost of less flexibility. Control may also impede physical availability, for example if a firm chooses to sell only via its own retail outlets it has complete control over its sale, but could possibly have much wider distribution if it sold through independent retailers.

Examples of strategy decisions made with a view to controlling the marketing mix are: selectivity, ensuring service consistency, negotiation and response, and centralised versus localised decision making.

Selectivity

This term means being selective in the appointment of distributors, using criteria such as the distributor's image or marketing mix. For example, signing only distributors that are 'up-market'. Intuitively one would think it would be bad for an expensive or luxury brand to be sold by down-market retailers because doing so would be injurious to the brand's image. Surprisingly, there is a lack of evidence this is necessarily a problem. For example, the premium champagne brand Dom Perignon sells more volume in Costco in the US than any other retail outlet (Loewentheil, 2017).

A more important aspect of selectivity is that a business will set standards for retailer or channel partners in that they must have the resources and capabilities to sell the product in the way the owner wants. For example, a maker of earthmoving equipment like Caterpillar might require a wholesaler or country distributor to be very knowledgeable and have, say, 10 years of experience in that particular field, as well as having a qualified engineering support staff and facilities. The distributor is very much the face of the brand in such cases, so selectivity is very important.

Ensuring Service Consistency

Franchising is an example of a distribution strategy in which the brand owner (say, McDonalds Corporation) is able to sell through thousands of retail outlets around the world, but those outlets must conform to strict standards. The standards relate to staff training and appearance, store appearance (cleanliness, signage, parking) menu and cooking procedures. McDonalds Corporation in this way exerts control over the way its brand is presented to the public in-store. McDonalds believes that a high-quality, standardised experience is an important success factor in fast food. People do dine at different McDonalds' restaurants over time – partly because they know what to expect. Therefore, it is extremely important that the experience is consistent across stores.

Negotiation and Response

Salespeople's or account managers' ability to respond to price negotiation requests is an important marketing factor that needs to balance control with flexibility.

Take the example of a sales representative in a B2B marketing context, for example, selling IT equipment to businesses. It might be the case that the salesperson prepares a tender or bid worth tens or hundreds of thousands of dollars to a client, and the client discloses that a competitor has underbid for very similar equipment. Can the salesperson or even their immediate manager decide to match or better the competitor's offer? If the business gives the salesperson or their manager the flexibility to respond, then what tends to happen is the average price for products falls – salespeople 'give in' to requests for price reductions too easily. Sometimes buyers bluff and play one salesperson off against a rival to get better deals, which is why firms enforce pricing controls (i.e. lower limits on pricing). But the cost of doing so is that sometimes business might be lost because a competitor has genuinely undercut price and the business does not respond to the price cut.

Centralised versus Localised Decision Making

In many large organisations, there can be many different people and business units that conduct marketing activity. This could be within a country or even a local region. For example, we earlier mentioned the example of Suzuki. This company makes cars, motorcycles and small trucks. Each of these product lines will likely have its own team responsible for marketing in a country or region, for example, there could be a team for cars, one in South-East Asia, one in North America, one in South America, then Europe, Africa and so on. Then the same structure for motorcycles, then again for trucks. That is a lot of different marketing teams – perhaps 20 or more of them! And then, there could be consumer teams and corporate (business customer) teams as well, and then a global team responsible for the overall Suzuki brand. In a situation like this there would be a lot of complexity and co-ordination needed such that each team can adapt what it does to its local market, but doesn't create a marketing mix that is counter to what the larger business wants. Global companies need to be very careful that what they do in one country doesn't make a mess for some other country team. For example, suppose the North American Suzuki team creates an extremely generous incentive scheme for dealerships in that country, more generous than what dealers get anywhere else. This scheme might make it very difficult for the other countries if their local dealers learn that US counterparts are getting far better deals. This highlights the importance of control in a global marketing strategy but can apply to more localised examples as well.

Self-test Question

How would you know if your marketing strategy, in particular your pricing strategy, was erring too much on the side of control, or too much on the side of flexibility? Consider the scenario of a B2B company selling irrigation equipment to farmers, horticultural businesses and retailers in Europe. The company employs a dozen sales representatives and three sales managers, in an extremely price-competitive market. (Hint: what sorts of messages received from the market, or your team, might indicate too much control or too much flexibility).

Risk Reduction

There are two aspects to risk: how likely it is that something bad will happen, and how bad it would be if it did. The concept of risk reduction is commonly associated with investment decisions. For example, conventional wisdom is to invest in, say, six stocks rather than one because it reduces the unique risk with any specific investment that could decline in value; or, to invest not only in stocks, but in real estate and some interest-yielding deposits – this spreads the investment risk and if there is a disastrous downturn the investor's portfolio is not as damaged as it would otherwise be. But risk reduction is also a desired outcome of many business decisions – often implicitly, in other words, the business might not necessarily think of what it is doing as risk reduction.

Deciding to employ a seasoned, well-known person in your industry might be a risk reduction decision. Risk reduction more broadly is any action that reduces the likelihood of future events damaging the business or its brand. Building brand assets – awareness, familiarity and relationships – is said to reduce the uncertainty, or risk attached to future revenue for a business (Srivastava et al., 1997).

One simple example where a business should think about risk reduction is where it has an over-reliance on one or a couple of key customers. Consider a business that achieves, for example, 50 per cent of its sales from two key accounts – it is in severe danger if one of them curtails its business (say, a supermarket delists a particular small supplier). A variation of this over-reliance is where a firm only sells through one specific channel. A business that the author worked with over several years manufactured premium sunscreens. It consciously decided to sell only through a particular distribution channel – that steadily accounted for a smaller and smaller proportion of total category sales. Moreover, it thought that since it had the support of this channel it did not need to advertise any more. Its sales were entirely dependent on this channel, which then over a period of a few years altered drastically due to the arrival of new entrants. The big new players had no need for this manufacturer, it was delisted and ceased operations. It had failed to see the inherent risk in (a) sticking with a small, declining channel and (b) failing to build consumer familiarity for its brand.

Another form of risk is where a firm has a very narrow product line. This can be seen as particularly risky if a competitor has, or will have, very similar products in the future. More generally, a business selling through intermediaries or channel partners should always consider the question: do our resellers need us as much as we need them? If the answer is no, the business is in quite a risky situation. It needs to create a situation whereby its channel partners do need it; or it needs to find a way of selling directly to consumers.

Self-test Question

Could the concept of risk reduction be applicable to marketing activity? In other words, can marketing activity act as a risk-reducer to the firm or a brand? Think of specific examples other than those discussed above.

Information Value (for Firms)

The value of information for making good decisions cannot be underestimated. There are innumerable examples where a lack of information (or, good quality information) has led to disastrous decisions; and where getting good information has led to spectacularly good decisions. And these examples can come from all sorts of situations In World War One, during the battles in France, an allied general was continually exhorting his troops to advance at Ypres. The troops were being killed by the thousands each hour, but the general kept insisting on an advance. The general and his staff at HQ could not understand why the objective was not achieved. What they did not know was that the troops were trying to advance through an enormous sea of mud, so it was simply impossible to do what the general wanted. The men were trapped in waist-deep mud and simply being slaughtered. This sad example shows the danger of making decisions without adequate information on the situation. More generally, governments spend hundreds of millions of dollars on gathering information as a basis for decisions. Worldwide, the market research industry that constructs and sells information to business about buyer behaviour, knowledge and sentiment is worth billions.

Returning to a marketing context, the whole idea of doing the internal and external analysis of the global and market environment is to provide relevant information for decisions. But more specifically, we can zero in on the idea of generating *insights* from that information. Basing marketing strategy on insights about buyers can be particularly beneficial. Here is an example from Germany.

Nivea: Using Social Listening to Develop a New Deodorant

Nivea is an international beauty and personal care brand based in Germany and owned by the firm Beiersdorf. Nivea uncovered a uniquely valuable buyer insight from monitoring social media discussions between consumers. It learned that consumers on various online forums were complaining about deodorant leaving stains on garments. This was a factual problem: apparently, when residual sweat and particles of deodorant mix in with chemicals in laundry detergent, it leaves a yellow stain that is very difficult to remove.

As a result of this netnographic research (ideaconnection, 2012), Beiersdorf identified that there was a sizeable market opportunity presented by this consumer problem. It developed a new non-staining deodorant, which was most useful for white clothing. It tested the new product with a large panel of users, which led to another buyer insight, namely that consumers were worried about deodorant leaving light-coloured stains on dark garments. The development team at Beiersdorf refined the product and it was marketed as 'Nivea invisible for black & white'. The company claimed this was the most successful product launch in ten years (Gordon et al., 2016).

This case illustrates the strategic value of marketplace information in the form of insights. It also highlights a new way in which firms can get these insights, from monitoring consumer discussions and forums on social media.

Self-test Question

In which parts of the analysis section of a marketing plan (global environment, market environment) are you most likely to find valuable insights?

Signalling

Firms communicate to the market and to buyers in various ways, but there is an additional communication concept called 'signalling' in the strategy, marketing and economics literature. This concept means that firms send 'signals' to the market by what they do and how they choose to communicate. A prominent aspect of signalling pertains to quality.

A difficult task for brands or businesses is to signal their level of quality. Suppose that different brands or firms in a market differ somewhat in quality, but consumers find it hard to tell which are better. Where there is more uncertainty about quality among buyers, and the consequences of poor quality are severe, signalling by sellers becomes more important.

However, most business say, explicitly or implicitly, that they offer good quality – just look at car dealers. Therefore, it can be difficult to judge quality in advance. Firms try to signal quality in various ways. Advertising is usually an implicit signal of quality, if we recognise a firm's advertising it reassures us that the business has existed for a time and is likely to be acceptable. There is a school of thought that says very expensive ads carry a strong quality signal to the market: our product must be very good, otherwise we would not have spent this much money on an obviously extravagant ad.

There are other specific quality signals that businesses can use. One is accreditation – being accredited by an industry body. Universities spend large sums being tested and accredited by bodies such as Equis and AACSB. Accountants use bodies or titles such as Chartered Accountant as a quality signal. Qualifications of key staff would be a strong quality signal for many firms, from allied health to financial advice. Another is building a link to a test that strongly signals quality. An example is car makers being involved in Formula 1, or the Paris–Dakar rally. Testimonials are a quality signal, particularly from clients who are well known, or have characteristics that imply they would be demanding. Showcasing past and present clients is another signalling tactic. There are numerous other possibilities, including highlighting the brand's heritage or awards received. The important take-out is that a firm should consider if it is adequately using quality signalling and if there are more effective tactics it could use.

Signalling is not only restricted to quality. Firms sometimes want to signal low price: over and above just having low prices, they try to build a perception of low price. An example is that Costco in the US has sold a hot dog and soft drink combo in its forecourts for the same price for 35 years. While some commentators say that by doing this it loses money on every meal, charging this low price helps cement the retailer's reputation as being very cheap.

Signalling can also have a strategic interpretation, in that firms send signals to the market via major initiatives or events that confirm their commitment to a market. For example, a new airline entering a country market could buy naming rights to a major sporting stadium. Doing so would signal (a) it is prepared to invest for the long term and (b) it wants to be seen as a 'local' member and contributor to the community.

Self-test Question

Peruse the website of some manufacturers of surgical instruments or surgical supplies such as www.utilita.it or www.dentag.com. What are some of the ways they are signalling quality?

STRATEGY CONCEPT CHECKLIST

We can ensure that we are using, or at least recognising, any of these strategy concepts that are applicable to us in our marketing plan and strategy by completing this checklist, as per Table 8.2. Checklists seem simple, however, using them has been shown to result in superior outcomes. In medical practice, for example, using checklists reduces diagnostic errors that arise from doctors' cognitive biases and mental shortcuts (Ely et al., 2011).

TABLE 8.2 *Strategy Concepts – Checklist*

Strategy Concept	Business Assessment Questions
Principally about features of the firm and its activities	
Efficiency	Are we focused so much on efficiency that it is degrading our effectiveness?
Effectiveness	Are we making the most of the opportunities present in the environment?
Leverage	Are there features of the business or activities from which we can gain leverage?
Economies of scale	Do we benefit from economies of scale? Will our marketing strategy bring about, or use, any identified economies of scale?
Economies of scope	Are there potential economies of scope that can be captured from our marketing activities?
Complementarity	Does our range of products or services exhibit complementarity? Would we lose complementarity if we cull certain products? Are there products we could add that would offer complementarity?
Principally about features of the market	
Barriers to entry	How high are the barriers to entry in this market? Are there barriers to growth for small players? If so, what are they, and how might they be overcome?
Threshold effects	Are there any thresholds of effectiveness in our market? Are we operating at levels of diminishing returns in any of our marketing activities?
Network effects	Are there network effects in our industry? If so, are there identifiable networks of buyers or users that we could prioritise?
Information imperfection	Is the level of buyer uncertainty about the merits of competing offers low or high?
Switching costs	Are there switching costs for buyers in our market? What are they? How trivial/severe are they?
Principally about features of the firm's decisions	
Opportunity cost	Are we sense-checking that our strategy choices are better than an alternative?
Pre-emption	Are there competitor initiatives that we should attempt to pre-empt? Are competitors trying to pre-empt us?
Irreversibility	Are we taking care that decisions which are irreversible are carefully considered with adequate information?

(Continued)

(Continued)

Strategy Concept	Business Assessment Questions
Control and flexibility	Do we understand the main aspects of the business that require flexibility and the ones for which we need to prioritise control?
Information value	Do we have information, or insights, to back up the major marketing decisions that we make?
Risk reduction	Are we prudently reducing the risk that our products or brands might not continue to generate future revenue?
Signalling	Are we capitalising on effective ways to signal quality?

Going through this strategy concept checklist makes it less likely that important aspects of the marketing strategy or features of the marketplace are overlooked or ignored.

Once the full checklist has been completed (the entire list does not need to be included in a marketing plan document), you write a summary. The summary as per Table 8.3 is then inserted into the plan.

TABLE 8.3 *Strategy Concepts – Summary for the Marketing Plan*

Type of Strategy Concept	What Strategy Concept Has Been Identified and How Does the Firm's Stated Marketing Strategy Relate to It?
Feature of the business	
Feature of the market	
Feature of firm's decisions	

Marketing Plan Case Study: Marketing Strategy Template

Use the following template to construct the marketing strategy objectives for Remedy Physiotherapy.

Marketing Objective

Re-state the marketing objective. Stated in terms of either revenue, customers, market share.

What Markets to Compete in (and Those Not to Compete in, if Relevant)?

Outline the chosen market (defined by geography, buyer type, etc.)

Which Buyers Will We Sell to?

Outline the particular characteristics of the buyers we are aiming to acquire. Are there different buyer groups to consider separately?

How Will We Compete?

That is, how we will win customers.

How Will We Represent the Business/Brand?

The broad themes we want to communicate to buyers.

How Does Our Strategy Relate to the SWOT?

How we will use our strengths/compensate for or resolve our weaknesses/capitalise on opportunities/minimise the possible impact of threats.

Strategy Concepts Employed or Assumed in the Plan

Summarise identified strategy concepts, one each where relevant for: business, market and firm's decisions.

Note: Highlight Your Logic

Note that in the description of the firm's marketing strategy, you should link the strategy decisions to the outcomes of your internal and external analyses and audits. For example, link your decisions in terms of how they build on strengths, remedy weaknesses if possible, capitalise on opportunities, mitigate threats. And also, in your strategy you point out how you will use or leverage your insights from the market, customer and competitor audits. Some examples of the type of logic statement are:

> We will do <this> – which capitalises on the insight that buyers are often showing <this need/behaviour>.
>
> We will invest more in <this> because of the finding that it is more cost efficient than <that>.

CHAPTER 9 Marketing Programme

In this section of the marketing plan, we list out the specific aspects of our marketing mix: communications, product, pricing and distribution. Following that we construct a programme timeline, which details when our activities will occur.

Note that this section comes before the budget section in the plan. The question might arise, how can we construct the marketing programme before the budget? In other words, how can we map out what we're going to do, before we know how much money there is to spend? The answer is that the marketing director will have an estimated figure in mind. This budget figure may have emerged from assessing the task required to achieve the sales objectives. Or it might be based on past spending levels. Or the CEO has already allocated how much money is to be made available. The programme is then constructed, which allows a sense-check and possible adjustment of the estimated figure. Following that, a detailed budget specifying the exact amounts spent on each marketing activity is put together.

COMMUNICATIONS DECISIONS

This section closely links to the one on how we will represent the brand.

Here, the plan lists out the choice of media (paid media, earned media) that will be used, along with targets for reach. For example, we may choose to employ paid Facebook advertising that over the course of a year, at our level of spending, will reach 2,000,000 consumers. Earned media can also be planned out in relation to reach – for example Twitter readily reports the number of impressions for a Twitter account over a time period; other social media report visitors, followers and so on.

First, the communications plan must be predicated on having a clear link between the advertising, the brand and what the good or service actually is. In other words, what products it provides to buyers; or at least what category it is in. This seems so obvious that readers could think it should go without saying, but many pieces of communication fail to link the brand to what it sells. It doesn't mean every piece of communication must be 'busy' or hard sell. Some communication can be brand building without getting into the specifics of products, but a beer company still needs to convey in its ads that they're for beer, an insurance company needs to impart the message that it provides insurance – not just say, for example, 'we make lives better' or some similar vague brand-purpose statement.

Second, the communication should make links between the brand and some prevalent Category Entry Points or CEPs. CEPS are the situational contexts, need states or consumption requirements (e.g. Romaniuk, 2003) that coincide with buying or using the product category. We talked about these in the customer analysis section.

To reiterate a point made earlier, it's easy to get confused between CEPs and what's thought to be important to buyers. If you try to rely on what buyers tell you is important, your advertising may be ineffective at creating memory links. Suppose you are a marketer for a brand of bread called Tiny Tim's. If you ask people what's important for them when they buy bread they'll say something along the lines of freshness, doesn't go stale quickly, a competitive price. So, using this approach, your marketing communications might say, Tiny Tim's White Bread – it's fresh, long-lasting and not expensive! Which might not be very effective in building mental availability for the brand because this is not necessarily what's on people's minds, it doesn't link with the cues they're receptive to when buying bread. You don't know what's in their minds because that's not what you asked about – you asked about importance, which is an evaluation, not a memory link. Now suppose you had asked people what they are buying bread for, and the most common answers were, say, for their children's school lunchbox or for making toast in the morning. If your advertising featured these usage situations, then arguably it would be more effective at building mental availability because the advertising message is aligned with the most commonly thought-of buying or usage cues. You would never uncover these CEPs asking buyers about what is important.

Third, communications must feature some distinctive brand elements to help it be noticed and correctly attributed in the competitive clutter. Brand elements are things like: logos, stylised colour schemes, taglines or characters (Romaniuk, 2018). To some business-people, spending time developing logos and so-forth might seem trivial, but these have an all-important function, which is to help buyers know 'that brand is yours'. Consider the example of a party hire company that provides goods such as chairs, tables, cutlery and crockery for parties and social functions. Many of the businesses in the industry have the words 'hire' or 'hiring' as part of their brand name. And indeed, so did this company – it had a very generic brand name (i.e. it merely sounded like the category). The owner of this particular business found that some buyers mistakenly purchased from their competitor, due to name confusion. One issue we discovered from talking to the business was that it had no distinctive brand elements. It would be reasonable to think that developing brand elements – by using a distinctive font or colour scheme – not only on the business website and brochures, but on its delivery vehicles and the packaging that some of its goods was delivered in – would provide a memory anchor such that those with previous experience with the business would remember it more easily ('oh, yes the one with the yellow!'). And of course, it would make these activities and facets of the business more memorable to prospective clients. The moral of the story is, the brand name doesn't necessarily have to be unique or different or meaningful for it to 'stand out' in the market – the way it is visually represented can do that for it. Over time and after repeated exposures, buyers get to know what sort of brand it is, they form their own set of associations with it.

Visual Identity System

A very common practice in business is to create what is called a visual identity system, which means a set of standards for how the brand's elements are produced and presented.

This system will usually specify very precisely the font and colours to be used in the brand's name, colour and shape of the logo and other supporting elements – whether they appear on a sign, an ad, in the office, on a letterhead or email signature. The value of having a system like this (in small companies it can be called a 'style guide') is ensuring the brand is always consistently portrayed. It can be surprisingly difficult to ensure consistency in the way the brand is represented to buyers. This is because people outside the marketing department may have occasion to 'use' the brand or its elements in some activity (a business event, a speech, a press release, a presentation) and these people may not recognise the importance of consistency in branding or may not realise they can access standardised communication resources (letterheads, PowerPoint templates, banners, signs and so on). For example, the head of finance wants to give a talk at a business association and goes ahead and creates their own PowerPoint badged with some images of the company they plucked from the internet. These sorts of occurrences are quite common and highlight that a task for marketing is to remind everyone in the business that branding consistency is important and resources to do so are easily available.

The visual identity system should also communicate the key themes the business wants to portray or project. Using the example of the accountancy firm mentioned in the previous section, the attributes obliging, honest, smart about money are central – a graphic designer would usually be contracted to make a palette of colours, shapes and fonts that visually communicates these attributes. Whereas a party hire company, while also wanting to communicate generally desirable attributes such as obliging and honest, may want to visually portray the concept of fun and celebration.

It sometimes also happens that a business changes its brand elements, but due to budget constraints cannot afford to change everything. For example, a small business might decide its logo is outdated and change its website and other easy-to-alter communications tools such as business cards and stationery. However, it also has an expensive sign that will cost $5,000 to change. The upshot is, the firm ends up with inconsistent branding. Therefore, before changing brand elements, take the time to compile a full inventory of everything that would need to be changed in order to calculate the full expense and the time to change it all.

Examples of brand identity palettes on Pinterest can be found at:

www.pinterest.com.au/rnhsieh/visual-identity-system-vis-design/

The importance of having a visual identity system is more easily appreciated when we consider a global brand – in dozens of countries, across a multiplicity of media. Let's consider Toyota. Go to the Toyota website:

www.toyota.com/brandguidelines/introduction/

The Toyota system provides detailed guidance to country-marketing teams in terms how their advertising should, and should not, use the Toyota brand elements. The importance of consistency in use of these elements becomes apparent in some of the examples where Toyota shows how *not* to combine two elements of the brand. Its examples of 'do not do this' look jarring, because we never see any lapses in Toyota's consistency.

PRODUCT DECISIONS

Here we summarise what range of products will be offered. We would list out changes to the range including new introductions, deletions, improvements and when they will occur.

Under this heading we might also discuss what is sometimes called the 'augmented product' – the ancillary products or services that complement the core products we sell. In some cases, this might simply be phrased as customer service. But simply categorising augmentations of the product offering as customer service will probably not capture the full range of possibilities. For example, the party hire company mentioned earlier not only took orders and delivered tables, chairs, tablecloths and crockery/cutlery, in many cases the manager would meet with clients and help them plan their event, in terms of 'look and feel', and figure out the best positions for placing equipment at an event. This interaction helped the hire company to form good relationships with some larger business clients who repeatedly staged events. It also reportedly resulted in word of mouth recommendation. However, this client interaction tended to be informal, and simply arose from ad hoc client contact. A marketing plan for the coming year would outline how this service could be formalised and communicated to current and potential clients. In addition, if the business anticipated extra demand for such services, the plan would nominate who in the business would do it and, if necessary, how it could charge appropriate fees.

PRICING DECISIONS

This section summarises the price levels that each product will be offered at. That might not mean the price for every single product is listed out (obviously it would not be feasible for a restaurant to state in January what the prices for every entrée, main and dessert will be for the year). Rather, the plan would specify ranges or families of products and their price average and range. For example, a home builder might operate in the 'mid-range' of the house construction market, with two broad specifications of homes. For argument's sake one home might be called the Classic, priced between \$220,000–\$260,000 depending on options; and the Luxe would be priced between \$280,000–\$320,000. For each of these products, there could be options such as an extra room for \$25,000. First, the value of setting out these expectations of what price will be is that the prices to be set should be based on some sort of market-based rationale – based on the various micro and macro analyses, so everyone knows what they are and why they are at that price. Second, this pricing information creates a logical link from price per home, to expectations about how many homes will be sold, and then to revenue.

This section would also identify if there will be temporary discounts or specials and if so, what criteria will qualify clients for discounts. A simple example might be a winery that sells to selected retail outlets, offering prices by the bottle, lower prices for full cartons of 12 bottles, and lower again for a pallet load of cartons. The criteria for getting the discount is the quantity ordered.

Another example might be a private school that offers annual fees of \$8,000 per year from the first year of secondary school, up to \$12,000 per year for the final year. But it also offers a limited number of scholarships, 10 per year, to students with either musical genius, unusually high sporting prowess, or from a low socio-economic background. In the education industry, scholarships are essentially a discount, but selectively given to students who meet certain criteria. Usually, this is that they have a reduced ability to pay, or they have some quality that the school can use to make itself look good (good musical performances and sports success are desirable attributes for schools).

Books such as Nagle and Holden's (2003) *The Strategy and Tactics of Pricing* discuss myriad ways in which discounts can be structured.

DISTRIBUTION DECISIONS

Here we will describe the channels that clients will use to buy or use our product/service. For example, a bank might sell loan products through its own branch network, via online applications and through a mortgage broker. A gourmet pet food manufacturer might sell via veterinary clinics and smaller independent pet food stores (but perhaps not through the large supermarket chains, because it lacks the scale to supply them or maintains supply contracts with the vets or independents because it doesn't supply supermarkets).

However, we want to go further than just listing out channels that we sell to. We want to consider how we can increase our sales through them. We can either expand our distribution coverage with new or improved channels (finding a new channel, perhaps) or improve our distribution coverage within the existing channels. It is also worth noting that channels can be virtual as well as physical, for example website purchasing or information sources. We refer back to all the work we did on the channel audit as the basis for this section.

Distribution Is Closely Related to Physical Availability

Distribution relates closely to the concept of physical availability; but there are some aspects of physical availability that aren't quite the same as distribution.

A challenge for the marketing team is to make the good or service easier to buy and use. In some cases, it might not seem feasible to make something easier to buy – for argument's sake a retail shop is in a 'fixed' geographic location. Take a florist shop in a shopping arcade as an example. Can it increase its physical availability? Yes. Longer opening hours, expanding its display area into the walkway in front of or close to the entrance, internet ordering, and of course home or workplace delivery are all options. Having the right portfolio of products is itself an aspect of making the company easier to buy from, and so (while an overlap with the 'product' part of the marketing mix) is part of physical availability.

As another example, take a bank that offers transaction accounts, loans or investment products. It has physical locations but it can increase the ease with which it can be purchased (or used) – its presence on price comparison sites, the extent it appears from keyword searches, mobile bankers, phone apps and so on are all aspects that increase physical availability.

It is often the case that increasing physical availability is an investment (opening a new store, investing more in adwords, a deal with Uber Eats, adding more staff to a call centre). In many cases the business would dearly like to increase its physical availability via striking a deal with a distributor, but it cannot because it doesn't have a compelling enough business case, or the distributor doesn't need it as much as it needs the distributor. For example, a small winery might endeavour to obtain distribution via a retail chain, but the retailer already deals with 200 suppliers and doesn't need a 201st at the present time. In such a scenario, the supplier has to (a) keep working on building mental availability of its brand to make it a more attractive option for the retailer in question, or other retailers, and (b)

TABLE 9.1 *Illustration of a Marketing Programme Timeline for a Private School*

Month	**J**				**F**				**M**					**A**				**M**				**J**					**J**	
Week	**1**	**2**	**3**	**4**	**5**	**6**	**7**	**8**	**9**	**10**	**11**	**12**	**13**	**14**	**15**	**16**	**17**	**18**	**19**	**20**	**21**	**22**	**23**	**24**	**25**	**26**	**27**	**28**
School newsletter				x				x					x				x				x					x		
School tours																												
Email follow up non-enrolees																												
Scholarship programme announced (for following year)																												
Scholarship applications open																												
Scholarship interviews & awards (10 @ $6,000 each)																												
New signage on school fences			x	x	x	x	x	x	x	x	x	x	x	x	x	x	x	x	x	x	x	x	x	x	x	x	x	x
Graduation ceremony Year 12																												
Year 12 Merit awards					x																							
Principal speak at government- sponsored education convention																		x										
Total																												

*consumables, attendance fees, venue hire, printing, guest food/drink and other incidentals.

Month			A				S					O				N					D					
Week	**29**	**30**	**31**	**32**	**33**	**34**	**35**	**36**	**37**	**38**	**39**	**40**	**41**	**42**	**43**	**44**	**45**	**46**	**47**	**48**	**49**	**50**	**51**	**52**	**$ Spending***	**Person**
School newsletter		x				x					x				x					x				x	$500	Maria
School tours														x		x		x							$200	Tim
Email follow up non-enrolees																			x	x						
Scholarship programme announced (for following year)							x																			
Scholarship applications open								x																		
Scholarship interviews & awards (10 @ $6,000 each)									x	x															$60,000	Maria
New signage on school fences	x	x	x	x	x	x	x	x	x	x	x	x	x	x	x	x	x	x	x	x	x	x	x	x	$2,500	Maria
Graduation ceremony Year 12																x									$1,000	Maria
Year 12 Merit awards																									$500	Maria
Principal speak at government-sponsored education convention																									$300	Maria
Total																									$65,100	

keep looking for product options that might enable it to offer the retailer something that would particularly add value to its retail assortment.

MAPPING MARKETING ACTIVITY IN A TIMELINE

Next, we map out the timeline for all these aspects of the marketing mix for the next 12-months, showing when changes or activities will occur.

This process will allow the marketer to see the entire year's sequence of activities all together. The benefit of doing so is that one avoids things like scheduling too much activity in one time period and nothing in another. And of course knowing that a major activity is planned for, say, June makes it more apparent that the preparation for the activity needs to be completed by the end of May. Other reasons for creating a clear programme are to communicate with channels and the sales force exactly when activities will occur, so they can plan ahead. Indeed, external partners who need to book media spending, or need to create content for your marketing communications, will find this programme helpful, aiding them to plan their own work and thereby get yours done in time. Lastly, the programme allocates people to tasks – it is a way of ensuring everyone is clear on what they have to do, and by when.

Earlier in the book we raised the question, how can the marketing programme be constructed before the budget figure is known? The answer is, the head of marketing will often have an estimated figure in mind. This figure can be adjusted after constructing the programme, because the programme helps to identify if there is enough activity planned to actually meet the marketing objectives.

We show an example of a marketing programme timeline for a private school to illustrate the idea – see Table 9.1. The school employs newsletters, school tours, a scholarship programme, signage, special events such as graduation, as well as attendance at education-related events to promote itself. Some of these activities are arguably more scholastic rather than marketing. But they all involve communication between the school and various stakeholder groups. For example, scholarships costs are not necessarily a marketing expense, but they do fulfil a marketing purpose. The key thing is that this programme shows all the marketing activities that are planned to occur, when they will occur, and how much they will cost.

Self-test Questions

1. Can you think of an example where a marketing activity planned for one month in a year might mean that it is crucial to complete some other activities earlier in the year?
2. Why might it be desirable to use a marketing programme to avoid having multiple activities occurring at the same time? Give an example.

Marketing Plan Case Study: Marketing Programme Template

Use the following template to outline decisions about product, pricing, advertising and other communications activity (community engagement, social media, etc.), and distribution for Remedy Physiotherapy.

Recall that earlier, in the objectives section, we calculated what Remedy clinic's marketing spending would be if it spent in line with its market share objective. This figure gives us a good idea of the scope of activity we can include in the programme.

Marketing Mix Summary

Product

What will be offered to buyers, detail of changes or improvements.

Pricing

What major decisions on pricing will be made?

Advertising Media (Defined Broadly, Including Things Like Sponsorship)

What media will be used to reach buyers/audience?

Advertising Content

What specific messages and CEPs will be emphasised?

Distribution

What channels will be used to make the goods/services available?

Summarise These Activities in a Table

Enter the planned series of marketing activities and actions for Remedy Physiotherapy into Table 9.2. This summarises all the marketing activities and when they will occur. For example, if you plan on making a new product or service available sometime in the year, note in which month/s this will occur. Simply enter the required information into the header row and indicate when the activity occurs with an X or shading in the month cells. Later, in the budget, the cost of these activities is entered. The reason for having this programme, as well as a budget, is that some activities do not have specified costs (like, making a change to prices or making a new product available).

It there is not a specific activity or change relating to an aspect of the marketing mix, simply leave it blank or enter NA.

TABLE 9.2 *Marketing Programme for Remedy Clinic*

Marketing Activity	Jan	Feb	Mar	Apr	May	Jun	Jul	Aug	Sep	Oct	Nov	Dec	Total Spending	Person Responsible
Product decisions														
Pricing decisions														
Advertising														
Distribution														

CHAPTER 10 Marketing Budget

It is worth briefly considering the different ways that the budget component of a marketing plan can be created. One school of thought is that in a market-led business, the budget for the entire business is created *by* the marketing team. The basis for this idea is that since marketing is the interface between the organisation and its served markets, then marketing is in the best position to estimate likely demand and what its activities can achieve. But bear in mind this line of thinking places a huge responsibility – and esteem – on the marketing management team. In practice, it is unlikely the marketing team will be solely responsible for budget setting. Take the example of the private school in Table 9.1 – enrolments are obviously not simply a function of marketing activity, they depend on location, the facilities, the school's long-term reputation in terms of student character development and scholastic achievement, teaching staff and so on.

At the other end of the spectrum, marketing might have almost no responsibility for budget creation. The finance department, probably in conjunction with the general manager, creates the budget for the business, and marketing is simply allocated a certain amount of money to spend (perhaps based on history, or the percentage of sales method outlined below).

Given there are these differences between firms in the extent to which the marketing department is involved, there are several different ways in which a marketing budget is created. We now talk through the ones that marketing commentators usually discuss: the percentage of sales method, the task method and the competitive method.

Then we contrast those with another common method, which is simply how much money is available to spend on marketing.

One point to note: a question that can arise during the construction of the marketing plan is whether the salary costs of the marketing team go in the marketing budget. In general, salary costs are not considered part of the marketing budget. Other costs such as media spending certainly are.

PERCENTAGE OF SALES METHOD

In this method, some proportion of sales revenue is allocated to marketing activity. For example, a company with sales of $2 million might allocate 5 per cent of its revenue to marketing. But where does the 5 per cent figure come from? The answer is history or precedent, the past experience of managers, or some collective understanding in the business about how much similar businesses spend. But an important point is, the marketing team to a great extent gets 'told' how much it can spend, rather than formulating its own idea of how much it should spend in order to grow the business. Another point is that if sales go up, in theory marketing expenditure should go up, which seems sensible since the business is larger now. However, it has the capricious problem that if sales go down, automatically the amount devoted to marketing will go down, when logically it might need to be preserved to try to recover from the downturn.

To help guide percentage of sales spending decisions, there is published information on what is called the advertising–sales ratio, which is the proportion of sales spent on advertising. Some examples of the average advertising–sales ratio among firms in various industries are shown in the Table 10.1. These figures are for the US (WARC, 2017) but they can give some sort of guide to managers in these industries in other countries.

TABLE 10.1 *Advertising–sales Ratios*

Industry	Advertising as % of Sales	Industry	Advertising as % of Sales
Cosmetics	21	Banking/loans/credit	4
Cleaners/detergents	11	Restaurants/takeaway	2
Toys/games	9	PCs/computing	1
Wine	7	Airlines	0.7

These figures likely do not include other marketing expenses such as sales or marketing department personnel. The clue is that the percentages are quite small for markets like banking, but banks tend to have quite large marketing departments, so if staff were included the proportion would be higher. However, they are useful as a broad guide for businesses that have no clear idea of how much they should spend on advertising (which means principally, spending on paid media).

TASK METHOD

In this method of budget creation, the marketing team examines the size of the task required and calculates the amount of money necessary to accomplish it. For example, a company wants to launch a new branded snack product in Australia. The objective is to sell five million units, or $8 million worth, in the first year. In order to do so, the brand will need to gain distribution in the two big supermarket retailers that command 80 per cent of grocery sales. In turn, for those retailers to agree to stock the product they wish to see the brand launched with a four-week national media campaign that would reach 80 per cent of households. Moreover, the brand would be required to provide $200,000 in 'co-operative' funds for the retailers to feature the brand in their own media advertising. The task approach would therefore be based around the estimated cost of the launch campaign, plus the co-operative funds and associated costs such as merchandising to ensure the new brand enjoys in-store presence in its launch period.

The ideal situation in which the task method would be used is to know the sales outcome of certain levels of spending. For example, if a company spends $200,000 on a digital campaign for a new tourist resort, how many bookings will result, over and above what would have occurred if it had not spent that money? Unfortunately, detailed knowledge about sales response to advertising/promotions like this is usually not readily available. However, if a business has been very astute in cataloguing its advertising campaigns, when they occurred, and how much they cost, as well as the associated sales effects, it may be possible to develop quite reasonable estimations of the outcomes of ad spending. This is probably easier for businesses which can readily identify and count their customers – such as, say, banks or insurance companies. For argument's sake, if a bank has traditionally run four or five bursts of advertising each year, it can ascertain the extent to which customer enquiries and new memberships increase during or immediately after those bursts (and obviously this would be harder to do if the bank runs continuous campaigns). Or, the same institution could run direct mail or digital campaigns and monitor the short-term sales results. Of course, such approaches will probably underestimate the total effects of the marketing communication because some people will have been reached who are only ready to buy months or even years later, but their familiarity with the brand has been shaped by that communication.

COMPETITIVE METHOD

Here, the business looks at what competitors spend to get a benchmark for how much money the business should allocate. Of course, one has to adjust for the fact that competitors can vary massively in revenue or market share. For example, suppose a company with $2 million revenue looks at three other competitors: A has $6 million revenue and spends around $500,000 on marketing; B has $7 million revenue and also spends around $500,000, and C has $11 million revenue and spends around $1 million. The business is one-third the size of A. This implies an equivalent level of spend of about ($500,000 x ⅓) = $160,000; using the same approach for B yields $140,000, and for C it would be $180,000. The average of the three competitors (adjusting for the fact they are all bigger) is around $165,000.

Related to the competitive method is the 'share of voice' concept. Share of voice means the spending by the business on advertising (and other advertising communications) divided by the total spending by all players in the industry. In other words, the company's spending as a proportion of all spending in the industry. If you decide that your share of voice should be about the same as your share of market, implicitly you are using the competitive method of spending allocation.

'HOW MUCH MONEY DO WE HAVE AVAILABLE' METHOD

While this method tends not to be mentioned in textbooks, it is a very common approach with small business, and not-for-profits. Some businesses simply do not have money for marketing or, more specifically, for marketing communications activity. In our interactions with small local businesses in the UniSA Marketing Clinic, we have heard many times, 'we want to achieve certain growth objectives, but somehow we have to achieve them with almost no funds'. Or 'We have some great ideas for a marketing campaign but no money to do it'. The reason some organisations have no spare funds is simply that they are running very close to breakeven. Or that the senior management of the business just will not allocate money for marketing over and above employing some staff. We had a sports club that wanted to spend some money to attract more female participants – its request was unfortunately blocked by the solely male board of the club! Therefore, the female club members have resorted to doing some marketing activity with no club money being spent.

Therefore while 'money available' may not be the logically soundest choice for deciding on spending level, in many cases it is the only option the marketing manager has to work with. The task is therefore to figure out the best way to spend it. A general rule is to fix the firm's worst marketing weakness first.

WHICH METHOD TO USE?

It is quite likely a business would use some combination of all these methods. In relation to the percentage of sales method, common sense tells us that if marketing expenditure has tended to be, for example, 8 per cent of sales, and the business has enjoyed acceptable growth, then this figure should be a good basis for the new marketing budget. It likewise seems sensible to spend approximately what competitors spend, adjusted for company size, and perhaps outspend somewhat if the business is pursuing a high growth target. And of course, calculating the necessary expenditure to accomplish a marketing objective is a logically sensible way to do things. The end outcome should be a budget that has a rationale – the marketing manager can make a case that it is appropriate for (a) the size of the business presently, and (b) the growth goals of the business; which in turn both relate to (c) the magnitude of the marketing task to be accomplished.

Therefore, included with the budget can be a summarisation of the total spending as a percentage of company sales: for the forecast period as well as previous years, as well as what the industry average is. Also included can be the estimated share of voice. These figures provide a rationale for the level of spending. Of course, the budget is an estimate of what sales will be, and it is based on either what the business has told the marketing team it has to accomplish; or what the marketing department has said it can accomplish given the amount of money it has been allocated. Therefore, there is always a bit of circularity in budgeting, and in the justification for marketing spending.

For example, the narrative written for the budget could include a rationale statement like this:

For the year 2022 budget period we calculate our marketing expenditure will be 7 per cent of sales revenue. This is very close to last year's level. We calculate the industry average to be 8 per cent of sales, so our level of spend is conservative. We have 2 per cent market share currently and our best effort to calculate our share of total industry spend is 1.9 per cent, therefore we are spending approximately in line with our company size.

What if the Business Has No History of Marketing Spending?

Suppose there is a situation whereby the business has never spent money on formal marketing activity before. The question might arise, does it need to now?

Certain businesses may not have spent money on what might be called formal marketing spending, such as advertising or other forms of marketing communication. An example might be a small business with a local catchment – an accounting firm, a retail store, a tradesperson business. In this scenario, the managers of the business might be tempted to think that if the business has survived for so long without advertising or marketing communications, therefore perhaps it is not needed now? There are two answers: first, the mere existence of a business has some communications impact – having a shopfront with a sign is like a local advertisement. A tradesperson's business, such as a plumber with signed vehicles that people notice in traffic, or parked in the street, is engaging in some default non-zero level of marketing communications. Therefore, it's not the case the business has survived without any advertising, these elementary pieces of communications have been a form of advertising and they have obviously worked otherwise the business would not exist. Second, if the business wants to grow, it has to apply some more resources to generate additional business. And one of these resources is spending money to communicate the business to a larger pool of potential customers than before. But the challenge is that one may have little idea how much to spend to get to a higher level of sales if there has been no history of spending on paid advertising.

If the business is in this situation it has to decide in a somewhat arbitrary manner how much to spend on marketing. The recommendation is to be conservative and lean towards underspending rather than overspending. For a small business with little history to go on, the best approach is to pick the smallest increment that would have some sort of measurable impact, such as $1,000, allocate that to the medium that will have the broadest reach among category buyers, and see if there is any discernible impact after a quarter. If there is, continue or increase the spending level. If there isn't, keep the spending up but try a different medium.

WHAT IS 'ZERO-BASED BUDGETING'?

In the last ten years there has been a lot of discussion about a budgeting approach called zero-based budgeting. In short, this means that the staff involved in preparing a budget cannot simply base it on previous years with some increment, such as 'last year we spent €200,000 on advertising, this year because the sales budget is 5 per cent higher, we will spend 5 per cent more on advertising'. Rather, there is no assumption that any expense is 'entrenched' or gospel; rather, everything has to be justified. The idea is that spending has to be based on actual needs, not precedent. It is meant to avoid what is an often-times blind nature of budget preparation where people simply add some percentage increment to last year's spending, which in turn was based on the year before and so on. While the term 'zero based' implies all spending is set to zero and a case has to be made for it to be non-zero, many consultancies suggest this is not how it is usually done. It more correctly means that a business does not assume that because it has been spending money on certain activities that it should continue to do so. Therefore, zero-based budgeting is actually fairly similar to the task method described earlier.

MARKETING AS A COST, OR CAN IT PAY FOR ITSELF?

There has been debate for decades about the idea of marketing accountability. In short, this means whether the marketing department is able to quantify the financial return of its marketing effort (investments). At face value this sounds straightforward – calculate the sales response to various marketing activities, determine the incremental profit or contribution per sale and from that, arrive at some sort of payback equation – such as, for every dollar spent on marketing we get back $1.20. If only it were that simple! In practice this is very difficult. The business has so many different things going on at the one time – new products, price changes, new stores, new campaigns, digital, TV, outdoor and radio all happening together – leaving aside the activities of competitors, one's own sales force and so on. As well as that, sales are not entirely dependent on what the marketing team does. Why does Barclays in the UK sell billions of dollars of banking products each year? Not only because of its marketing team! It has a huge branch network, for one thing, as well as an army of advisors and retail salespeople and relationships with loan brokers – most of these are not in the control of the marketing department. But that's not to say marketing should have no responsibility for sales, or that it should simply be consigned to be a cost. One way to make the marketing department more motivated, and more accountable, is to offer it some ability to 'earn' its budget. The way this can be done is to say that each new customer, for example, results in a monetary bounty or allocation to offset the costs of marketing expenditure. That bounty could be a calculated fraction of the average revenue-per-customer over, say, a three-year period. For example, if a bank determined that an average new customer was worth $1,000 over three years – and that marketing has some influence on customer acquisition – then marketing is allocated 10 per cent of that sum, i.e. $100 for every new client. Then it has a real incentive to do things that acquire new customers.

A Marketing Budget in Which Activity Is Linked to Short-term Sales Results

In some cases, the marketing team will develop a budget that not only includes weekly or month-by-month marketing activity (and its costs), but corresponding estimates of the resultant sales revenue in those time periods. And indeed, if the marketing team can work out what the sales figures will be over the budget period, and also knows the costs of supplying the product or service, then it can work out the 'contribution' week by week or month by month. Contribution is a proxy for profitability, or more specifically the profitability of a product – before fixed costs are paid for. Contribution is calculated as selling price minus variable costs. For example, if a jeans brand sells for $98 per pair and incurs $25 variable costs each, then its contribution is (98 – 25) $73 per pair. From this information, we can start to understand how marketing activity is contributing to financial performance.

Another benefit of creating a budget as described here is that it indicates when demand will be higher, and why. For example, the marketing team plans to sell a lot of jeans in April and September, so the business knows when to have additional stock available.

Indeed, if the task of reaching an overall, annual budget is going to be challenging, it would be beneficial to map out the weekly or monthly activity, estimate the likely short-term effect on sales of each – which then is a logical test to determine if all the activity planned for the year will be enough. An example of a budget with a link to sales results is shown next, for a hypothetical brand called Madison Chic jeans. The brand sells jeans online direct to consumers as well as through a select few retail outlets.

Let's briefly examine this budget as shown in Table 10.2.

In this example, the marketing team creates the budget based partly on last year's sales results as a baseline. The team has also factored in that its total spending on digital advertising will be approximately the same as the last couple of years, which underpins budgeted sales figures that are similar to last year plus a small increment reflecting the firm's broad growth objective. The marketing team has also identified that running consumer promotions has a big, temporary effect on sales. It has decided to run these promotions over two months in the coming year.

Therefore, we see in the budget there are estimated units and revenue figures for each month. In turn these are based on the assumption that if the brand runs the budgeted advertising on Facebook and Instagram, as well as co-operative advertising and POS with retailer partners, it will achieve these sales figures. Moreover, if the brand runs two large promotions during the year, sales will more than double while they run. The size of this sales spike is based on what has been learned in the past. Likewise, the brand team plans to run one price reduction of $9 discount per pair in November. It has learned that discounts of this magnitude result in sales increases of around 25 per cent over the normal level. As we can see, projected sales in November are 5,730 pairs, the normal level is around 4,600 per month.

Once all these planned activities are factored in, if the units and revenue estimates look acceptable, the team can conclude it has built in enough activity and spending for the year for the brand to reach the required sales objective.

The budget then adds up the revenue, deducts the cost of all the marketing activities, as well as taking out the staff costs for the marketing team. What is left over is the brand's contribution. Then, once other fixed costs are taken out (rent, other salaries) the firm's net profit is shown.

The question arises, if it is possible to estimate with some reasonable accuracy the sales effect of doing certain activities, why not double or triple the investment in those activities – to achieve very fast growth? The answer is, these are informed estimates, or forecasts; so to the actual results still have to be checked against forecasts. But if a budget of this type is created and it turns out to be quite accurate – then a decision would probably be made to up-weight the marketing investments, as long as there is capacity in the business to cope with increased demand. Alternatively, creating a budget of this type represents a quite good test of the marketing team's ability to stimulate demand. If they predicted quite a sizeable increase in sales from doing certain activities – and they were wrong – then this is valuable feedback and can be used in the next budget iteration next year.

WHAT IS A SENSITIVITY ANALYSIS?

In some marketing plans there will be a budget that draws a direct causal link between some marketing activities and sales. In other words, it says when we do this activity, it will have that much effect on sales – or perhaps profit, or a proxy for it such as 'contribution'. A budget like this is in effect a forecast of the future. And all budgets have to make some assumptions – such as, for example, that advertising or promotions will have some short-term effect on sales, based on what has happened in the past.

In cases like these, a manager may want to do a sensitivity analysis. A sensitivity analysis is a way to test how 'sensitive' the end result of the plan is to changes in those assumptions. When you hear people saying things like 'they modelled the budget', this is more or less saying the same thing, i.e. some analysts have tested various scenarios on a bottom-line result. For example, if we change an industry growth forecast from 3 per cent to 2 per cent, does the anticipated profit result collapse into a loss, or remain relatively unscathed? What if we had made an assumption that we could increase price by 2.5 per cent with no loss in sales? What if that assumption was not quite correct?

In the Madison Chic example, the marketing team determined or estimated that for every $1,000 spent on a consumer promotion, the brand would sell around 150 extra pairs of jeans; and that a price cut of $9 would result in about 800 extra pairs sold.

However, these are only an estimate of what will happen in the future. A sensitivity analysis could be used to see how much of a difference would be made to the total budget it that estimate was a bit different – suppose the additional sales from consumer promotions were only around 3,000 units per month instead of 4,000; or that the price discount of $9 resulted in a smaller uplift of only 600 instead of the expected 800 extra pairs. Will these slightly more pessimistic assumptions result in a small change in the overall expected result, or a big, problematic change?

In summary, a sensitivity analysis tests how much of a difference to financial projections there is if we change certain assumptions. Doing this will increase the firm's confidence in the marketing plan.

Self-test Questions

1. What is 'contribution', and why is it a useful measure for budgeting?
2. Why is it difficult to accurately calculate the 'payback' equation for marketing activity?
3. In your own words, explain 'zero based budgeting' and why some firms implement it.
4. Consider the budget for Madison Chic jeans. The brand is budgeting for big sales uplifts in April and September. If you were on this team would you be wondering about the projected sales figures for May and October, and why? (Hint, what is 'purchase acceleration'?)

TABLE 10.2 *Marketing Budget: Madison Chic Jeans*

	Jan	Feb	Mar	Apr	May	Jun	Jul	Sep	Oct	Nov	Dec	CY Total
Units	4520	4670	4670	10330	4480	4480	4520	10670	4670	5730	4670	63,410
Average sell price	$98	$98	$98	$98	$98	$98	$98	$98	$98	$89	$98	$97.20
Revenue $000's	$442,960	$457,660	$457,660	$1,012,340	$439,040	$439,040	$442,960	$1,045,660	$457,660	$509,970	$457,660	$6,162,610
Direct variable costs (totals)	$113,000	$116,750	$116,750	$258,250	$112,000	$112,000	$113,000	$266,750	$116,750	$143,250	$116,750	$1,585,250
Marketing expenses												
Advertising:												
Digital (Facebook and Instagram)	$25000	$25000	$25000	$25000	$25000	$25000	$25000	$25000	$25000	$25000	$25000	$275,000
Co-op with retailers		$15000	$15000		$15000	$15000		$15000	$15000		$15000	$105,000
Other:												
In-store POS and focused support to retailers	$19000	$10000	$19000				$19000	$19000	$19000		$19000	$133,000
Consumer promotion				$40000				$40000				$80,000
Marketing salaries	$29000	$29000	$29000	$29000	$29000	$29000	$29000	$29000	$29000	29000	$29000	$319,000
Total marketing expenses	$73000	$88000	$88000	$94000	$69000	$69000	$73000	$128000	$88000	$54000	$88000	$912,000
Total contribution	$256,960	$252,910	$252,910	$660,090	$258,040	$258,040	$256,960	$650,910	$252,910	$312,720	$252,910	$3,665,360
Not included fixed costs												
Fixed cost allocation												$3,200,000
Net result												$465,360

Note: this is a simplified example to illustrate the idea of a marketing budget with a link to product sales. We see that brand sales go up and down in the short term depending on the extent of marketing activity. Monthly sales estimates are based on last year's average, plus increments according to whatever promotion activity is being conducted during the month. In this example marketing salaries are deducted from revenue. Some small business owners may wish to do this if they want to see the net financial result once all marketing expenses are deducted. Note that a budget like this makes no account of marketing activity having a longer-term effect on sales.

Marketing Plan Case Study: Budget Template

In this section, we calculate Remedy clinic's overall marketing budget, and the budgeted figures for each aspect of Remedy's marketing mix. The timing of marketing expenditure is also mapped out, as well as anticipated client visits and resultant revenue per month.

Task

Confirm the anticipated marketing budget for Remedy clinic. Josh and Sarah decided they would use the approach of spending in line with their intended market share. Calculate the required figures using Table 10.3, to confirm your results from Table 7.3.

TABLE 10.3 *Anticipated Overall Marketing Spending for Remedy Clinic*

1	Market share objective for the next 12 months is:	%
2	Total spend by all providers in the market presently	
3	Planned marketing budget: row 2 multiplied by row 1 Make sure you're expressing the market share objective as a fraction, like 0.03 or something similar (hint: sense-check your result, the budget figure should be a small proportion of the total spend by all providers)	

Next, insert the anticipated cost of each marketing activity into the marketing budget, see Table 10.4. These costs will principally relate to advertising spending. Check the total is not more than the planned budget figure. Leave some funds aside for market research if it is planned to do some; re-calculate the total spend after including that line item. Then enter the anticipated number of new customers and repeat visits, and the anticipated revenue for each month. Check that the total revenue figure here corresponds with the revenue objective.

TABLE 10.4 *Marketing Budget for Remedy Clinic*

Marketing Activity	Spending $												
	Jan	Feb	Mar	Apr	May	Jun	Jul	Aug	Sep	Oct	Nov	Dec	Total

(Continued)

(Continued)

Marketing Activity	Spending £												
	Jan	Feb	Mar	Apr	May	Jun	Jul	Aug	Sep	Oct	Nov	Dec	Total
Budget total spend													£
New customer visits													
Repeat customer visits													
Anticipated revenue (total visits x price paid)													£

CHAPTER 11

Key Metrics and Market Research

The marketing plan is to a great extent a forecast of the future, and no one knows exactly what the future will bring. Therefore, it is vital that the business obtains updates on key metrics to ensure the plan is progressing. A metric is simply a measure used either to monitor business success – usually in units sold or revenue gained, to gauge the health of the brand, or to indicate the level of activity that is occurring.

There is obviously a close link between objectives and metrics. Metrics are essentially the measurement of objectives. If we have an objective pertaining to numbers of new customers acquired, then there is a direct link to the metric, which is the count of the number of new customers acquired. And we would look at this metric every month to see how well it is progressing against our objective. Having a regime of measuring and reporting key metrics focuses the team's attention on the objectives and how they can achieve them.

If the marketing team can receive metrics at certain intervals (quarterly, six-monthly, etc.), it can adjust the marketing plan if the metrics are not at the level expected.

The plan outlines the key metrics that will guide the plan's progress. We now explain in more detail the specific kinds of outcome and activity metrics.

END-RESULT METRICS

As the name suggests, these are the end result of marketing activity. There are potentially a large number of such metrics, but common ones are:

Sales: sales can be measured in units (like loaves of bread, or hotel room nights), or in revenue (units x average price). Sales are always evaluated for a particular time period such as a month, quarter or year. Sales itself can be a key metric but also increases in sales (e.g. an 8 per cent increase in sales units in the next 12 months) is a common metric.

Market share: market share is a useful metric to supplement the sales metric. Sales (units, revenue) is obviously a crucial metric for almost any organisation, but it is possible that sales are increasing because the category the business is in is growing. Management might be disappointed if sales increased by 3 per cent knowing the total category increased by 5 per cent (because this would mean the business lost some market share). Therefore, market share controls for the fact that the category may be growing, or declining.

Market share of current business: in some market sectors, such as banking, market share is calculated as: our total number of customers x the average number of products they hold with us, as a proportion of all customers in the market x their average number of products. A problem with this scenario is that since only some customers actually enter the market and buy a product, switch between providers, or stop using a certain provider in a time period like a year, overall market share is quite inert to these changes. Therefore, a useful supplement to (overall) market share is market share of the business conducted in the current year. For example, a brand's share of all the home loans, personal loans, credit cards and other banking products purchased, cancelled or switched during the current calendar year. An analogy is a car brand's share of all the cars actually on the road, versus its share of all the cars sold in 2021. It would be naive for a car brand to use the former measure as it reflects sales from many years past.

Number of customers: this sort of metric would be appropriate for a business that can actually identify its customers. An example would be a bank or insurance company that can count the number of individuals (or businesses) that have an account with it.

Number of new customers: many businesses are not only interested in the total number of customers they have but the number of new ones they have attracted. To continue the example of a bank, it might have 300,000 customers – and it sets an objective to attract 20,000 new ones over the next year.

Average purchases/spend per buyer: average number of purchases made, or average number of products used in the case of businesses like telcos, banks or insurance companies. An example from tourism is the average number of days spent in a country by tourists and the average amount they spend while in the host country.

These outcome metrics above all directly – arithmetically – relate to sales.

MARKET-BASED ASSET METRICS

The second type of metric is market-based assets. These don't arithmetically link to sales, but sales now and in the future will depend on them. Therefore, these are also important metrics to monitor, as they are additional indicators of the health of the business.

There are two principal market-based assets, namely mental availability and physical availability. We discuss these, then examine a third type of market-based asset which is based around buyer's evaluation of the firm or brand.

Mental Availability

Brand Mental Availability

This general term means the overall propensity to evoke the brand in memory over a range of potential cues, prompts or need/usage situations, including the name of the category – refer to Romaniuk (2013) and Romaniuk (2016). There are three specific measures of mental availability, namely mental market share, mental penetration and network size. We discuss these, then turn to the related metric of brand awareness.

Mental Market Share

This is the 'share of mind' that a brand has over a range of usage, benefit or product cues. For example, suppose we wished to measure mental market share for a pain relief brand such as Panadol or Tylenol. We conduct a survey of 1,000 people (say), and showed them five brands. The cues we decided to use were, say, need something fast acting, for strong pain, which is gentle on the stomach, and OK for kids. We then asked them, of these brands ... which ones are fast acting. Then ... which ones are for strong pain. And so on. A brand's mental market share is its share of all the responses to these brand/cue questions. An example of how one would derive this measurement is presented in Table 11.1.

TABLE 11.1 *Mental Market Share Example*

	Number of People Linking Brand to This Attribute				Total Number of Responses	% % of all Responses	N % Linking Brand to at Least One Attribute	Average Number of Attributes Linked to This Brand
Brand	**Fast Acting**	**For Strong Pain**	**Gentle on Stomach**	**OK for Kids**				
Adzove	157	112	92	67	428	33	367	1.2
Blinke	105	91	78	54	328	25	298	1.1
Zamoc	88	74	62	41	265	20	231	1.1
Hyzerc	55	48	39	31	173	13	147	1.1
Xanyl	49	32	20	21	122	10	117	1.0
Total	*454*	*357*	*291*	*214*	*1316*			

We add up all the brand attribute responses for each brand and calculate each brand's proportion of all the associations. This is its 'mental market share'. Therefore, in Table 11.1, Adzove has 33 per cent share of what we can think of as the 'brain space' or mental associations for this category. How did we get 33? Answer: Adzove received 428 out of the total of 1,316 responses across all brands.

Self-test Question

What is the 'mental market share' of the brand Hyzerc in Table 11.1?

Mental Penetration

This is the proportion of people who associate a particular brand with at least one cue. To continue the example above, a sample of 1,000 people are shown five brands and then given the first cue, need something fast acting – which brands come to mind? Then for strong pain – which brands come to mind? And so on. Suppose of the 1,000 people, 231 mentioned the brand Zamoc for at least one of these five cues. This is the brand's mental penetration, which would be 23.

Mental Network Size

This is the average number of cues or associations the brand is linked to. For example, in Table 11.1 above, of all the 265 people who mentioned Zamoc for at least one cue, the average number of cues they linked the brand to was 1.1. This is analogous to purchase frequency in brand buying metrics. Network size can tell us if our brand has a too-narrow network size. In other words, if it is linked to a small number of cues or associations. In general, a bigger network size is preferable because it means the brand is on average linked to a broader range of usage situations.

Brand Awareness

Brand awareness can be unprompted ('name some brands of …') or prompted ('have you heard of brand —'). Awareness is a useful measure if buying situations involve thinking about the name of the product category as a buying cue, for example 'I need a coffee' or 'I need car insurance'. But the category name may not be the only cue that people evoke when they have a need or buying situation. Or they might not think 'the category' at all, rather they might think in terms of benefits, features or usage situations. For this reason, many marketers have embraced the broader, more sophisticated memory-based metric called mental availability.

Physical Availability

Physical availability is how easy the brand is to notice and buy in buying situations (Romaniuk & Sharp, 2016). It is a market-based asset because it is a valuable resource that accrues to the firm from marketing activity, and exists 'out in the market' rather than inside the firm.

An important point is that while the term 'physical availability' has a connotation of bricks-and-mortar retail stores, physical availability is a relevant concept for the online world.

Metrics for physical availability include:

- The sheer number of stores, physical sites or online sites where intending buyers can purchase the brand. An example is a pet food manufacturer: at how many grocery stores, specialist pet-food retailers and even veterinary clinics is its product available to buy? Taking the example further, how many online stores offer its brand for sale?

- The number of businesses that act as referrers for the brand. For example, a small financial planner might receive referrals from taxation accountants and lawyers. A financial services firm could sell its car-loan products via a wide network of car dealerships.
- The number of third-party information sites or recommendation sites that feature the brand. For example, banks offer mortgages, and there are a plethora of recommendation sites that examine the relative merits of mortgage products. The more of these that include the mortgage products of a particular brand (Barclays, HSBC, Santander and so on), the wider is that bank's physical availability.
- The extent to which the firm or brand appears in search engine results. Take the example of a small legal firm. What proportion of the time does its name appear when users type in relevant keywords?
- Opening hours, and even availability of staff can be considered an aspect of physical availability for a small business. If a hairdressing salon decides to open for longer hours, or makes more staff available, it is potentially making itself easier to buy from, therefore it is boosting its physical availability.

These physical availability metrics all pertain to what is called presence – being present in buying situations.

There are other aspects of physical availability too, one of them is prominence (Romaniuk & Sharp, 2016: Ch. 8). Prominence is the extent to which the firm is noticeable in buying situations. A firm can be present, but not necessarily very noticeable in such situations. Metrics that pertain to this aspect of physical availability include:

- How visually prominent or distinct is the firm's premises? This may be an especially important metric for small retail businesses. If a business is visually recognisable from a long distance, this can make it easier to find and therefore buy from.
- How visually prominent are the firm's products in reseller stores or websites? Take the example of a cosmetics brand sold in department stores. Is it easily visible once one enters the cosmetics department? How much 'real estate' is allocated to the brand in the department, and is it in high foot-traffic locations?
- In the case of online search results, what proportion of the time does the brand appear in the first half-dozen results, as opposed to further down the page or even not on the first page of results at all.

Evaluation

A third type of market-based asset is buyer's evaluation of the firm or brand. Two common evaluation metrics are customer satisfaction and willingness to recommend, which is popularised as the 'Net Promoter'.

Customer Satisfaction

Customer satisfaction is one of the most widely used measures in market research. Of course, it is an evaluation measure, not an indicator of mental availability. Customer satisfaction – at the individual level – is certainly important. If customers are disappointed it is reasonable to think their chances of buying again are lower. That said, the research on satisfaction and actual customer retention is rather thin. The evidence that does exist is mostly based on what people say in surveys – people who give a high satisfaction score also tend to say they're going to be more loyal in the future. The problem with this is an effect called response bias – saying one thing in a survey actually influences the answers to later questions. It could be that people say they're going to be highly loyal partly because they've just said they were very satisfied, as per the heavy response bias reported in De Jong et al. (2012). Another study shows the big influence of response bias: Seiders et al. (2005) reported the correlation between satisfaction and repurchase intentions to be r = 0.53, but the correlation between satisfaction and actual later purchase was only r = 0.07.

It might be surprising to learn that there is no well-established association between satisfaction and market share. In other words: bigger brands don't have customers with higher satisfaction levels. In fact the relationship is actually slightly negative (Fornell, 1995) and no one really knows why. What about changes in satisfaction with a brand over time – do they link to changes in market share? A recent study of more than 30 brands, over 10 to 15 years found the correlation between changes in ACSI scores (American Customer Satisfaction Index) and sales revenue was – zero! (Dawes, 2020a).

This line of argument is certainly not saying managers can ignore satisfying their customers. Satisfaction should be measured and high scores are certainly not a bad thing! But these findings indicate that if your main focus for business growth is increasing customer satisfaction scores, it will not be enough.

Willingness to Recommend: the 'Net Promoter Score'

Arguably, willingness to recommend indicates a buyer's favourable evaluation of a brand. Willingness to recommend is usually measured by something called Net Promoter Score. Businesses all around the world use the Net Promoter Score (NPS) as a key marketing metric. This is because it has been sold very effectively as 'the one number you need to grow' (Reichheld, 2003). The inventor, Fred Reichheld, a senior partner at the big consultancy company, Bain & Co. Reichheld, wrote a very popular book that argued brands will grow by cultivating loyal customers, who will then recommend them to other people.

The way NPS works in this. Clients are surveyed and asked how likely they are to recommend the product or service to a friend/colleague. Scores are given from zero to ten. The scores of 6 and under are subtracted from the scores of 9 or 10. People who give a score of 9 or 10 are thought to be definite recommenders, those giving 6 or less are thought to be detractors (who will give negative word of mouth). Subtracting the 9 and 10 from the 6-and-under-scores gives the 'net' score.

Net Promoter is very popular. But lots of people have argued that it has flaws. Therefore, it's worth discussing it. First, it assumes people who give a low intent to recommend score are detractors. But that's only an assumption. Second, people often give high willingness to recommend scores, but actual recommendation comes from being aware that another person would be interested in the recommendation! We might be highly willing to recommend that new vacuum cleaner we just bought but why would we think we need to tell our friends or colleagues about it? So, typical Net Promoter scores highly inflate the actual amount of recommendation that would occur in a market. Third, the promulgators of NPS say it is linked to business growth. However, some of the examples of this supposed link use past growth, not future growth (Keiningham et al., 2007; Shaw, 2008), in other words the Net Promoter scores were obtained after growth had occurred.

But, marketers might say – people who give us high Net Promoter scores buy more from us!

A fairly common rationale among businesses that do use NPS is that there is 'proof' it works, in that individual clients who give higher scores buy more from the business. And this might be true, but it doesn't mean the NPS induces them to buy more. It could well be that clients who buy more tend to give higher Net Promoter scores! Let us explain this a bit more.

A robust finding that has been around since the 1960s is that users of a brand say more positive things about it than non-users (Bird et al., 1970; Bird & Ehrenberg, 1970).

We can take that original finding a step further, to see that heavier buyers of a brand say even more nice things about it than light buyers or non-buyers of a brand. In Table 11.2 we show the average number of positive brand attributes linked to four insurance brands, by non, light, medium and heavy buyers. Plainly, the heavy buyers say more positive things about the brand: 3.5 positive attributes compared to 3.1 for mediums and 2.4 for lights. Now, we can understand why it might be the case that clients who give us high Net Promoter scores apparently give us a lot of business: it's the other way around! Clients who deal with us more, also say more positive things. And those positive things likely include higher willingness to recommend.

TABLE 11.2 *Brand Attribute Responses among Non, Light, Medium and Heavy Brand Users*

	Average Number of Positive Mentions for the Brand for These Attributes: Good Coverage, Convenient Branches, Simple Policies, Will Pay Claims, Price Competitive				Row Average: Number of Positive Things Said about the Brand
	N	G	A	Z	
Non-user	2.2	0.8	1.6	1.0	1.4
Light user	3.0	2.3	2.2	2.0	2.4
Medium user	3.5	2.6	2.3	1.0	3.1
Heavy user	3.7	3.2	-	-	3.5

Source: Author data. Brand names disguised.

Overall, there is a strong argument to avoid using the NPS as a marketing metric. It is presented as a metric that indicates, or drives, future growth but the evidence on this is far less than decisive. It implies growth comes from service excellence, or customer loyalty, or recommendations. These are all desirable factors, but we also know that they are not the principal drivers of growth. Lastly, willingness or intention to recommend is not the same as actually recommending. Most people who give a high intention to recommend don't actually end up recommending (Kumar et al., 2007).

PRECURSORS TO SALES METRICS

Next, there are other metrics that are precursors to sales. One is the number of enquiries that buyers make to the firm.

For many businesses, a sale is preceded by an enquiry. For example, a mobile phone company might have customers who come into stores, or call asking about prices or terms, then buy later. If enquiry levels tend to be a leading indicator of sales, then enquiry would be a very worthwhile metric to monitor. Enquiries might be measured by face to face, telephone, texts ('how much would it cost for you to come and fix my leaking tap' for a plumber), email or website hits, or enquiry forms submitted. The fact that enquiries are often very closely linked to sales a week or month later means that businesses should have good systems for tracking them. This helps the business (a) know if recent marketing activity has been working, (b) have the capacity to handle the enquiries and (c) if enquiries increase, start building some capacity to handle the upcoming increase in business.

Making a link between specific precursors to sales and end-result metrics means the firm is better informed to implement marketing activity to boost these precursors. For example, specific activities to generate phone enquiries or website visits.

Some commentators suggest that it can be enlightening to examine Google searches for one's brand, and perhaps also for the category. In fact, it has been strongly implied that 'share of search' can predict future sales for a brand (Swift, 2020). While there is a lot of work to be done to determine the extent to which this claim is correct, certainly knowing about search levels for one's brand and how it varies over time would be an important enquiries-type metric.

ACTIVITY METRICS

It is also important monitor certain marketing activities. It might not seem intuitively obvious to do this, because arguably a business could do a lot of activity that does not translate into sales results. Or it may be very difficult to discern a clear relationship between certain activities and sales. However, the point is to count activity that should (logically) lead to sales, or improvement of market-based assets, which that will lead to sales later on. Counting activity is a good way for marketing to demonstrate its value to the business. It may not be possible to show (via some sort of statistical analysis) that activity A, B or C 'drives' sales. However, it is good for the marketing team to show what they accomplish in terms of activity from the funds and personnel they are allocated. For example, the marketing team might say something along the lines of: 'with a smallish budget of $5,000 we managed to reach over a million potential buyers with a message about our business, on three occasions this year on average'.

Activity Metrics Inventory

There is a wide array of possible activity metrics. For business to business firms, this metric can include client presentations or proposals written. By a proposal, we mean a written 'pitch' for a potential client's business, such as an accounting firm trying to win a contract to do the book-keeping and tax returns for, say, an air conditioning installation firm.

Activity metrics can also include number of weeks or days 'on air' (in which a news story mentions the brand) or in which some communications activity occurred. As an example, for a small consultancy firm, this could be the number of days of the year in which a client presentation, conference talk or some PR exposure occurred. Social media posts could also be included here if this is relevant to the business. Activity metrics can also include things such as the number of clients in the company's database or the accuracy of all the client records in the company's database. One could verify the accuracy of these records from bounce-backs.

For firms which sell through distribution channels (say, a vitamin maker that sells through retail pharmacies and small grocery retailers) activity metrics could be number of sales calls made each week, or the number of its retailer partners who feature particular point of sale material.

For organisations that sell services, such as education, the number of visits to their events such as open days or information sessions would be an important metric, as they logically are a lead indicator of future sales and the extent to which marketing communication is being noticed by potential buyers. Getting potential buyers to come to an event can be an important source of marketing intelligence too – having marketing or customer service staff chatting to customers and answering their questions helps the business to understand what's on buyer's minds. One should split a metric like this into two parts: the number of events, and the attendances and enquiries arising from those events.

A SIDENOTE: MARKETING RETURN ON INVESTMENT

It has become very fashionable to talk about marketing return on investment (ROI), which means the short-term financial gain from each dollar of marketing spending.

While the idea seems sensible (after all, the concept of return on investment is a fundamental one in business finance) it has some severe shortcomings for marketing. A big problem is that if you identify an activity with a high marketing ROI it strongly implies you should shift money from your low ROI activity into the high ROI activity. But businesses don't just need to earn a high rate of return on their marketing dollars, they need high absolute sales. And high marketing ROI tends to come from small-scale activity. If you find you can spend $2,000 on some digital activity that earns a marketing ROI of 150 per cent, you get $3,000 back – but if you're in a business that has a turnover of $2 million, this is an immaterial amount. The $2 million in turnover very likely depends on a much larger amount of marketing spending, accumulated over years, that might not have necessarily earned a short-term ROI at all. Making decisions to transfer spending to apparently high ROI activity might jeopardise the things that built the business.

To expand our thinking about marketing ROI, consider a completely different context: the case of an urban shopping centre spending $2 million on upgrading its entrance. Why is this being done? The owners of the centre judged that the centre would benefit in terms of visual appeal, and so decided to spend this large amount of money. And indeed, they could be quite right. But it would be virtually impossible to calculate the ROI of this investment in terms of increased customer numbers or sales revenue for the centre. This is because it just might not have any short-term effect (shoppers begin to patronise a shopping centre because it renovated the entrance?); and trying to disentangle the effect of the entrance upgrade from all sorts of other factors in the longer term would be fruitless.

But the entrance upgrade is a necessary investment to maintain and improve the shopping centre's visual or aesthetic appeal. Without this spending the centre would gradually look dowdy, run-down and out of date. In other words – the shopping centre is a valuable asset, which needs periodic investment to maintain its value. And indeed, marketing directors may need to make similar decisions – without needing to justify them by recourse to ROI; but simply by logic – 'we need to spend money on our valuable asset to preserve its value'. One can know that the spending was 'worth it' but trying to figure out the ROI of that spending can be obtuse.

MARKET RESEARCH

The marketing plan should list out what market research is needed for the following year. The reasons are: (a) so the cost of the research gets allocated into the budget and (b) so the timing of the research can be planned for. It does take time to get research projects commissioned. A rationale for doing the research is also needed – what doesn't the business know and why does it need to find out? Or what information needs to be updated? It may be the case that specific pieces of market research are needed to obtain certain metrics – for example, brand awareness. Or the business might not feel it has adequate information on customer needs, therefore a survey could be planned to acquire the information.

Self-test Questions

1. Explain the link between objectives and metrics.
2. Why are we interested in market share as well as sales? Surely it is sales that produces our actual revenue?
3. Explain the concept of market share of current business. How is this different from market share?

There is one more section to be included in the plan: a summary of information sources.

BIBLIOGRAPHY/INFORMATION SOURCES

In this section of the plan you list out information sources, as well as the detail that sits behind your analyses in the current marketing situation. The idea is that you put the headline content, and the important 'take-outs' in the actual plan and relegate the detail to this bibliography and information sources section. That way the plan doesn't get bogged down in detail.

The value of explicitly listing out information sources is: first, we all have fallible memories, and it will be extremely frustrating and non-productive to find information relevant to your plan then forget where it came from and second, these information sources can be re-used and updated for the next iteration of the plan.

Marketing Plan Case Study: Metrics, Market Research Template

Use the following template to construct the metrics and market research section of the marketing plan for Remedy Physiotherapy.

Metrics

End-result Metrics

Outline the end-result metrics, how often they will be reviewed, and by whom.

Market-based Asset Metrics

Outline the specific market-based asset metrics, how often they will be reviewed, and by whom.

Precursor to Sales Metrics

Outline the specific precursor metrics, how often they will be reviewed, and by whom.

Activity Metrics

Outline the specific precursor metrics, how often they will be reviewed, and by whom.

Market Research

In order to obtain key metrics, it is likely that the firm may have to commission some market research. Describe what market research is considered necessary for the following year.

Topic or Metric to Be Researched

Outline the specific issues that need research.

How will the information be obtained and when?

Specify how the relevant information will be acquired (survey, secondary data, observation) and when (what time in the year).

Reminder: Now Write the Executive Summary

Now that you have completed all the sections of your marketing plan from the internal analysis through to controls, you write the executive summary following the guidelines at the start of the book. Place this at the start of the plan.

The next section covers the important topic of how to construct good tables and charts for your plan. By 'good' we mean they look attractive, and they communicate a key message you want to impart.

CHAPTER 12 How to Construct Good Tables and Graphs for Your Marketing Plan

A marketing plan involves an assembly of facts, together with lines of thinking, which presents a reasoned course of action. Facts often come in numerical form, and so people writing marketing plans will often use tables and graphs. A problem arises in that many marketing plans, indeed many marketing and business documents, do a poor job of presenting data in tables or graphs – which means the real storyline is lost, managers do not properly understand certain facts and perhaps the plan is not supported. Therefore, this chapter goes through some fundamentals of presenting data in tables and graphs. It cover these points:

- How to clearly present numbers and the 'story' they tell in a table.
- What graph to use for different sorts of data.
- Why and how to write clear storylines or captions for tables and graphs.
- Why clear labelling of tables and graphs is important, and how to do it.

Many of the recommendations and ideas in this section are based on Andrew Ehrenberg's famous book *Data Reduction* (1974), available for free at www.empgens.com.

The key concept to keep in mind when presenting data is that you're using it to tell a story, for the audience or reader to get a 'take-out'. They don't need to retain a memory of exactly what the numbers you presented were, what they should have is an understanding of what those numbers told you.

GOOD PRACTICE FOR PRESENTING DATA IN TABLES

To illustrate good practice for tables, let's first consider an example of a poorly constructed table, as shown in Table 12.1. We'll then apply these rules for data presentation: ordering, rounding, clear headings and a *storyline*, to pre-empt obvious questions that might arise from the information in the table. Suppose we are a producer of snack foods and one of our products is nuts. We produce a table showing the retail sales of nut types as in Table 12.1.

TABLE 12.1 *Retail Sales of Nuts, Unnamed Country*

	Year 1	Year 2
ALMOND	762,309,599.68	735,935,714.87
OTHER NUT	25,816,456.08	23,362,326.67
CASHEW HALVES	250,988,970.67	243,016,198.44
CASHEW WHOLE	526,802,065.81	558,284,045.06
CORN KERNEL	14,288,910.50	14,295,165.40
MACADAMIA	38,555,853.08	42,113,107.98
MIXED NUT DELUXE	376,013,581.37	367,065,873.19
MIXED NUT REGULAR	314,316,823.17	299,773,722.77
PEANUT	788,204,646.75	746,734,446.27
PECAN	49,375,549.59	58,529,411.02
PISTACHIO	618,266,536.45	745,360,249.83
PUMPKIN/SQUASH	54,620,247.97	54,898,628.39
SUNFLOWER KRN/SD	171,361,162.16	156,012,976.23
TRAIL MIX	748,987,890.87	745,573,969.21
WALNUT	39,062,711.42	38,779,018.79
Grand Total	4,778,971,005.55	4,829,734,854.11

Source: Author data.

The problems with Table 12.1 are, first, we don't know what exactly the figures represent. We know from the table header that the figures relate to sales, but is that sales in units, kilograms or dollars? In fact, the figures are dollars, but a reader would not necessarily know this unless it is explicitly mentioned. One needs to make it clear exactly what is represented by figures in tables. The second issue is that the table has no meaningful order. We can 'eyeball' the figures and identify that some nuts are hugely more popular than others. But why make it difficult to comprehend this information? We can make that much easier by ordering it by size, that is, with the biggest sellers at the top and the smallest at the bottom. This would make the story far easier to comprehend. Next, the data has unnecessary detail – we certainly do not need to know these figures to the exact cent or even dollar or hundreds of dollars. So, the data can be divided by one million to make it easier to comprehend. We should also make a meaningful table title to go above the table. Note that table titles should not go underneath the table! Occasionally people do this, but it looks terrible. The table title should also have a number, because your plan might have dozens of tables and it is far easier to handle queries or check them if they are all numbered.

Lastly, in its present format we do not know what the row headings, such as 'Nutrition', 'Almond' and so on mean. The answer is they represent nut types as well as seeds, or products (like trail mix), which includes nuts and seeds, but a reader may not necessarily know this. This table is based on an industry classification of what is considered to be the snack nut category, which comprises both nuts as well as products made primarily from nuts. Therefore, we need to make it clear to a reader, who may not be familiar with the market or these nuances of definitions, what the row descriptions actually mean. We'll now practise these tasks. The table in its original format is available in Excel, at study.sagepub.com/dawes. You can use the version on the website to complete these tasks.

Practice Tasks

Ordering

Order the nut types in Table 12.1 from largest to smallest sales in Year 1. Keep the grand total row at the bottom.

Rounding

Round the sales figures to millions (so that 39,062,711.42 becomes 39). Rounding helps us focus on the story that is in the data, without being distracted by long numbers that in this context have unnecessary precision.

Calculate Growth

While this table tells us about how sales dollars vary according to product type, we are probably also interested in which products are growing or declining. Therefore, we should calculate the percentage change from year 1 to year 2. We can do that to the table in Excel using a simple formula such as =(B2-A2)/A2*100 where the first year's sales figure is in cell A2 and the second year's sales figure is in B2. Calculate this yourself and insert the growth figures into the table.

Format Row Headings

Also, while the data came with the product names in ALL CAPS this is not a reader friendly format. Fortunately, Excel has a great feature, which is a formula: =PROPER(cell address) which converts all caps to 'normal' font. Use this now to replace the all caps row headings. Copy and paste your new row headers from Excel.

Create Clear Column Headings

Write clear headings for the columns including year.

Write a Storyline

Lastly, we need a storyline – what is the one-line 'take-out' of this data? Write what you think it is.

After making all these changes the revised table (minus the storyline, that's for you to write) now looks like the table in Figure 12.1. This version is much more readable. It tells us two key pieces of information. First, we get a good sense of the magnitude of difference between the product types: some sell over 700 million dollars per year, others sell under 50 million. Second, the two biggest sellers, peanuts and almonds are declining. Another big seller, pistachios, is growing at a very fast rate. If we were a business involved in the marketing of snack nuts and seeds, this is absolutely vital, basic information that would feature in our marketing plan. The question might then arise, what nut products do we sell: do *we* have products that align with the ones that are experiencing growth?

FIGURE 12.1 *Good Practice in Presenting Tables*

Informative column headings

Clear heading above table including table number

Note, you normally identify the actual years in a plan i.e. 2022 etc.

Table 41. Retail $ Sales and Growth of Snack Nuts and Seeds, Year 1 – Year 2

Nut/Seed Type	$ Sales (millions) Year 1	$Sales (millions) Year 2	Growth year 1 to
Peanut	788	747	–5
Almond	762	736	–3
Trial Mix	749	746	–0.5
Pistachio	618	745	21
Cashew Whole	527	558	6
Mixed Nut Deluxe	376	367	–2
Mixed Nut Regular	314	300	–5
Cashew Halves	251	243	–3
Sunflower	171	156	–9
Pumpkin	55	55	1
Pecan	49	59	19
Walnut	39	39	–1
Macadamia	39	42	9
Other nut	26	23	–10
Corn kernel	14	14	0
Grand Total	**4,779**	**4,830**	**(Avg.) 1**

Storyline for the table.

Rounding and ordering

'Storyline' for the table

Use totals and averages

WHAT SORT OF GRAPHS TO USE

Graphing the Association Between Two Variables

Graphs feature in most marketing plans and we need to consider the best choice of graph for what information we are working with.

Sometimes you will have data on two variables, and you want to show if and how they are related to each other. Perhaps when one is bigger, the other one tends to be bigger, or maybe when one is big, the other one is smaller. We call a pattern like this an 'association' between two variables. A 'variable' just means something of interest – for example the age of consumers can be a variable, and we could see if it has an *association* with some other variable, like their favourite brand of toothpaste, or which banks they use.

You can readily show associations like these in a table. Here is an example, Table 12.2, using coffee brands from a Western country. The information is masked to some degree for commercial confidentiality. The table is ordered in descending order of market share. The other variable is the brand's distribution coverage (the percentage of all retail outlets the brand is present in). Note that the table header tells us what the information in the table pertains to. Of course, the actual country and year would be mentioned in a real plan. Note that market share is listed to one decimal point, while distribution coverage has no decimals. This is because much of the market share information is less than 10 per cent, so arguably it is appropriate to show one decimal point for accuracy.

TABLE 12.2 *Brand Market Share and Distribution*

Brand	Market Share	Distribution Coverage
Starbucks	20.4	88
Folgers	14.7	87
Maxwell House	7.1	76
Dunkin' Donuts	6.6	79
Green Mountain	4.6	47
Peet's Coffee	3.3	43
McCafé	2.9	50
Nescafe	2.6	71
Eight O'Clock	2.0	35
Donut Shop	2.0	46
Gevalia	1.8	59
Average	6.0	62

Source: Author data.

You can also portray this relationship or association between two variables in a graph called a *scatterplot*. Here is the data from Table 12.2, translated into a scatterplot. The question arises as to which variable to put on the X axis (the horizontal one), and which variable on the Y axis. The conventional approach is to consider which of the variables we are primarily interested in and put that one on the Y axis. The other variable, which we think might help us understand the primary variable, we put on the X axis. Access the table in the book's website and create a chart in Excel like Figure 12.2. Make sure to label the axes and create a graph title. As well, write a caption that says what the 'take-out' from the chart is.

FIGURE 12.2 *Market Share and Distribution, Store Bought Coffee*

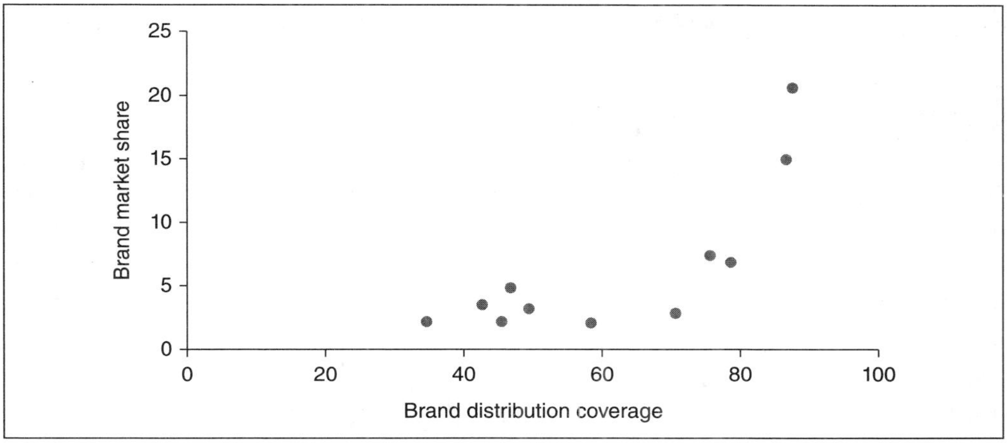

Source: Author data.

Tasks

Make your own Excel chart that looks like Figure 12.2 above.

Write a very brief storyline for it.

GRAPHING REPEATED OBSERVATIONS OF A VARIABLE OVER TIME

Suppose you have some information that shows repeated observations of some item over time. For example, total sales of clothing items per week for a clothing boutique in Paris, over a 104-week time period. You want to examine over-time trends, and whether there are seasonal ups and downs. The generally accepted way of visually showing this data is via a line graph. One would normally put time on the X axis, and the variable of interest on the Y axis. Let's work through an example to do this. Table 12.3 shows data for four-week unit sales for a type of alcoholic spirit in France. A unit in this instance is a 9-litre case. This data is also available via the book's website.

The data uses 13 x four-week periods in a year. Using four-week periods is better than using calendar months, because some months have fewer days in them than others, which means monthly sales can be higher or lower. Note the table heading describes what the data represents.

The data is arranged into these multiple columns simply to save space. The data that is in the book website is stacked vertically, ready to be graphed. The line graph of this data is shown in Figure 12.3. Note how the graph axes are both clearly labelled.

Tasks

Create your own line graph in Excel using this data.

Write a storyline about what the graph shows.

TABLE 12.3 *Four-week Unit Sales of Alcoholic Spirit Product, France*

Period (4-wk)	Year	Unit Sales	Period (4-wk)	Year	Unit Sales	Period (4-wk)	Year	Unit Sales
Period 1	1	290,072	14	2	297,053	Period 1	3	293,434
Period 2	1	311,266	15	2	312,975	Period 2	3	314,620
Period 3	1	310,108	16	2	311,707	Period 3	3	321,898
Period 4	1	326,840	17	2	336,276	Period 4	3	333,754
Period 5	1	317,462	18	2	332,137	Period 5	3	341,323
Period 6	1	328,713	19	2	334,101	Period 6	3	334,297
Period 7	1	317,431	20	2	310,459	Period 7	3	309,625
Period 8	1	313,932	21	2	324,425	Period 8	3	297,861
Period 9	1	328,768	22	2	323,071	Period 9	3	322,742
Period 10	1	301,442	23	2	345,851	Period 10	3	328,302
Period 11	1	365,489	24	2	343,432	Period 11	3	347,985
Period 12	1	347,569	25	2	349,176	Period 12	3	352,582
Period 13	1	474,277	26	2	499,711	Period 13	3	469,053

FIGURE 12.3 *Four-week Unit Sales, Alcohol Product, France*

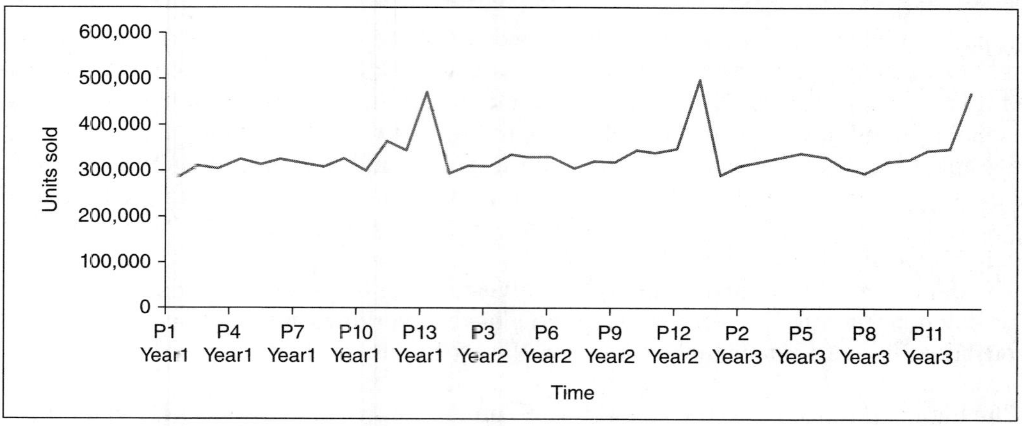

Source: Author data.

Graphing to Show a Recurring Pattern in Data

In some cases, we may want to use graphs to visually reinforce a point about a recurring *pattern* we have discerned in some data. An example is shown in Table 12.4, using banking data. Brand names are disguised. The overall story is that each of these banks shows the same pattern, namely that a large proportion of their buyers use the bank for only one financial product, and only a small proportion use them for many products. This pattern may be important for a marketing person to communicate to their colleagues, as it has an implication for how a banking brand is likely to grow. Therefore, it could be shown in a series of column graphs, one for each bank, and all on one slide to show the pervasiveness of the pattern. A challenge for the audience watching the presentation could be to guess which particular graph is for the bank they work at.

TABLE 12.4 *Percentage of Bank Customers with 1, 2, 3 or 4+ Products (UK, Financial Services)*

		% of Bank Customer Base with 1, 2, 3 or 4+ Products			
Brand*	**Penetration**	**1**	**2**	**3**	**4+**
B	34	55	21	15	9
H1	33	61	23	10	6
S	29	56	30	9	5
Na	28	60	21	11	8
L	20	54	21	14	11
Na	19	59	22	11	8
H2	17	49	26	16	9
T	14	77	19	3	1
TS	8	74	14	7	5
Average	22	61	22	11	7

Source: Author data. Bank names disguised.

Tasks

Create column charts for the biggest four brands from Table 12.4. Figure 12.4 shows the style. Present them on a PowerPoint slide.

Explain what pattern is obvious in these graphs.

Don't Use Spider Charts

Spider charts, also known as radar charts, are terrible. They do not aid understanding of the data they are derived from. The recommendation is to not use them. Here is an example in Figure 12.5. The data is client ratings of a firm on certain brand attributes such as 'accessible', 'community oriented' and so on. Scores are included for 'our firm', a particular competitor and the market average.

FIGURE 12.4 *Percentage of B Bank's Customer Base Using It for 1, 2, 3 or 4+ Products*

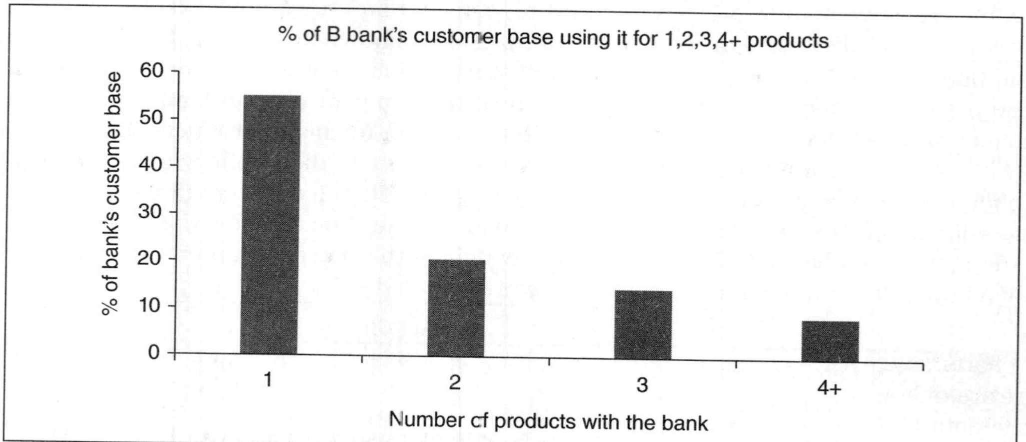

FIGURE 12.5 *Comparison of Key Attributes: Spider Chart*

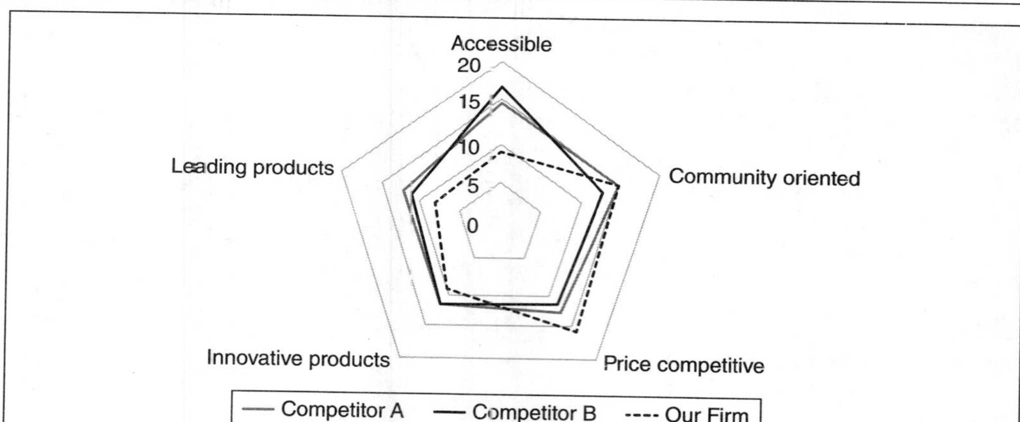

The story from the data is far clearer if we just present it in a simple table, as per Table 12.5. Note how the table is ordered from largest to smallest in both rows and columns. Now we can potentially see the story better.

Task

What is the main story from the data in Table 12.5?

TABLE 12.5 Comparison of Key Attributes

	Accessible	Community Oriented	Price Competitive	Innovative Products	Leading Products	Average
Competitor A	15	15	13	12	12	13
Competitor B	17	13	12	12	11	13
Our firm	9	15	16	10	8	12
Average	14	14	14	11	10	-

Source: Author data.

Don't Use Pie Charts

Pie charts are used to show the percentage splits in some factor of interest. Sometimes there are only a few of these splits, sometimes there are many. If we have only three splits of the data for instance, why is there a need to use a pie chart? You could just state the information in words. And if you have many data splits, the data is too finely graded to use a pie chart because the detail of the small percentages is lost. Pie charts convey less understanding of data than a well-designed table would. Here is an example of a typical pie chart. The data comes from UK survey data obtained by the author.

FIGURE 12.6 Percentage of UK Consumers Saying This Is Their Mobile Phone Plan Provider: Pie Chart

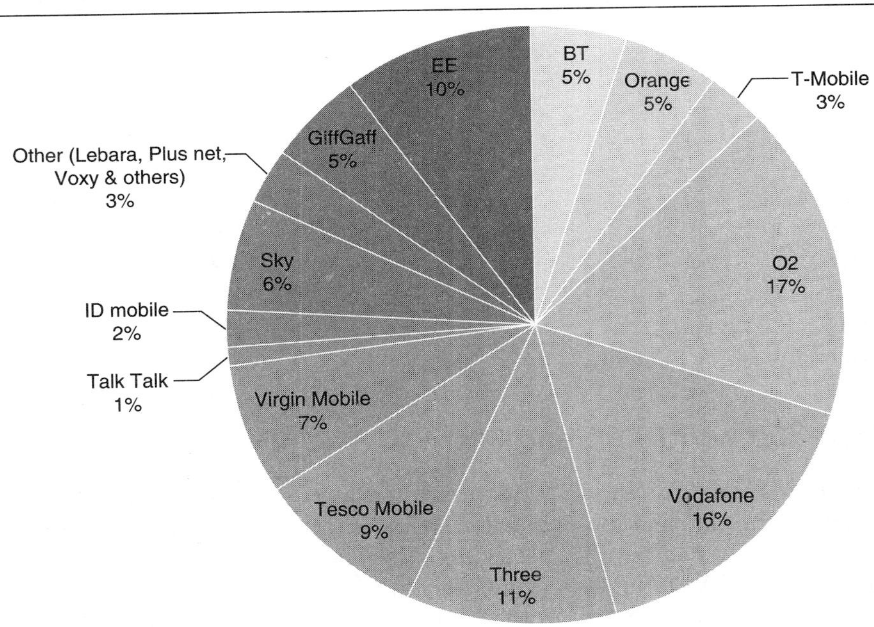

Source: Author data.

This data could have been presented more clearly and simply by using a table. The information from the pie chart is shown in Table 12.6. It is ordered in descending market share. We can clearly see the main things that need to be communicated: O2 and Vodafone are by far the market leaders with around 18 per cent penetration and there are a variety of small brands with up to 3 per cent penetration.

Task

Re-create the table in a word document. Re-order the data alphabetically (keeping the total row at the bottom). Compare the table ordered alphabetically with the one ordered by consumer usage. Which is easier to interpret a storyline or 'take-out' from?

TABLE 12.6 *Percentage of UK Consumers Saying This Is Their Mobile Phone Plan Provider*

Brand	% of UK Consumers Using This Brand
O2	17
Vodafone	16
Three	11
EE	10
Tesco Mobile	9
Virgin Mobile	7
Sky	6
BT	5
Orange	5
GiffGaff	5
T-Mobile	3
Other (Lebara, Plusnet, Voxy & others)	3
iD mobile	2
Talk	1
Total	100

Source: Author data.

Don't Use Stacked Bar Charts

It is quite common for information to be presented in complicated 'stacked' bar charts. This term means the information is stacked inside a bar or column in the graph. These graphs are popular but can be difficult to interpret – as you can see in Figure 12.7. This sort of approach for presenting data is counterproductive, because the idea of summarising data is to inform people, to tell a story that people can use to make better decisions. If an audience struggles to even comprehend what a graph shows, it cannot be informative.

The example chart shows the proportion of people who have been a client of their mobile phone provider for periods of one to ten years. But can we discern the principal story to be told from this chart? It seems more difficult to do than it could be.

FIGURE 12.7 *Length of Time People Have Been a Customer of Phone Provider: Stacked Bar Chart*

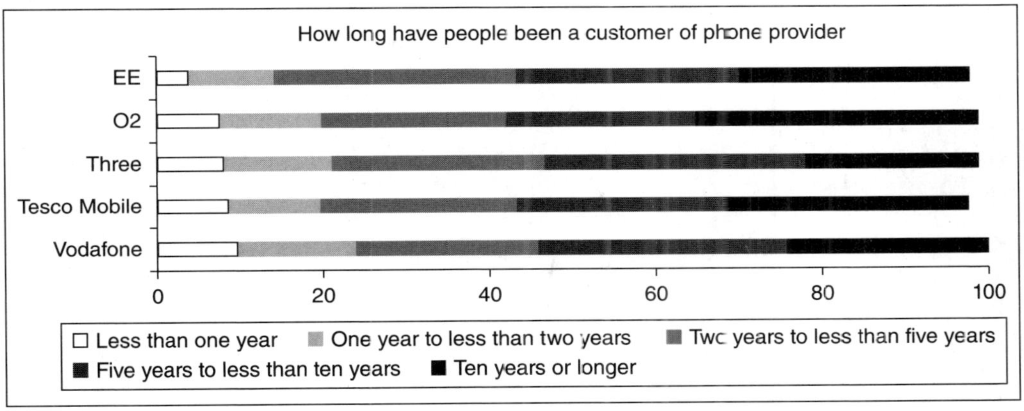

If we simply put the data into a table and order the rows numerically, we can more easily see a pattern. Table 12.7 more clearly shows that all these providers have a minority of their customers who have been with them less than a year or between one and two years. Moreover, it shows that EE has the lowest proportion of brand-new customers, and Vodafone has the largest, which implies it has grown a lot lately.

TABLE 12.7 *Length of Time People Have Been a Customer of Phone Plan Provider*

	Time Period with Phone Plan Provider					
	Less than One Year	**One Year to Less than Two Years**	**Two Years to Less than Five Years**	**Five Years to Less than Ten Years**	**Ten Years or Longer**	**Total**
Vodafone	10	14	22	30	24	100
Tesco mobile	8	11	24	25	29	97
Three	8	13	25	32	21	99
O2	7	12	22	23	34	98
EE	3	10	29	27	28	97
Average	7	12	24	27	27	-

CHAPTER 13 Marketing Planning Scenarios, with Tasks

MINI CASE 1 – MARKETING FOR A SMALL, NOT-FOR-PROFIT ENTERPRISE

You have taken a marketing placement/internship as part of your final semester. Your internship is with a very small non-profit enterprise operating in a city of one to two million people (the precise city is irrelevant; this same scenario is repeated in many places). The organisation works with aged care. In particular, it finds nursing home places for elderly people who have suffered an incident (a fall, a stroke, heart attack), been admitted to hospital and cannot return home. The situation surrounding such incidents is obviously highly emotional for the person's family, who are usually dismayed to hear their loved one cannot return to their own home (reason being, they need a high level of care and monitoring and a purpose-built environment). Added to that emotional aspect is the fact that hospitals generally prompt the older person's family to find a nursing home placement quite quickly – within about a week or two of the incident. Unfortunately, finding an appropriate nursing home place is not an easy task as they are often expensive and come with all sorts of complications such as organising power of attorney, liaising with doctors, possibly selling the family home and so on. These issues take some dealing with, as well as the fact most people want their relative to be well cared for so would like to look at several homes and meet the management and some staff for reassurance. So often, the family needs some help and advice.

The organisation you are interning for charges €500 to help the family navigate its way through the complexity of this process. It is very familiar with all the nursing home providers in the local market (the city and its immediate suburbs, approximately a circular city around 20 kilometres from side to side), as well as the other players involved in the process such as social workers, nurses and discharge officers (the latter are people who sign off that the patient can leave hospital and has an appropriate destination to go to). It uses this €500 per 'client' to pay for at least some of its staff (it employs eight staff, five of which are volunteers) and pay its expenses such as rent. The organisation survives from earning around €50,000 from these placements as well as a government grant of €20,000 per year, which is likely to expire in the next 18 months. It also offers other services oriented towards elderly people such as advice about managing money, accessing personal services and housing options. It would like to earn more money from offering this nursing home sometimes people have actually tried to do the repairs themselves, which can be dangerous, for example if the springs fitted to a heavy door break, they can cause serious injury to a person or their car. Gary sometimes thinks it would be good to make some very short videos in which he explains how he does things, to showcase his expertise. But he has never got around to doing it, being constantly busy actually doing the work. And he has little idea of how to use any form of communications media to get his message across.

Once Gary has looked at the client's job, he then emails a quote to the client, usually the next day. Gary is very experienced, and clients mostly find him pleasant and competent in understanding their repair problem and getting a quote ready. Out in the market, higher disposable income and the affordability of new doors means the new-door market is growing.

A repair job for Gary often involves ordering parts from fabricators in a nearby city. Gary orders parts for a client and awaits their delivery, which is usually within three days, but sometimes longer. On Thursday, one of his clients calls to follow up on a repair job. The client was anticipating the parts would be delivered the day before (on Wednesday) with the repair slotted in for Thursday. The client is calling to find out if they have been delivered and when Gary will perform the repair. Upon listening to the client, Gary replies, 'Ah, they didn't come yesterday! I thought they should have. I don't know when they'll come exactly, I'd hope by tomorrow'.

The client rings again on Friday to follow up. Gary says, 'No they still haven't come, they're on a truck somewhere but I don't know exactly where it is … yes, I will try to find out which transport company it's coming on'. After he finishes the call, Gary says to himself, 'Man, I'm sick of clients hassling me for details like that!' Added to his frustration is the fact that he has noticed an advertisement by a national franchise chain looking for franchisees for skills including lawnmowing/gardening, fencing, paving, painting and repairs to all sorts of domestic items including garage doors.

Tasks

Gary enquires with a university about hiring a final-year marketing student to help him with some marketing advice, and you are selected to work with him for two weeks. You decide to follow the tried and trusted approach you learned in your marketing planning course.

First, identify an internal factor about Gary or Gary's business that is favourably impacting on it acquiring or keeping customers. Use a format along the lines of: X is occurring which means that Y outcome is happening.

Next, identify an internal factor about Gary or Gary's business that is negatively impacting on it getting, acquiring or keeping customers.

Then move on to the external environment. Determine an aspect of the global environment that is favourably impacting on Gary's business. Then do the same, but for an aspect of the market environment that is favourably impacting on Gary's business.

Also, identify an aspect of the market environment that is unfavourably impacting on Gary's business.

Write a half-page summary of what you have found along with a course of action you would recommend to Gary. That is, apart from getting better information from the transport company.

Part 2

Gary is chatting about how his business is doing with a friend, Xandra, who is a bit of a technology enthusiast. Xandra is telling Gary about how she had her little Dahon bicycle repaired recently. It required a bike-shop service, as well as replacement of several broken spokes in the front wheel. Apparently, the spokes were a special size that needed to be shipped from interstate and then hand-cut to size by the bike repair shop. The proprietor of the bike repair shop told her that all their parcel deliveries feature a tracking code, and this enables the transport company to constantly know the geographic location of the parcel (in the warehouse of the fabricator, en route to the local truck depot, etc.). Furthermore, the trucking company gives each item a special code and supplies it to clients, so they can log in and view the location and status of their delivery very easily. Xandra is mildly chiding of Gary for his apparent ignorance about marketing and especially social media. She says to him, not for the first time, 'Gary, you should be on Instagram and your own site. It would allow you to show, in short videos, how you repair stuff, explain the technicalities and dangers of self-repair, show to people how good you are, show the installations, and maybe testimonials'. Gary has heard of the growing popularity of Instagram and is aware that browsing suppliers on the internet is very widespread and growing. But being a bit 'old hat', as he describes himself, all he says is, 'Yeah, one day'.

Tasks

Identify an aspect of the global environment that is potentially relevant to Gary's (hint: technology).

Identify another aspect of the global environment that is relevant to Gary's (hint: could be classified as technology or socio-cultural trend).

Identify an aspect of Gary or Gary's business that is unfavourably impacting on his ability to win or keep business (from the part 2 narrative).

PART II

Readings and Knowledge Base

The next section of the book presents some broader marketing issues, concepts and empirical knowledge. We start off by examining the important concept of marketing ethics. This is followed by Chapter 15, in which we examine several prominent strategy models, and assess their usefulness. Following that, we outline a series of empirical generalisations – a 'fact base' that marketers can use to make more informed decisions. Finally, we consider a series of management biases that can hinder good decision making, along with prescriptions for how to avoid those biases.

commentators, or what can be thought of as micro-journalists, to publicise corporate misdeeds. These commentators are not limited by editorial decisions of major newspapers or a small number of TV stations, as was the case in the past.

Is Business Education to Blame for Ethical Lapses?

Some commentators suggest that business education is responsible for the seeming lack of ethics in business. The idea is that business school students are taught the general canon that the priority of a business is profit – and therefore, by implication, people come second. However, a large-scale study in the US showed no differences in moral philosophy between business students and non-business students (Neubaum et al., 2009).

High-profile Corporate Misconduct

A series of high-profile cases of spectacular instances of poor business behaviour is likely to have brought the issue of business ethics to the forefront. Consider these events.

GFC

In the period 2007–2009 there was an event called the global financial crisis. This crisis was sparked by a downturn in the US housing market. What had happened was that house prices had been rising buoyantly, and this led to people and property developers borrowing large sums to build more and more housing. Many such loans were for amounts larger than the houses were worth. Risky mortgage loans were re-packaged and on-sold from one bank to another. In turn, the banks increased their levels of borrowing to feed the lending frenzy. When house prices dipped, everyone started to lose lots of money. There was an explosion of consumer loan defaults. A large US financial firm, Lehmann Brothers, went bankrupt and this triggered a panic in financial markets around the world. Banks stopped lending to each other, and also stopped lending to businesses, because they were afraid the lender would fail. Millions of people became unemployed, hundreds of thousands of families had their homes repossessed. This event, and the subsequent expose of unethical behaviour in the finance sector, left an enduring cynicism among many people about big business.

Fatal Supply Chain Events

There have been some highly publicised, tragic events such as the factory fire in Bangladesh in 2012 that killed over 100 workers. This factory was linked in the media to several US retailers including Sears and Walmart. This event brought considerable scrutiny onto the supply chains of large corporations. Another widely reported story was high suicide rates at the Foxconn factory in China. While there were subsequent debates as to whether the suicide rate was actually higher at Foxconn than in China generally (Heffernan, 2013), the extremely arduous working conditions at Foxconn were highlighted.

The Volkswagen Emissions Scandal

Volkswagen was found to have put software in some of its diesel car models to defeat emissions tests. It had previously trumpeted about how its cars performed extremely well on emissions. As a result of this discovery, Volkswagen had to recall hundreds of thousands of cars and had to pay a fine of over $4 billion. The company said it regretted the incident, which it felt had lost the trust of consumers. This was a news story that played out over a year, earning the car maker huge amounts of negative publicity. The ethics of the senior management team at Volkswagen was scrutinised, and the CEO was forced to resign.

Fyre Festival

Fyre Festival was meant to have been a luxury music festival held in the Bahamas. It was highly publicised by famous celebrities and influencers – many of whom were paid to do so but didn't tell people they were being paid. The festival was a terrible experience for guests, with failures in accommodation, food, security and medical services. In fact, it was so bad, the organiser received a prison sentence on a charge of fraud. The saga was heavily reported in the news, and several documentaries were made about it.

Opioids

There has been a terrible drug problem in the US (and other countries) relating to opioid addiction since 2000. Hundreds of thousands of people have lost their careers and homes – and many, their lives – by becoming addicted to opioid drugs. There are many reasons, one being that the prescription rate for drugs containing ingredients such as codeine have for many years been massively higher in the US than other countries. As well, there has been a markedly increased use of illicit drugs, such as heroin and fentanyl. Another drug, oxycodone/OxyContin, became widely used as a recreational drug. In turn, this problem was seen to be at least partly caused by the marketing policies of a certain large pharmaceutical company. Eventually, the US government launched legal proceedings against that firm. The crisis, and the legal case, received huge media attention around the world. In turn, this publicity raised the general issue of how businesses should conduct their activities in an ethical manner (Strickler, 2019).

Price-fixing

Less prominent in the news, but certainly serious, have been instances of price fixing. This term means that businesses have somehow agreed with each other to artificially raise prices. Such practices are illegal. A recent alleged example is a federal investigation into price fixing in the US chicken industry (Bunge & Kendall, 2020); another concerns a conspiracy to hike the price of insulin (Silverman, 2020). Such prosecutions happen reasonably often and are regularly reported in business and mainstream news.

Over time, the coverage of all these types of events has sparked a desire among policy makers, business educators and many consumers that ethics receive a higher priority in business.

THE COMPONENTS OF MARKETING ETHICS

The definition of marketing ethics was listed earlier in this section. The key words are: transparent, responsible, trustworthy, integrity (which encompasses the concepts of independence and fairness, among others). These are certainly all desirable at face value. Let us consider what they might mean to a business in practice.

Transparency

This means being open with others about marketing policies and practices. A simple example is clearly stating policies for returning goods or giving refunds, or listing ingredients in products and where the product is made. Business are also facing an environment in which there is more pressure to be transparent in relation to what data they possess about people and how it is stored. There is also a requirement that banks in the UK, for instance, publish their customer satisfaction scores (Anthony, 2019; Competition and Markets Authority, 2020).

A corporate policy of being transparent sounds fine at first, but it can be a challenge to know which things a business is transparent about and which it is not. A business can be quite justified in keepings its proprietary technology to itself, for example in-house developed software, or manufacturing methods. A marketing example is that Samsung, for example, will not want to disclose the details of how it will be promoting its new phone products planned for launch next year – until it is ready to! A fashion label will keep its new lines under wraps until it is ready to show them to the world. Therefore, is it obvious there are some things that a business cannot be transparent about, if it wants to compete effectively. The test of appropriateness hinges on whether an external party or stakeholder has a right to know something about the business. One thing that external parties do have a right to know about is what data is being kept about them by a firm (Intersoft Consulting, 2020). Another pertains to the completeness of information for buyers or prospective buyers to allow them to make an informed decision. Factors such as order deliver times, conditions under which lower or higher prices apply, and warranty limits are aspects of being appropriately transparent.

Responsibility

This means being aware of the outcomes of one's actions, taking care that they do not harm or impinge on other parties. A simple example would be the serving of alcohol in bar or nightclub – taking care that children, or obviously intoxicated persons, are not able to purchase it. The point at which a business is or is not responsible for other parties becomes more difficult in many situations. For example, suppose a manufacturer of paint tries to increase its market share by cutting prices by 20 per cent. This action has the outcome that a competitor suffers a poor financial result for the year and has to shed staff. Is the price-cutter responsible for this loss of jobs? It is doubtful many people would think a business has to take care not to hurt its competitors, but where do we draw the line? Another example is that price wars break out between firms, and sometimes they harm suppliers because lowered prices at retail generally mean lower prices for suppliers. A milk price war in the UK around 2015 resulted in thousands of farmers having to quit the industry. The same happened in Australia, with one retailer deciding to use milk as a weapon to drive store traffic and signal low prices for other items in the store. The other large competitor responded (no surprise) with the result that both retailers were selling milk 30 per cent lower than they were before. And of course, these lower retail prices placed a lot of price pressure on suppliers. The fallout was again very severe on the dairy sector. Of course, it is difficult to generalise from these milk examples to say a business cannot ever take actions that impact negatively on suppliers. In some cases, the suppliers might be more powerful and earn much higher margins than the retailers! But in general, it would seem that a responsible management team would first consider what impacts their actions are likely to have on supply chains, particularly ones that are already financially vulnerable.

Responsibility also means being prepared and able to handle situations where products or services are faulty. Another important aspect of responsibility relates to the fact that a business usually has a power advantage compared to an individual person. For example, suppose a business launches a lawsuit against an individual person – or threatens to launch one. For the staff in the business, this is not a big deal – they can go home and not worry about the outcome – there is no personal implication. For the individual person on the other end of the lawsuit, however, there could be a huge personal implication – the potential of losing their livelihood or their home. This situation could destroy their mental state and leave them worried and anxious for months or years. Businesses should therefore consider the personal implications of their decisions against individual people. They should remember that they usually have a tremendous power advantage over individual people and employ that power only when it is really necessary and with prudence.

Trustworthiness

This concept is quite straightforward, it means being truthful in conveying information. That information flow could be within the firm – from managers to staff – or from the firm to customers or channel partners or other stakeholders. A business may not necessarily have an obligation to answer every question asked of it by a stakeholder. However, it does have an obligation that what it does say is correct. Operating under a policy of trustworthiness means that claims made about products or services are accurate.

Integrity

This is a concept that we recognise when we see it, but it can be hard to define. Integrity can be more easily understood by explaining some more specific components that, collectively, describe it. These components – independence, honesty, consistency commitment and fairness – are adapted from Robinson (2016).

Independence: the ability to stand apart from competing interests. For example, suppose a marketer in a business was choosing between two providers who are bidding to build a customer app. One provider has a well-established relationship with the business, but its app is not quite as customer friendly as the other. An independent decision about which provider to use would be less influenced by the existing relationship, and more by the app quality.

Honesty and transparency: transparency has been discussed already; honesty is self-explanatory.

Consistency: this means applying criteria to decisions in a similar way over time or across situations. If a marketing director decides that a marketing priority is promulgating a quality image, then all decisions need to be consistent with that view. It would be wrong, then, to decide to sign a new distributor or accept a contract to produce low-price, low-quality goods that detract from the firm's quality image.

Commitment: this means having a well-considered viewpoint and sticking to it. For example, if a senior marketer decides to pursue an evidence-based approach to marketing, then they should consistently base decisions on evidence, not just some of the time.

Fairness: this means that one's treatment of people is impartial and consistent with community expectations (Rubin, 2012). As a general notion this appears unarguable. However, in practice sometimes businesses can do things that might seem unfair. For example: should Brian pay more than Darlene for the exact same hotel room on the same date? Perhaps, but perhaps not if one booked some time ago when future demand was slow, while the other booked later when there was limited availability. Or we notice that in times of shortage, prices increase. Is this fair? The answer might depend on the specific situation. Pushing prices up to take advantage of a shortage, or limited supply, seems unfair. This appeared to be the case when the infamous Martin Shkreli raised the price of a drug by 5,000 per cent (Pollack, 2015) overnight. In this case the drug wasn't actually in a shortage situation but was the standard medication to treat a serious medical condition. In other cases, the market simply bids up, or pushes prices up, when there is a shortage. Imagine a banana supplier, when a hurricane wipes out a significant crop: retailers will immediately begin calling to secure supply, knowing there will be a shortage, and will implicitly bid against each other to ensure they obtain stock.

While it is reasonably easy to comprehend what concepts like fairness and integrity mean, it might be harder to ensure a business actually operates in line with ethical action. Therefore, it is useful to have a checklist of specific questions that make it easier to discern if the business is operating ethically.

MARKETING ETHICS CHECKLIST: DOES OUR MARKETING STRATEGY INCORPORATE THESE POINTS?

- Do we have well-understood criteria by which clients can purchase goods or services at different prices or terms? For example, a customer can receive lower prices for booking early, or for buying larger quantities.
- Are the claims we make about our products/services truthful and accurate?

- Do we provide enough information about our products for buyers to make an informed decision? That is, no important aspects or shortcomings are left out.
- Do we have the ability to answer and fix legitimate complaints about product or service failures?
- Are we protecting data gathered from buyers such that it is not used by other firms, or used in a way that is inappropriate?
- Do we have an understood policy in relation to the way we provide entertainment or rewards to clients, such that our dealings are legitimate? More specifically, are we sure we do not offer money or other favours in a corrupt attempt to get others to do something we want?
- Are we ensuring our activities to promote our goods and services do not result in harm to vulnerable buyer groups, or indeed to buyers generally?
- Is our treatment of suppliers fair, particularly considering if we are comparatively more powerful than they are?
- Do we know whether our suppliers engage in responsible activities in relation to supply chain management?
- If a well-qualified, impartial external party such as a lawyer or other expert could examine the details of our marketing plan and our internal discussions about it – would they be dismayed or alarmed by any aspects? If yes, we need to consider changing those aspects.

ETHICALLY CHALLENGING SITUATIONS: WHAT IS THE ISSUE AND WHAT WOULD YOU DO?

Now that we have covered what ethics means in principle and examined some examples of very poor lapses in corporate ethics or conduct, let's look at some real-life examples of ethical quandaries. See if you can identify the ethical issue – there could be more than one! Put yourself in the situation described and reflect on what you would think and do.

Scenario 1

You have been working in the in-house advertising team for a car brand for the past month or so. One of your roles is managing an ongoing email campaign. In this campaign, prospects are emailed an invitation to visit a dealership near them to receive a small incentive to test-drive a new model. The prospects are targeted such that they are likely to be in the income range necessary to feasibly afford the car, and they live in the geographic area of the dealership. As well as that, they may have exhibited some online interest in motor vehicles. As part of this process, you have been negotiating with providers of database lists. These providers are businesses that supply names and email addresses of consumers that are likely to match the criteria needed for a targeted campaign. Each month your team receives a list of 3,000 contacts. You are having a conversation with a colleague who has been working in the business for several years. You ask, 'Where do these lists actually come from?' Your colleague looks at you as if you are slightly stupid for asking the question, and replies, 'The list bank of companies, of course!' – but you persist, asking – 'Sure, of course I know that, but how do they get the names and contacts?' Your colleague says, 'As far as I know, they just buy them from some wholesale source. Does it matter? All we're doing is an email, if people don't like it, they can delete it'.

Question

Is there an ethical issue here, if so, what is it? And what, if anything, would you do?

Scenario 2

You are a marketing graduate for an international company that produces alcoholic beverages. The company sells to large retail chains, as well as via wholesalers to bars/pubs, nightclubs and restaurants. It has worked to ensure its marketing of alcohol to consumers is responsible, for example visitors to its website need to vouch they are 18 or over, it does not advertise on free to air television before 8.30 p.m., it does not engage in any intentional target marketing of youth. The company has given you a series of confidential market research reports about consumers' consumption of alcohol in general, and more specifically, your brand. The market research company managed to survey people aged from 16 years and over, and it is a fact that the legal age for purchasing or drinking alcohol in this country is 18. The general content of the reports is all quite conventional, but you are going through the appendices and notice that a figure of 22 per cent of respondents aged under 18 said they had bought or consumed your brand in the past 12 months. In fact, it is one of the more popular brands among underage drinkers. You have been asked to make a presentation on all the research material to the brand and category management team next week.

Question

Is there an ethical issue here, if so, what is it? And what, if anything, would you do?

Scenario 3

You are going over your new website analytics with a software consultant. He points out that it is possible to identify site visitors according to their source. Some come direct to you, some come via price comparison sites. On average he says that research shows people who come though price comparison sites are more price sensitive. You need to make a recommendation to your marketing director: should we offer lower prices to people who have come via a comparison site, and higher for people who haven't?

Question

Is there an ethical issue here, if so, what is it? And what, if anything, would you do?

Scenario 4

Some researchers claim they are able to discern people's personality type and even perhaps their frame of mind – outgoing, confident; or anxious, fearful, depressed – from their social media profile and posts. You work for a pharmaceutical company as the marketing director. The head of insights in your firm has been discussing working together with a consultant firm that has developed a way to scrape internet information to successfully identify five broad types of personalities. That is, it could identify the personality type of individual people. Moreover, it could create ads tailored to these different personality types, and selectively target each type with a specific ad. With the result that the campaigns would be extremely effective. Would you proceed with a test campaign?

Question

Is there an ethical issue here, if so what is it? And what, if anything, would you do?

Scenario 5

You are a recent MBA graduate working for a global accountancy firm with a regional headquarters in London. You've been seconded to work with a senior B2B marketer for a month. His name is Emile and he's your 'lead' for this assignment. The organisation's clients are finance managers and treasury principals in big corporations. One of your tasks at present is to assist Emile with running several corporate hospitality events. You have been running an invitation-only corporate event, whereby your firm invites 30 clients and potential clients to a beautiful hotel with its own golf course. The clients play golf, eat very well, and enjoy fine wine for a day and a night – all paid for, naturally, by your organisation. It is Sunday morning, and the clients are in the process of decamping back to their homes. One client, however, is staying on. He is the CFO of a €5 billion turnover company that operates all over the world. Your boss tells you he has organised a private golf lesson for him with a world-ranked golfer for the morning, he is then staying on an extra night after also being treated to a special dinner prepared by a TV cooking show chef. Your eyes goggle a bit at this news, and you say, 'Wow that must be costing a lot!' Your boss looks at you and says, 'Oh it sure is, about €5 thousand. But we're chasing this person for a big auditing and compliance contract worth €6 million a year so the cost is very cheap stacked up against the reward'. You digest this news over a croissant and coffee and chat with Emile about the next event to be organised. In about a week, your assignment with Emile and his events is complete and you will resume your normal role. In fact, you have an annual performance appraisal with HR in two weeks. You wonder how that conversation will go and what sorts of things you will discuss.

Question

Is there an ethical issue here, if so, what is it? And what, if anything, would you do?

Scenario 6

You are the marketing director of a hotel chain. You and your main competitor have been fighting an intense battle for market share, which has meant price levels have dropped 25 per cent and profits are down. In fact, your job is looking a little precarious. You attend an industry association lunch and find yourself sitting next to your competitor. She passes you a note saying, 'Why are we fighting each other? A return to normal pricing levels will benefit us both. Talk after this'. What do you do?

Question

Is there an ethical (and, legal) issue here, and if so, what is it? And what, if anything, would you do?

CHAPTER

15 Prominent Strategy Models in Marketing

GENERIC STRATEGIES: TIME TO STOP!

In the 1980s, management author Michael Porter presented the idea of three so-called generic business strategies. The three strategies were: differentiation, defined as providing a superior or unique product, which would allow the business to earn high prices and therefore high profit margins; low cost, which would allow the business to still earn better margins than rivals because its costs would be lower than theirs; and finally focus, which was defined as catering to a 'niche' or under-served part of the market, the reward for which would again be higher margins, because by focusing, the business would be in a special position to cater to specific client needs very well.

These strategies were claimed to be the only ways in which a business could achieve a 'competitive advantage' over its rivals. They have been written about and prescribed in hundreds of management, strategy and marketing textbooks since then. Recent publications still prescribe them.

Unfortunately, Porter's generic strategies are difficult for marketers to implement. This is because to a large extent the strategies are true by definition, in that the definition of a profit margin is the difference between cost and selling price, so if differentiation is synonymous with higher prices, then logically differentiation should mean higher margins. But the firm's overall profitability depends not only on margins, but on how many items it sells. Moreover, having low costs is at face value desirable because it could mean high margins, but as a route to high profitability is incomplete because again company profit depends on how many items are sold; simply having low cost is no guarantee of success, for example if the product is out of date or inferior, then its low cost is irrelevant. Presenting a choice between low cost and differentiation as marketing strategy alternatives is unrealistic. No marketing manager this author has ever spoken to has raised the notion that low cost versus differentiation are marketing options.

Porter also presented the three generic strategies as mutually exclusive: a business had to pick just one, because trying to do more than one led to being 'stuck in the middle' with neither superior differentiation or lower costs. His casting of the three strategies as mutually exclusive implies that a business can simply have the lowest costs in an industry and that would virtually ensure its success (i.e. all you need are the lowest costs). Now, how do you think a car maker or an airline would cope, trying to compete solely on the basis that its costs were lower than all other competitors? The answer is, it would not survive more than a month. That's because this idea completely disregards the requisite quality of the offering. Would passengers fly on an airline that they were unfamiliar with, because it never advertised? Indeed, how would they even know it existed, because Porter would say marketing spending is 'differentiation' and adds costs. And what if adding features to a product, and investing in advertising it, leads to sales increases, which allow the business to enjoy economies of scale and thus lowers per-unit costs. Here, differentiation, in the sense of a product being less perfectly substitutable with others, can result in lower costs, not higher ones. Lastly, the idea of focus is said to be distinct from low costs or differentiation because focus is meant to mean the business focuses on a specialised niche allowing it to offer a superior (customised, informed) product for that part of the market. This sounds like differentiation! Therefore, the Porter strategy trichotomy of low cost, differentiation or focus is not particularly helpful for the creation of marketing strategies.

GROWTH-SHARE MATRICES – USEFUL OR UNHELPFUL?

From the 1970s onwards, a number of consultancies and business thought leaders presented the idea of matrices as an aide to help business decision making. A matrix in this context is simply another word for a drawn 2 x 2 'box'. On the horizontal or X-axis is usually the market share of a firm or a brand, on the vertical or Y-axis is usually the growth rate of the market that that firm or brand is in. This basic matrix is known as the BCG matrix. The idea is to represent business strength and market attractiveness in a simple arrangement. It can be used for a firm's portfolio of products as well: suppose we have three products, this tool could show us more clearly that we have one strong product in an unattractive market, one weak product in an attractive market, and one strong product in an attractive market.

While a little out of fashion now in the 2020s, this idea has been hugely influential in marketing and strategic management for at least 40 years. So, it is worthwhile for marketing planners to be at least aware of the idea and its documented usefulness and also shortcomings. The logic of the BCG matrix is partly linked to the idea of relative costs. Around the same time the BCG matrix was introduced to the world, there was another important business idea called the experience curve. The experience curve basically showed that as the cumulative volume of a product made by a firm doubled, its per-unit costs dropped, sometimes quite markedly by amounts such as 20 per cent.

The BCG logic is that having a larger market share is indicative of your firm's (or that product's) cost position relative to competitors. If you have a large share, according to the logic, you have larger accumulated volume and therefore an almost unassailable cost advantage over rivals. And if you have a cost advantage, then the product is more likely to produce profit, or what BCG called it, cash flow. Indeed, the BCG matrix is predicated on the assumption that there is a causal link between market share and profitability, e.g. firms with higher market share earn higher rates of profit (e.g. Buzzell & Gale, 1987). While it has been found there is a correlation between market share and profitability, there has also been vociferous argument among researchers about whether this was a causal link. Indeed, it seems brave to assume that the mere possession of market share makes a business more profitable.

The Y-axis of the BCG matrix indicates market growth, which it uses as a proxy for attractiveness of the industry or product category you are operating in. Higher growth means more attractiveness, although being in high growth markets probably means the firm or product needs more monetary support to keep going (i.e. to keep up – to maintain market share in a growth market needs more effort because rivals are attracted to growth markets). So, tools like these are competitiveness/attractiveness matrices.

The BCG matrix featured names for products or brands in each of the four quadrants, for example products in the low share, low growth quadrant were called 'dogs', that is, they were undesirable for two reasons – supposedly uncompetitive and in unattractive markets. Whereas products in the high share, high growth quadrant were labelled 'stars', implying they were the stars in the firm's portfolio because they would generate ample revenue and profit.

TABLE 15.1 *The BCG Matrix*

Market growth rate (a proxy for market attractiveness, but also requirement for funds)	High	Question Marks: low market share in a high growth market	Stars: high market share in a high growth market
	Low	Dogs: low market share in a low growth market	Cash Cows: high market share in a low growth market
		Low	High
		Market share (a proxy for competitive position)	

There are several aspects of the BCG matrix to critique. First, some researchers have done experiments where they asked graduate students to make investment decisions using the BCG matrix. The findings were that using the BCG matrix led to poorer decisions (Armstrong & Brodie, 1994). The reason was apparently that the BCG labels interfered with the way that the students appraised the decision. That is, if an otherwise good investment was presented so as to be for a 'dog' product, students were less likely to support that investment, even if at face value it was profitable.

Another criticism is the assumption that market share indicates competitive position, via a cost advantage to the large-share firm. The idea is that a firm with more market share has accumulated more experience in making the product. There was evidence from World War Two onwards that the costs of manufacturing things (like planes) dropped a lot as one went from making, say, the first 10,000 to the second 10,000 and the third 10,000 items. But relying on the idea of accumulated experience being the key to costs is actually a dangerous assumption. For example, a smaller player with innovative technology might readily turn out to leapfrog a larger competitor on cost reduction.

Another criticism is that using market share and market growth as proxies for competitive position and market attractiveness, respectively, is too simplistic. For example, a business with large market share might still be in a precarious competitive position. It might be large at the present because of the legacy or long-term effects of past investments or entry barriers, but will soon succumb to new players. Likewise, a growth market might be unattractive if it has very low margins.

In response to these problems, other matrices were developed using multiple indicators of competitive position and attractiveness. For example, for competitive positioning one could use a combination of market share, relative costs and relative quality. And for market attractiveness one could use growth rate, margins and long-term barriers from new competitors. Some people refer to these sorts of matrices as the GE matrix, the Shell matrix or the directional policy matrix.

In general, the use of matrices like these has died out in the last decade. But they are still discussed in sources such as Investopedia; and are still a staple in many business courses. It is therefore useful for marketing students and practitioners to know these critiques about them.

THE ANSOFF MATRIX: A LEGENDARY TOOL, BUT WITH TWO LOGICAL PROBLEMS

Introduction

The Ansoff matrix has been widely taught as part of business education for over 50 years. It is a tool designed to help managers think through the options for growth that are available. It portrays growth options as a 2 x 2 matrix of options, with the horizontal axis representing products (existing/new) and the vertical axis representing markets (existing/new). Two logical problems arise from the matrix. Both problems relate to assumptions or interpretations pertaining to newness. If we assume a new product really is new to the firm, in many cases a new product will simultaneously take the firm into a new, unfamiliar market. In that case, one of the Ansoff quadrants, namely diversification, is redundant. Alternatively, if a new product does *not* necessarily take the firm into a new market, then the combination of new products into new markets does not always equate to diversification, in the sense of venturing into a completely unknown business – which the model, and many subsequent interpretations of the model in textbooks, assumes.

The Ansoff Framework

The Ansoff matrix will be familiar to almost anyone who has done a business strategy or marketing strategy course in the last 50 years. It has prominently featured, and still features, in marketing strategy/planning texts (e.g. Hollensen, 2010; McDonald & Wilson, 2011) and business planning and strategy texts (e.g. Campbell et al., 2011). The matrix is a simple tool for strategic planning. It portrays business growth options as a 2 x 2 matrix with axes being: products – existing and new; and markets – existing and new. By market, Ansoff meant the product's mission, i.e. 'the job which the product is intended to perform' (Ansoff, 1957: 113). Combining the 2 x 2 axes creates four potential strategies, summarised below.

> **Market penetration**: 'increasing volume of sales to its present customers or finding new customers, without departing from an original product-market strategy' (Ansoff, 1957: 114). In other words, selling more of the same product to the same market.

Product development: 'retains the present mission and develops products that have new and different characteristics' (Ansoff, 1957: 114). In other words, selling new products to the same market.

Market development: 'adapt its present product line to new missions (Ansoff, 1957: 114). In other words, find a new market for the same product or one with minimal adaptation.

Diversification: 'a simultaneous departure from the present product line and the present market structure' (Ansoff, 1957: 114). That is, selling new products into a new market.

The Ansoff matrix is shown as Table 15.2.

TABLE 15.2 *Ansoff Matrix*

New Markets	Market Development	Diversification
Existing Markets	Market Penetration	Product Development
	Existing Products	**New Products**

Using of the Ansoff Matrix: Example 1

Ansoff made use of an example in the original 1957 publication to illustrate the basic idea of the matrix. The example was an aircraft manufacturer currently producing planes for commercial aviation. The physical item, namely an airplane, was the product. Its current mission was said to be commercial passenger aviation, that is, transporting consumers. Adapting the companies' passenger planes to transport cargo was stated as an example of a market development strategy. That is, the altered product was very similar to what the business made already, but a new market (transporting air cargo rather than people) was found for it.

A Problem with Subjectivity

First, a potential issue with the use of the matrix is the subjectivity involved in determining what constitutes one strategy versus another. Using Ansoff's example, for example, one could argue that an aviation company would sell its planes to airlines, many of which operate in the commercial passenger market, but would also offer airfreight. In which case the client list for the airplane builder's cargo planes might be many of the same airlines it currently sells to. Therefore, the *product mission* – providing a transport vehicle to commercial airlines – would hardly change at all, but the product itself would be arguably different (planes with no passenger seats or windows, but rather, full of cargo bays). Therefore, the example used by Ansoff to illustrate a market development strategy might therefore arguably be classified as a product development strategy if we consider the altered aircraft a new product. Alternatively, if we did not classify the altered aircraft as new (which is a reasonable proposition, since it might only entail internal modifications), then this strategy might even be considered a market penetration strategy, if the major clients, namely airlines, offered passenger transport and airfreight. These issues highlight the subjectivity involved in using the Ansoff matrix. The next section illustrates other issues with the Matrix, using a typical example of its use in a marketing textbook.

Using of the Ansoff Matrix: Example 2

Kotler et al., (2007: 90–91) provide this example of how the Ansoff matrix can be used, using the consumer goods multinational Unilever. The interpretation of the matrix in Kotler's example, and the resultant strategies, are consistent with Ansoff's original descriptions. The example is then utilised to highlight two logical inconsistencies in the matrix.

Kotler et al. (2007: 90–91) suggest that Unilever Foods could potentially consider four growth strategies. This company sold products such as margarine and ice cream. The growth options were:

Market penetration: more sales to existing customers without changing products. For example, cutting the price of its branded margarine or increasing its advertising.

Market development: identifying new markets for current products. For example, review demographic groups such as kids, teenagers, young adults, to see if any of these groups could be encouraged to buy, or buy more of Unilever's ice cream. Or, restaurants, food services or hospitals to see if sales to these buyers could be increased. It is notable that while these authors portray this as a market development, it is quite likely Unilever would already sell to all of these groups or client types so why this is cast as identifying new markets is unclear.

Product development: offering modified or new products to current markets. Unilever Food's products could be offered in new sizes or new packaging, or new products could be launched such as Flora cholesterol lowering margarine. Note that in this example the products are new, but quite within the scope of Unilever's product line and production and marketing competencies.

Diversification: as stated by Kotler et al. (2007: 90–91), under this strategy Unilever could start up or buy businesses entirely outside its current products and markets. For example, the company could move into the growing health and fitness industry, which includes gym equipment, health foods and slimming programmes. Why these specific industries were chosen rather than space exploration, oil drilling or sportswear was not explained (since the idea was moving into businesses 'entirely outside' current products and markets).

A Problem with Logical Inconsistencies

We now discuss two logical inconsistencies in the Ansoff matrix that are made apparent by this example. In short, they are:

1. If the definition of a new product encompasses 'mildly' new-to-the-firm additions such as a food company adding new package sizes or product formulations, then the

strategy of diversification, defined as new products and new markets, is not necessarily a 'break with past patterns ... and an entry onto new and uncharted paths' (Ansoff, 1957: 113), nor necessarily inherently risky.

2. If a firm develops, acquires or sells a *really* new product – that is, something as yet unfamiliar to the firm – arguably this simultaneously takes the firm into a new market. In which case the matrix cell of diversification is redundant.

These points are now discussed in more detail.

Diversification?

In the Kotler et al. example above, it is suggested Unilever could develop new products – incrementally new – to sell into its existing markets, customer groups or segments. The strategy is therefore new products/same segments, which equates to a product development strategy. However, the problem with this logic is that if we accept that new products can be incrementally new, then the strategy of diversification – a combination of new products and new markets – is not necessarily a risky break with past patterns. To reiterate the Unilever example: the product development strategy involves new sizes or packaging; and the market development strategy is chasing additional sales in demographic groups or institutional buyers. Therefore, the combination of new products (product development strategy), and new markets (market development strategy) – which the matrix classifies as diversification – should logically involve both these initiatives. But doing these initiatives in tandem does not sound like a marked break with the past, nor highly risky.

However, offering new sizes or altered products to different client groups does not at all resemble the actual example given by Kotler et al. (2007) of diversification for Unilever. Rather, their example involves venturing completely outside Unilever's scope of business expertise, to try running gyms or selling fitness equipment. It appears that when authors such as Kotler et al. use the term new products for the product development strategy, they consider mildly different products but when they consider new products for the diversification strategy, they use examples of completely different products from what the firm currently sells. This may be because the original definition of diversification by Ansoff included the idea that it necessarily involved a risky break from the past.

Really New Products?

One might argue that the example of new products given by Kotler et al. (2007) – packaging or formula changes – are rather trivial and therefore do not constitute 'new'. Therefore, let us now consider Unilever Foods launching a product that is much more 'new' to it. Suppose Unilever Foods decided to sell vitamins. At face value, according to Ansoff, this is a new product development strategy – new product with different characteristics, same markets (consumers, grocery retailers and so on). The logical problem that arises now is that there is an assumption that a business can venture into quite a different product without its market changing. Arguably, Unilever knows nothing about the vitamin market, and the needs, wants or influences of consumers when purchasing vitamins. It could learn about these issues, by hiring relevant staff and doing research, but the key point is that by launching or adding a really new product to the business, the company has simultaneously moved into a new market. In which case the diversification quadrant of the Ansoff matrix is redundant.

To summarise, there are two logical inconsistencies embedded in the Ansoff matrix

1. If we accept that new products can be incrementally new, then the combination of new products and new markets does not necessarily equate to a risky break from the past, as written by Ansoff (1957) and echoed by other authors for example (Gilligan & Wilson, 2009; Westwood, 2005).
2. If we reject the notion that new products in the Ansoff matrix can be incrementally new, and must be really new (to the firm) then it is very likely that developing or adding such a really new product simultaneously takes the firm into a new market. In which case there is no need for a separate strategy called diversification.

These shortcomings, as well as the apparent subjectivity involved in classifying the various Ansoff strategies, should be recognised by the academics who include the Ansoff matrix in their marketing or strategy curriculum.

The Ansoff matrix, like the BCG growth-share matrix, is now a bit dated. But it still emerges in many present-day online information sources such as smartinsights.com and www.quickMBA.com. So, it's worth knowing at least something about the tool and its shortcomings.

THE RESOURCE-BASED THEORY OF COMPETITIVE ADVANTAGE

Earlier in the book we presented the idea that the concept of competitive advantage has been rather over-hyped. It may not be applicable to small businesses, and it seems difficult to see how multiple competitors in an industry can each have a competitive advantage (and what if the managers in each competing business all read the same books promising they can achieve one?). However, it is still instructive to understand a theory called the resource-based theory, which explains how businesses could build or attain such a state. It may be useful to substitute the idea of building a strong competitive position in an industry rather than a competitive advantage; or that a competitive advantage is not something a business has or has not but rather something that businesses can possess to differing degrees.

Over the past 30 years, there has been a lot of attention paid to a concept called the resource-based theory of competitive advantage (also known as the resource-based view or RBV). This is a theory that tries to explain why some businesses outperform their rivals over fairly long periods of time. The term 'outperform' in this context means, earn higher profits or earn a higher rate of return on invested money. The theory says that this superior performance boils down to possessing certain resources – or more specifically, resources and capabilities – that are valuable, unique, hard to build or copy, and not possible to substitute. But more subtly, the point is made that those resources still have to be appropriate for the market environment. Therefore, in a sense this idea builds very much on the traditional idea of strategy being a match between a company's strengths and weaknesses on one hand, and the opportunities and threats presented by the environment. The advances on past work lie in the heightened focus on the nature of the company's resources and capabilities. The following points are adapted from articles such as those by Collis and Montgomery (1995) and Srivastava et al., (1998).

The essential idea is that competitive advantage arises from the possession or utilisation of certain resources or capabilities. It may be that the concept of competitive advantage is too definitive, too 'strong'. It implies the business can 'beat all others' and is difficult to reconcile with the fact that we can observe multiple competing businesses in an industry, perhaps six of them doing very well and another ten not doing so well. Do all the six good performers have a competitive advantage? If so, an advantage over which other firms? These uncertainties mean we could perhaps replace the concept of competitive advantage with 'superior performance' or 'very good performance' or just 'ability to compete'.

Sometimes the resources that underlie superior business performance are physical. An example might be that a store is located in an incredibly good location, like Harrods in London (of course, Harrods' turnover is not just due to location, its brand is obviously a factor among other reasons). Another example could be that a business owns a patent, perhaps for a drug that has a unique ability to control a prevalent disease.

Sometimes these sorts of resources are intangible, such as having a brand that is widely known, with good levels of mental availability; trusted and established in the market. The links that exist in people's mind between various uses of the product category and your brand are indeed a resource, an asset (kind of like millions of tiny pieces of real estate, out there in people's heads). They favourably impact on buyer's propensity to buy your brand and can obviously last for very long periods of time if nurtured with advertising or other communications. Consider the brands that have been market leaders in their industry for 50+ years, there are innumerable examples – Ford, Kellogg's, Boeing, IBM, Hilton Hotels and so on. These benefit from intangible resources, in their widespread familiarity.

In some cases, the resource is some form of organisational learning.[1] Some businesses have learned, over time, to do particular actions very well. Take the example of the German-owned supermarket chain Aldi. The basic nature of supermarket operations is fairly apparent – it requires skills in real estate identification and development, finding and maintaining hundreds of good quality suppliers, inbound logistics, in-store merchandising and marketing skills. But doing this all very well takes very good systems and organisational knowledge.

Therefore, ownership of these resources – physical, intangible or learning-related – allows the business to perform activities – most specifically, produce and sell products (goods or services) – better, more efficiently or effectively than their competitors.

However, we also need to note that one cannot evaluate these resources in isolation, because the value of the resource depends on its interplay with the market. A resource that is very valuable in 2022 might be worthless in 2024 – perhaps technology has changed, consumer tastes have changed. Or perhaps what is good for one market isn't good for another. Tesco, like Aldi, has fabulous skills in running supermarkets but has failed at operating them successfully overseas, particularly in the United States. The same thing happened to the successful Australian hardware chain Bunnings – it could not transfer its skills

[1] Organisational learning is also intangible, you can't see it our touch it. But it's useful to split out intangible (which mostly refers to brands) and learning-related resources or capabilities.

and knowledge of (Australian) hardware retailing into the UK market. Or we could also take the numerous examples of companies that have tried to enter new markets via acquisitions. These ventures often fail because the skill set, or organisational learning (or brand or locational advantage), doesn't transfer into a new context.

Therefore, valuable resources and capabilities only lead to superior (or at least, 'good') performance when matched to the appropriate external environment.

There is a series of tests of a firm's assets that can help it to determine if they are really going to be the basis of long-term superior performance. These tests are now outlined.

The Test of Inimitability

Is it hard for competitors to copy? If your business owns or has access to a valuable resource that allows you to be very successful – competitors will want to copy it. Some resources are physically unique (Harrods store in London, the Great Barrier Reef).

In some cases, resources cannot be imitated because of what is called path dependency. This means, a series of circumstances led to their creation, and those circumstances might not occur in the same way again; or would take a very long time to re-create. For example, a brand name that is widely known and trusted due to a long history of good quality as well as marketing communications – such as BMW or Heinz or Sheraton Hotels. These brands have fairly strong and numerous perceptual links to their respective product categories, have many existing and past buyers who hold positive memories about them. One cannot re-create this mental 'real estate' quickly or easily.

Another reason for inimitability is what is called causal ambiguity – it is difficult for would-be imitators to figure out exactly what the valuable resource is (it's not visible, not easily definable) or perhaps the resource arises from a combination of factors that are difficult to comprehend or disentangle). For example, if we were Nestlé Pet Food division, we might discern that our biggest competitor, Mars, successfully deploys very good advertising. But how is Mars Corporation so good at putting high-quality advertising content on-air? Nestlé would find this very difficult to answer.

The Test of Durability

Is the resource something that will continue to depreciate fairly quickly? Some resources like brand recognition and brand image can last for decades, if there is ongoing investment in them. Other resources, like having a restaurant with a trendy look, are not as likely to remain as valuable for long periods.

The Test of Appropriability

In other words, is it us who can capture the value that the resource generates or creates? Or is it some other entity? Some resources are not necessarily appropriable. For example, a shop in a great location – the location might mean the shop enjoys a lot of customers and sales, but if a landlord owns the real estate they will quickly realise the shop should pay high rent, therefore the landlord appropriates the value of the location not the shop business manager. Another example might be that a business is very successful because of a key staff member (a great salesperson, a talented architect) – the individual in question realises the business is making a lot of money because of them, so they might either leave to start their own, or negotiate a significant pay increase. By contrast, if the business has built market-based assets – brand awareness, reputation, good distribution – not only does it 'own' them, but it can appropriate (keep) the value that they produce.

The Test of Substitutability

Can this resource be trumped by a different one? A valuable resource, one that allows the business to compete effectively and perform well in terms of sales and profits, might be able to be substituted by a different resource controlled by or employed by a competitor firm. For example, one might argue department stores in key retail locations such as malls and shopping centres had a locational resource that newer rivals could not match, but to some extent those locational advantages are not as supreme as in the past, due to the rise of online purchasing. In the past, free to air television broadcasters had semi-monopoly rights meaning it was very difficult for new players to enter the TV market. Now, that resource has been substituted at least partly with internet and cable accessibility.

The question for the marketing manager is: are the resources that we rely on to survive and compete easy or hard for competitors to substitute? If they are easy to substitute or will become easier to substitute, we need to change our resource base to include some new or adapted resources that are hard to substitute.

The Test of Competitive Superiority

It can be too easy for managers to do an internal analysis and determine the business does one or two things better than others, and conclude those things are either its core competency, its strategic assets or its key strengths, etc. What it should do is determine if it has resources, skills, competencies, intangible assets that are superior to competitors.

This is certainly the approach outlined in all works about the resource-based theory.

A Caveat about Competitive Superiority

It certainly makes sense to consider resources or competencies, and therefore strengths, in terms of how strong they are relative to competitors. Unfortunately, it may well be the case that the business identifies that it doesn't have anything that makes it competitively superior to its rivals. Imagine the manager of an Indian restaurant, writing a marketing plan. It has a staff of six – several good chefs, quite good waiting staff – and offers essentially the same sort of cuisine options as most other Indian restaurants, in a modest premises on a main road. Would it even be sensible to think about possessing or leveraging a competitively superior resource or capability? Perhaps not, at least at present. In this case a marketing plan would, in a sense, have to be based on what is available, without necessarily having real strengths – apart from the basic strength, which is that in its local area, it is the closest

Indian restaurant! That said, even this one strength could be the basis for a plan involving tactics to build its existing mental and physical availability to higher levels, as well as ensuring its competitiveness on pricing, perceived quality and customer service. There will always be incremental improvements that, when added up over time, could turn a moderately good business into a very good business.

The relevance of the RBV for marketing is that marketing activity creates market-based assets. These sorts of assets pass the tests described above. A brand – and its familiarity, image, mental structures in people's heads – is first and foremost inimitable. A competitor can build their own brand assets, but they cannot imitate your brand's assets. And this building is hard, expensive and risky, so if you've done it, and are continuing to do it, you are building something that will bring in revenue for a long time to come.

Therefore, marketing should not be seen only as an activity to create sales, but as an investment in creating and maintaining valuable, hard to imitate company assets. The financial value of these market-based assets can be seen in the fact that when investors buy a business, a large part of what they pay for is not money in the bank, real estate, trade secrets, patents – it is often market-based assets such as brand awareness or mental availability as well as established distribution arrangements with distributors which would be very expensive and time-consuming to build from scratch.

CHAPTER 16

Empirical Generalisations and Their Link to Marketing Planning

A marketing plan and strategy becomes more solid, more likely to succeed, if it builds on or acknowledges facts about how buyers behave, how brands perform, and how pricing and advertising work. Therefore, in this chapter we review a series of *facts* that have arisen from research – and spell out how they are relevant to marketing planning. This list of empirical generalisations starts with a series that have directly or primarily arisen from the work of Ehrenberg and colleagues: such as double jeopardy, the duplication of purchase law, the law of buying frequencies, users of competing brands seldom differ, or natural monopoly. These laws, of generalisations, are more fully discussed in *How Brands Grow* (Sharp, 2010) and *How Brands Grow: Part 2* (Romaniuk & Sharp, 2016).

DOUBLE JEOPARDY

The double jeopardy pattern is that small brands not only have fewer buyers, their buyers are somewhat less loyal to them, on average. This is one of the most well-known findings from Ehrenberg and colleagues (Ehrenberg, 2000; Ehrenberg et al., 1990). It has been found to apply in innumerable market contexts from consumer packaged goods (Dawes, 2008; Ehrenberg et al., 2004), to cars (Colombo et al., 2000), to banking services and even to political parties (Ehrenberg, 1991).

Double jeopardy is a simple empirical pattern or 'law', but it tells us quite a lot about why some brands are big and some others are small. Brands are bigger mostly because they have managed to do things that attract a larger customer base, not because they are intrinsically better or superior (otherwise, it might be the case that big brands get a lot more loyalty, or that perhaps some brands might be very big with only a modest customer base and very high loyalty). Next, double jeopardy tells us that loyalty is fairly predictable – since it is correlated quite strongly with brand size. This in turn implies that efforts to unilaterally increase loyalty, or strategies to have markedly higher loyalty levels compared to competitors, are misguided. While some brands have been found to be 'niche', that is, higher loyalty than they 'should get' given their market share, this loyalty is often due to structural factors such as that the brand has restricted distribution (so it is big/popular in some places, pushing up its loyalty in line with double jeopardy, but isn't available in other places, which pushes down its market-wide penetration, leaving it with comparatively high loyalty for a low level of penetration).

This is not to say loyalty doesn't matter – it does. A brand's 'sales equation' is: the number of buyers x how many times they buy in a period x how much they pay each time (adapted from Uncles and Ellis, 1989). Therefore, loyalty is directly, arithmetically linked to sales. Banks, for example, get roughly similar loyalty levels but they all have to work hard on customer service and good products and systems – as well as advertising and physical availability to keep up with their competitors. Loyalty is important, but the evidence is that growth comes far more from recruiting new customers or buyers than loyalty. Loyalty improves a little bit as brands grow, but penetration grows a lot more. This phenomenon is detailed in multiple studies (Dawes, 2016a; Nenycz-Thiel et al., 2018; Romaniuk et al., 2014).

Management Implication

Given double jeopardy, are we making realistic assessments about the extent to which we can achieve loyalty relative to competitors?

BUYERS BUY FROM REPERTOIRES OF BRANDS

Over time, buyers buy from a small selection of competing brands in a category (Banelis et al., 2013). This buying pattern has been widely documented for consumer goods such as diverse as coffee, to banking and insurance products. Here are two examples, banking and cat food, shown in Table 16.1.

TABLE 16.1 *Repertoire Size: Two Different Market Contexts*

Banking Buyers with This Many Banking Products	Deal with This Many Banks (Hong Kong)	Canned Cat Food Buyers Who Buy This Many Cans of Cat Food in a Year ...	Buy This Many Brands on Average
1	1.4	O to 10	1.3
2	1.9	11 to 20	2.5
3	2.4	21 to 30	3.4
4	2.8	31 to 40	3.8
5	3.2	41 to 50	4.2
6	3.4	51 to 60	4.7
-	-	61 to 70	4.5
-	-	71 to 80	4.7
-	-	81 to 200	5.5
-	-	201+	6.3
Avg. repertoire size	**2.6**	**Avg. Repertoire Size**	**4.1**

Source: Author data.

The fact that repertoires are generally fairly *small* tells us something about buyer behaviour. As we can see in Table 16.1, bank customers tend to deal with about two to three banks: consumer packaged goods buyers on average buy two to three brands in a year. Bearing in mind there are dozens of brands in those categories, actual repertoires are a very small subset of what is available. Repertoire buying – from smallish repertoires – tells us, first, that this is consistent with a worldview of buyers as 'cognitive misers', we don't want to think too much about solving problems such as which brand to buy; second, we use familiarity repeatedly to guide us in buying situations; and third, plainly we must screen out a lot of information about the virtues of other brands we don't buy (otherwise, we'd buy from a much broader selection of brands!).

The other point is that a buyer's repertoire size is systematically related to the amount of category purchasing the buyer does: frequent category buyers buy from more brands, light category buyers tend to buy far fewer brands, often only one.

Management Implication

Managers should understand the difference between 'switching' and simple repertoire buying. The fact that they can observe that many buyers buy their brand one time, then buy a different brand the next time, isn't necessarily a cause for alarm. It is a 'fact of life': buyers will buy from a selection of brands over time. The more successful brands get into more buyer's repertoires; so that should be the marketer's objective rather than getting more of a share within buyers repertoires, i.e. a loyalty strategy. There is also an implication from the observation of small repertoires, which is that brand loyalty is still a strong influence on buyer behaviour.

The fact that repertoire size is related to category purchasing rate means that it seems unlikely that a strategy to selectively target heavy category buyers and earn a lot of their business will work. This is because it goes against the natural tendency of heavy category buyers to spread their requirements out among multiple brands.

THE DUPLICATION OF PURCHASE LAW

We know from the previous law that buyers buy from repertoires, but there is an aggregate-level pattern in how this occurs. That is, brands share their buyers with competitors about in-line with the size, or market share, of those competitors. The word 'duplication' is perhaps an unfortunate one, being fairly opaque, but it refers to the fact that a single buyer can appear in the customer base of multiple brands, as if they were duplicated. Examples of this pattern are shown for restaurants (Lynn, 2013b), tourist destinations (Dawes et al., 2009), brands (Ehrenberg, 2000) and cars (Colombo & Sabavala, 2013). Here is an example analysis by the author, using the IRI academic dataset (Bronnenberg et al., 2008). We see that on average, more buyers of any of the brands also buy the other largest brand, namely Suave N – on average, 30 per cent; while the smallest brand, Suave P, attracts only 9 per cent of the buyers of any other brand. This is the duplication of purchase law in action.

TABLE 16.2 *Duplication of Purchase for Shampoo Brands (USA)*

	Penetration (% using)	% also using ...								
		Sua N	**Whi**	**Clai**	**Sua F**	**Alb**	**Lor**	**Pan**	**H&S**	**Sua P**
Suave N	15		27	21	34	23	17	9	7	10
Whiter	14	34		20	25	26	18	9	7	11
Clairol	13	27	20		15	17	22	14	9	8
Suave F	13	45	26	16		22	19	10	7	13
Alberto	12	33	30	20	25		18	6	7	6
Loreal	12	25	22	26	21	18		12	11	9
Pantene	8	20	16	25	17	9	18		7	7
H&S	7	19	14	19	15	12	19	8		8
Suave P	4	35	29	21	34	14	20	10	11	
Average duplication		30	23	21	24	17	19	10	9	9
Penetration		**15**	**14**	**13**	**13**	**12**	**12**	**8**	**7**	**4**

In some cases, groups of brands form a cluster or 'partition'. These brands will share some feature in common such as a formulation, for example in diet soft drinks. But these partitions only become apparent once one knows the general duplication pattern. Brands in a partition compete more intensely against each other, they are more closely substitutable with each other than with the other brands in the market. But even for a brand that forms part of a partition, there is still substitution/competition with all the other brands in the market. In Table 6.2 we see the Suave brands form a partition – buyers who buy one type of Suave (N, or F or P) know the brand, so they're more likely to buy other Suave sub-brands. We also see that Pantene and Alberto share buyers with each other far less than they do with other brands. This indicates these two brands tend not to compete against each other as much as expected.

Management Implication

Brands don't compete, or gain/lose sales to only one or two competitors, they compete against all other brands in the market, about in-line with the size of those competitors. Growth will come from getting a bit more cross-purchasing from the buyers of every other brand in the market. Therefore, planning to get growth by attacking one specific competitor brand isn't likely to work! The other implication is that if brand buyers share their purchasing with competitor brands in line with their size, it's unlikely a brand is bought for some special reason, or due to its unique image or positioning. If that were the case, it would seem odd that the brand's buyers substitute it with competitors – and not specific competitors usually, but rather all other competitor brands according to their market share. This seems more like buyers are seeing all the brands as reasonably substitutable with each other.

BUYING FREQUENCIES GENERALLY FOLLOW AN NBD PATTERN

The Negative Binomial Distribution (NBD) is a famous statistical distribution associated with the work of Andrew Ehrenberg and Gerald Goodhardt. The word 'distribution' here means the spread of observations around an average – for example, the normal distribution takes a bell shape. Other distributions, such as the NBD, can take different shapes.

Without going deeply into the maths, the NBD helps us understand how many buyers will purchase exactly 1, 2, 3 or more occasions in a time period simply from knowing the overall number of buyers who buy at all, and their average rate of purchase. The general pattern of purchases in markets such as consumer goods is that there are many infrequent or occasional buyers, fewer 'medium' buyers and far fewer again heavy or very frequent buyers. Examples of this pattern are shown in Dawes and Trinh (2017).

Researchers often refer to this pattern of many infrequent buyers and fewer heavy buyers as an 'NBD pattern'. We see this type of pattern in the banking data that follows.

Table 16.3 presents data from the UK retail banking industry. This is how we interpret the table: 34 per cent of people have an account with brand B. Of those, 55 per cent have one product with B (say, a transaction account); 21 per cent have two products, 15 per cent have three and so on. We can see plainly that the largest proportion of any of these bank brand's buyers is the group with only one product with the bank – 61 per cent on average.

TABLE 16.3 *Buying Rates for Bank Customers (UK, Retail Banking)*

		% of Bank's Customer Base that Has This Many Products with It			
Brand	**Penetration**	**1**	**2**	**3**	**4+**
B	34	55	21	15	9
H	33	61	23	10	6
S	29	56	30	9	5
N	28	60	21	11	8
L	20	54	21	14	11
N2	19	59	22	11	8
H	17	49	26	16	9
T	14	77	19	3	1
T2	8	74	14	7	5
Average	**22**	**61**	**22**	**11**	**7**

Source: Author data.

Management Implication

For a brand to grow, it has to attract many more buyers and most of them will be light buyers. A brand doesn't grow by selectively boosting the heavy buyer end of their customer base. But more generally, managers need to appreciate that a very large proportion of their customer base hardly buys/uses them at all – they're a small part of their customer's lives. In practice, many managers start thinking their customers are as 'into' the brand as they are.

USER PROFILES OF COMPETING BRANDS ARE USUALLY QUITE SIMILAR

The users of brand A in a category tend to be quite similar in all sorts of ways to the users of brand B, C, D within a category. This pattern was first documented by Hammond et al. (1996). A summary paper by Uncles et al. (2012: 252) reviewing data over many decades, countries and product categories concluded: 'Despite attempts by marketers to differentiate brands and provide customized features for distinct target audiences, the evidence of the current study confirms that user profiles of directly competing brands seldom differ'. Anesbury et al. (2017) confirmed that user profiles stay very similar over time.

Here is an example, in Table 16.4. Consumers in a Western country were asked a range of 'lifestyle' questions such as the perceived importance of healthiness, whether they considered themselves a good cook and so on. The proportion agreeing with the statements are tabulated for the user bases of a selection of brands in a food category. More people agree that a healthy life is important to them (46 per cent average), fewer agree that they work to a strict budget (28 per cent) or that brands are important to them (16 per cent). Reading down the columns we can easily see the buyers of each brand are about the same on these lifestyle attributes.

TABLE 16.4 *Competing Brands Have Buyers with Similar Lifestyles*

	% Agreeing with This Lifestyle Attribute				
Users of Brand ...	**Healthy Life**	**Good Cook**	**Little Time for Myself**	**Strict Budget**	**Brands Are Important to Me**
Store brand 1	44	40	31	27	16
Brand C	43	39	29	27	18
Store brand 2	47	42	33	28	17
Brand G	48	41	31	28	18
Store brand 3	42	40	29	30	15
Store brand 4	49	44	30	31	13
Brand D	49	43	30	27	18
Average	**46**	**41**	**30**	**28**	**16**

Source: Author data.

Management Implication

Managers should not think their brand's buyers are necessarily any different from competitor brands' buyers. It is likely that they look very much the same. And they should also remember this generalisation in tandem with the ones about repertoire buying and the duplication of purchase law – how could a brand's buyers be markedly different from competitor brands, when many of its buyers also buy those competitor brands?

This empirical generalisation also shows that to grow, a brand needs to increase its sales across the board, to buyers of the category, not to more tightly defined specific buyer sub-groups.

THE NATURAL MONOPOLY EFFECT

The natural monopoly (NM) effect mean that bigger brands tend to appeal to, or 'monopolise', light or less-knowledgeable buyers of the product category. In practice, we can see this effect by tabulating or graphing the average rate of category purchasing for each brand, alongside the market share or penetration of each brand. The natural monopoly effect is documented in a study by Dawes (2020b).

Figure 16.1 shows category purchasing rates for potato crisp brands in a European country. We see that buyers of the biggest brands buy the category around 18 times a year; while buyers of the smallest brands buy the category around 23 times a year. The correlation between brand penetration and category purchase rate in this market is r = –0.45, which is reasonably strong. The natural monopoly pattern has been documented by other researchers as well. Of course, this is not to say the people who buy big brands are different from those who buy small ones, many people buy both. But on average, the buyer base of a market leading brand has a lighter category buying rate.

FIGURE 16.1 *Natural Monopoly Effect, Potato Crisps*

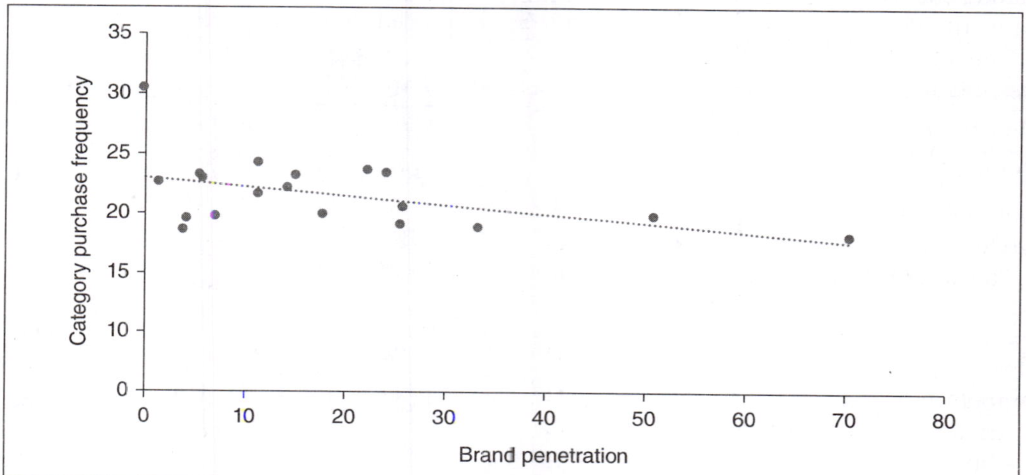

Management Implication

The NM effect helps us to understand why some brands are big and some brands are small. That is, the bigger brands have simply done a better job of reaching the vast pool of category buyers and creating familiarity among them. The NM effect implies that for a brand to grow from small to large, it must steadily appeal more and more to light/less knowledgeable buyers of the product category. In turn, this provides a rationale for mass-reach advertising. Moreover, the NM effect tells us that an undue focus on heavy buyers is inconsistent with the goal of becoming (or staying) a large brand.

COMPETITOR-ORIENTED OBJECTIVES ARE DETRIMENTAL

Part of the business/strategic management or marketing planning process is setting objectives. It appears the objectives set by managers have an impact on the long-term success of the business. Specifically, setting objectives to beat or harm competitors has a negative impact on financial performance. Armstrong and Collopy (1996) found evidence of this in a literature review, a series of experiments and an analysis of business data. In their experiments they presented graduate students with business scenarios in which a choice of strategy was required. The choice related to a 'low price' strategy in which the firm would make a certain amount of profit, and a 'high price' strategy in which the firm would make a different – higher – amount of profit. And for some participants, information about how much profit a competitor would make given the firm's strategy was also presented. So, participants could choose a profitable strategy in which competitors would also do well, or a less profitable strategy in which competitors would either make a loss or make much less profit.

What they found was that when participants were informed that their strategy would induce competitors to make much less profit than otherwise, they chose this strategy, even if it meant their own firm would make far less profit. For example, choosing a scenario in which their firm would make $40 million and competitors $20 million rather than their firm making $80 million and competitors making $160 million. Or, choosing lower profits if the competitor would make a large loss.

One might argue this sort of decision is logical because driving a competitor out of business might be good for one's own profit in the long run. However, the effect was the same even when participants were given a 20-year time horizon. Debriefs with participants seemed to indicate that profit relative to competitors seemed to be highly motivating, rather than the absolute amount of profit earned. So it seems that when people (managers) think about how their actions might harm competitors, or when they judge their outcomes relative to competitors, they make less profitable decisions.

The authors then examined a sample of 20 corporations for which information on pricing objectives had been gathered by another researcher. They analysed the firms' ROI for many years after the information on objectives had been obtained. They found those who had more competitor-oriented objectives had subsequently lower ROI (correlations between competitor orientation and ROI were around -.40 for up to 20 years afterwards).

Armstrong and Green (2007) summarised a number of other studies that corroborate this finding. A series of additional experiments with graduate students with slightly more complex pricing scenarios showed again that a high proportion of participants chose to harm their competitors at the expense of their own profit. The paper also summarised the results of a learning simulation in which student teams competed to earn profits. Participants were surveyed to measure the extent to which they believed in a competitor orientation (i.e. that results should be judged against competitors, that beating competitors was useful). The student groups with higher competitor orientation earned lower rates of profit.

Management Implication

Focus on profits and much less on market share. Avoid using sports or military analogies ('let's get out there and win the battle against competitor X') because they foster a competitor orientation. Do not set goals to beat or harm competitors.

CUSTOMER SATISFACTION IS IMPORTANT, BUT IT IS NOT WHAT DISTINGUISHES BIG FROM SMALL BRANDS

We all know that we expect and like good service, which leads to satisfaction. No one likes long waits, inattentive staff, inadequate information or poor facilities like a dirty hotel room. And we generally feel less inclined to use a service provider that has given us poor service. Therefore, it seems intuitive that good customer service and therefore high levels of customer satisfaction should correlate with happier clients, higher rates of repeat-purchasing from clients, and perhaps even more positive word of mouth from those clients. And extrapolating further, businesses with higher overall levels of customer satisfaction should be more successful – have higher sales or market share – than those with lower levels. Surprisingly, however, this is not the case. Fornell, the founder of the American Customer Satisfaction Index (ACSI), reported two 'empirical generalisations' about customer satisfaction. First was that it is invariably negatively skewed, meaning that scores are usually high, clustered around 7–8 on a 1 to 10 scale. That said, some industries differ a lot in customer satisfaction, for example cars had an average score of 77/100 while TV broadcasting had an average of 46/100 in Sweden in the 1990s (Fornell, 1995). For brands, taking cars as an example, current figures for automobiles in the US are: Lexus 88/100, Volvo 85/100, Lincoln (Ford) 84/100 and many other brands at around the 80/100 level. The lowest is Chrysler at 74/100, see www.theacsi.org.

The second major finding is that the relationship between customer satisfaction and market share is 'often not positive (and often negative) in cross sectional analysis' (Fornell, 1995: G203). Moreover, this result is not confined to any one country, the same pattern is shown in US, German and Swedish data. Somewhat surprisingly, other researchers find that customer satisfaction is positively linked to profitability (Anderson et al., 2004), albeit very weakly, and only discernible via using very complicated statistical modelling. It is apparently impossible to show the association clearly in a graph, which makes one dubious about the effect.

Why isn't there a stronger association between customer satisfaction and market share? It could be partly because rivals in an industry tend to have fairly similar customer satisfaction scores, yet the other factors that do dictate market share, namely mental availability and physical availability, tend to vary a lot more from one competitor to another. As well as that, market share comes from sales, but customer satisfaction often comes after a sale is made. For example, new-car owners are asked how satisfied they are with the car several months after they purchased it (they might also be asked about satisfaction with the dealer almost as soon as they buy). Therefore, the causal link between satisfaction and market share is not intuitive. That said, it seems reasonable that if your service is quite poor, you might repel enquiries or trials of your product, which will result in lower sales and therefore market share. But, of course, most satisfaction surveys like the ACSI ask people who have purchased a product (like a car) how satisfied they are with it, they do not survey people who just made an enquiry.

Management Implication

In simple terms, customer satisfaction scores between rivals in an industry tend to be usually positive, around 7 to 8 out of 10, or 70 to 80 out of 100, and usually bear little association with market share. Therefore – while it is important to keep your customers satisfied, there is often not a lot of room to improve your scores. That is to say, if you are getting, say, 82/100, you can't go much higher – probably no one gets above 90 in the industry. And if you do, there isn't actually any evidence it will pay off in market share. Therefore, a marketing plan should not predicate increasing sales or market share from a planned improvement in customer service, unless there is quite strong evidence that the business has a problem in the way it interacts with clients. Of course, this doesn't mean management let's customer service or customer satisfaction slide downward, it needs to keep working on it – but managers need to be realistic about how much growth can be predicated on it.

ADVERTISING DOES WORK, EVEN WITHOUT SHORT-TERM SALES LIFTS

Does advertising work? This question has been posed countless times over the past 100 years or more. The answer is yes, it does – on average. But the way in which the question is answered is very important. If one attempts to answer the question by seeing if advertising causes lifts in sales, the answer will often be no it doesn't appear to do anything. Indeed, many advertising campaigns have no discernible impact on brand sales – but that doesn't necessarily mean the advertising didn't work. That's partly because advertising also reaches people who may not be ready to buy the category until years after seeing the ad. So it's quite understandable that the effects of advertising on a brand's total sales (whether it be a brand of toothpaste, car tyres or accounting services) often are difficult to see, especially if you only track sales during and for a month after a campaign.

Many studies, what are called meta-analyses, have found advertising elasticity to be between 0.1 and 0.2. Elasticity is a multiplier; it signifies the change in sales for every 1 per cent change in advertising spend. So, based on these figures, if we increase advertising spending by 50 per cent, sales on average should increase by 50 x .1 = 5 to 50 x .2 = 10, between 5 and 10 per cent. However, a more recent, large study by Shapiro et al. (2020) found a much lower short-term (i.e. a sales effect over 3–4 weeks) ad elasticity of only around 0.03 – almost zero. They suggested the difference between their results and previous ones was that there is bias in academic journals to 'positive' results, and since meta-analyses can only rely on published results, their estimates are biased upwards. This is an example of a 'selection effect', which is mentioned elsewhere in the book. Note that these results about advertising elasticity tend to be for established packaged goods brands. And they are generally about short-term aggregate effects on sales, as in from a week to a month or so. Long-term effects were not considered.

Another point to recognise is that if you run advertising steadily all through the year, it can be working very efficiently, but the effects are hard to see because you have no 'control' condition when there is no advertising running, with which to compare.

Given there appears to be often very little relationship between turning advertising on and off in the short term, and sales – perhaps we need to look longer term. A project from the Ehrenberg-Bass Institute tracked brands that stopped advertising for a year or more. It found that after a year, those brands showed quite noticeable declines (Gelzinis, 2017). Therefore, if your sales drop some time (perhaps a year or more) after you cease advertising, then the advertising must have been working to maintain sales. But you can't necessarily see that effect if you are looking only week by week or even month by month. That said, some studies have been able to find short-term sales effects from advertising, using store sales data and ad spend. A large-scale recent study found the most effective ingredient in television advertising effectiveness for consumer grocery goods was the duration with which brand logo and product were shown (Bruce et al., 2020).

Management Implication

Managers should feel confident that if they invest money in advertising it will 'work' over the long term, even if it's difficult to see sales effects in the short term. But they need to check some key features of their advertising. First, is it prominently branded? i.e. easy for people who see/hear it to know which brand it is for. Second, does it link the brand to purchasing or usage situations?

SHARE OF VOICE IS RELATED TO MARKET SHARE

Another aspect of addressing the question around whether advertising works (and advertising used in a broad sense to mean all marketing communications) is the link between share of voice and share of market (or market share). Share of voice means the brand's spending as a proportion of all the advertising spending in the whole category.

Research has shown that an established brand's market share and its share of voice tend to be fairly closely related via what is called an advertising intensity 'curve' or line. Essentially, what this line shows, as per Hansen and Bech Christensen (2005) and Danenberg, Kennedy, Beal, and Sharp (2016), is that smaller brands tend to have a share of voice that is higher than their market share, and larger brands tend to have a share of voice that is lower than their market share. The tendency for smaller brands to spend proportionally more on advertising than would be dictated by their market share level is more pronounced in high-advertising categories such as fast-moving consumer goods. One notable caveat about this work is that a considerable proportion of brands in studies such as Hansen and Bech Christensen (2005) did no advertising, yet had some level of market share. These were reportedly private label and groupings of extremely small brands. These brands were not considered in the analysis.

In categories with overall lower levels of advertising – such as services, for example, we would expect that the association between share of voice and share of market would be much more linear. In other words, businesses or brands that spend at the level of 1 per cent of all market spend would be expected to have about 1 per cent market share, and those that account for around 10 per cent of all advertising spend would have about 10 per cent market share, and so on.

The other major finding from this work is, brands that increase their share of voice from one year to another tend to get a lift in their market share in the second year. The long time period, a whole year, is important – a brand might not get a discernible uptick in sales if it ramps up ad spend from one week to another, or one month to another. But on average, there are noticeable growth effects from increasing one's share of voice from one year to another. This is because the longer period allows the advertising effects to manifest among more people, since a lot of buyers buy only occasionally.

Management Implication

For the manager writing a marketing plan, the implication of this research is that there is a need to be realistic in thinking about market share or sales objectives. For example, if you manage a 1 per cent market share brand and have a goal to achieve 3 per cent market share and you cannot spend anything like 3 per cent of all the advertising spending, the goal just does not seem realistic. Second, this finding gives hope to managers who are thinking about a long-term up-weighting of their advertising spend: on average, raising share of voice tends to result in more market share – but not immediately.

PRICE ELASTICITY AVERAGES AROUND -2.5, AND VARIES ACCORDING TO KNOWN CONTEXTS

We have all heard the term price elasticity. It is the percentage change in sales for every 1 per cent change in price. Many studies have sought to calculate the average price elasticity for brands. It is –2.5 or so. Therefore, on average if a brand puts prices up by 5 per cent and competitor's prices stay the same, sales will drop by 5 × –2.5 = 12.5 per cent. Where does this evidence come from? Mostly from consumer packaged goods, we know far less about price elasticity for brands of services or durables. But here is a summary: Tellis (1988) summarised results from several dozen studies with over 300 estimates of price elasticity. The overall average was –1.8 but taking some biases into account and correcting for them (lack of information on factors like advertising and product quality, which can bias results downward) the estimated average was –2.5. Ehrenberg and England (1990) reported an average of –2.6 from a large research study involving a panel of households that purchased items from a visiting van over 12 fortnightly visits.

Many years later Scriven and Ehrenberg (2004) reported almost the same figure of –3.2 in a long-term study using a 'hall test' method (arranging brands on tables, inviting consumers to record which one they would buy, and manipulating the prices). This average was larger when a price change passed the price of the most popular brand in the category (–2.8 not passing, –5.6 passing). It was also systematically bigger when the price changes encountered by buyers were successive (seeing the price for the same item at a normal, then low, then high price – which meant the consumer remembered the previous price) as opposed to –2.5 for 'shopping trip' scenarios in which the previous price seen for the item was harder to remember. The 'shopping trip' scenarios were more realistic, so the –2.4 is a better reflection of in-market results. Elasticity was also higher when the price change was signalled to buyers (with a 'was X now Y' tag). Lastly, price elasticity was systematically smaller for large-share brands than for small brands (–1.9 for the very largest, –4.2 for the very smallest). Other research has also found lower price elasticity for large-share brands in a grocery context, for example Bolton (1989) and Bemmaor and Mouchoux (1991).

Another study, by Mulhern et al. (1998) analysed price elasticity for alcohol brands, finding an average of –3.5. They suggested the higher elasticity was due to the fact the price per item of alcohol (whiskey, etc.) is higher than for typical grocery items. It is also likely that price changes in this context were signalled to buyers, which, as Scriven and Ehrenberg (2004) found, leads to higher elasticity

Management Implication

We know price elasticity is negative for brands, and is around –2.5, so if the marketing plan involves price increases relative to competitors then sales will decline by around 2.5 times the price increase. Or, if prices are to be cut and competitors don't match, then sales will increase by something like 2.5 times the price cut percentage. However, in the real world competitors are likely to match price cuts. They might be relieved to see a competitor increase its prices and then follow soon after.

For a manager managing several brands that vary a lot in size, i.e. market share, these findings provide some context of what to expect from price changes. Price increases will hurt one's larger brand less than they will hurt a smaller one in the portfolio (in terms of sales), whereas the larger brand is expected to be somewhat less responsive in proportional terms to price cuts compared to the smaller brand in the portfolio.

Next, if a manager plans to cut price to increase unit sales, it would seem advisable to pass the price of a major competitor; whereas they should try to avoid passing a competitor's prices if there is a need to increase their own prices. Take an example where input costs have increased and there is a need to put prices up, but a 6 per cent rise would push the brand past a major competitor. The firm should settle for, say, a 4 per cent or 5 per cent increase. Also, one should signal price reductions, but try to avoid signalling or unduly drawing buyers' attention to price increases, within the bounds of expected ethical behaviour.

MARKETING COMMUNICATION HAS DIMINISHED EFFECTS FROM MULTIPLE EXPOSURES IN A PERIOD

Research shows that the greatest increase in a buyer's purchase propensity for a brand comes from their first exposure in a time period. This result has been reported in research studies by Deighton et al. (1994), Jones (1995a; 1995b), and Taylor et al. (2009).

How long a time period? It could be between a week and a month. Therefore, for argument's sake, a consumer has a 1 per cent probability or 'propensity' of buying a brand in the next couple of weeks if they see no advertising for that brand. If they see one ad in the next couple of days to a week, their propensity might increase to say, 1.1 per cent, which is an increase of 0.1. If they see two ads in that same period their increase in purchase propensity is bigger than 0.1: but it's not double, perhaps its only 0.15. And if they see three ads perhaps the total increase is, say, 0.18. So, the first exposure lifts propensity by 0.1, the second by 0.05, and the third by 0.03. Therefore, the argument is the money spent hitting that same person for the second and third time would have been better spent hitting two other people for the first time.

Management Implication

Do not accept media schedules that will expose buyers to your advertising multiple times in a short period, such as five times in two hours during a televised sporting event. This is wasteful.

Self-test Questions

1. Double jeopardy is a widespread empirical pattern, what does it tell us about how brands grow?
2. It's good to grow one's market share, therefore why should it be a bad thing to be competitor oriented?
3. There is a robust finding that brand buying frequencies follow an NBD pattern – usually more lights than heavies. But since heavy buyers are worth more each, should we not try to win more of them?
4. Which empirical pattern or law tells us that attacking one particular competitor is generally unlikely to result in brand growth, and why?

CHAPTER

17

Management Beliefs and Biases, and What They Mean for Marketing Planning and Strategy

Writing a marketing plan involves making decisions, and decisions can be influenced by all sorts of biases. A bias can lead to a lesser quality decision or course of action. Therefore, this section discusses a series of biases to alert the reader about them and how to reduce their effect.

CORRELATION AND CAUSATION – THE MISLEADING OF MANAGEMENT

A common phrase in science is that correlation is not causation. Correlation simply means that two things tend to be related – as this one gets higher or lower, that one gets higher or lower. For example, if unemployment gets higher, consumer confidence gets lower. Or high school GPA is correlated with university grades. A correlation varies between –1 and +1. The closer to –1 or 1 a correlation is, the 'stronger' is the association between the two variables.

Unfortunately, managers read and listen to countless articles, talks and perhaps pitches from consultants that make it sound like certain things cause other things, but they don't, the two things are merely correlated. Examples often relate to what people say in surveys about brands and what they do (or say they do) in terms of purchasing those brands. More specifically, some consultancy firms will survey consumers, and from their survey responses, obtain measures of brand equity – customer-based brand equity, that is. They then endeavour to show a correlation between firms' market-based brand equity and their financial performance (market share, share price) later on. This work is then presented to help sell the brand equity survey to firms on the basis that it predicts (causes) financial performance or share market movement.

But to reiterate, correlation is not causation. For example, the correlation between the number of pool drownings and the number of Nicholas Cage films released between 1999 and 2009 was 0.66 (Vigen, 2020). We can hardy conclude one causes the other. Indeed, pool drownings in the US also correlate quite highly with sales of ice cream. Does selling more ice cream cause pool drownings? Obviously not. In fact, they are both due to a third variable – namely the temperature. When it's hot, more people swim in pools, so the chance that on any day someone drowns is higher; and more people eat ice cream.

Therefore, what should a manager think when presented with a case such as, 'our brand equity monitor is the best because the scores we derive from it predict future market share and earnings'. Well, the overriding principle is to be healthily sceptical. There's nothing wrong with being sceptical, it's not a personal attack to be sceptical about a claim being made – especially if the claim is made with a motivation to sell a manager something. So, look for corroborating evidence. And consider there could be a third variable at work. Also consider that the causal claim could actually be the other way around: rather than A causing B, B causes A. For example, perhaps scores in brand equity surveys, rather than driving market share, are actually picking up that market share has already increased (due to new products, price changes, etc.). And firms that are currently increasing their market share are probably also enjoying an increase in their stock price. Lastly, be sceptical about claims made by agencies or consultancies that they have some mechanism which in effect means they can predict things like market share lifts or share price movement – they'd be billionaires from picking stock winners, not selling research.

Management Implication

Be sceptical of claims that because two variables are correlated, one causes the other. One should be especially sceptical if the information on the two variables is gathered at the same point in time (such as, a survey that asks about one thing, then another, determines that they are correlated, and concludes one *causes* the other).

THE HALO EFFECT

The halo effect is the tendency for our overall impression of someone or something to influence how we perceive specific things about them. For example, if we think a person is nice, or attractive, we also tend to think they are smart and or popular. This effect can influence our perceptions of ideas, decisions, firms, brands or people. The halo effect results in us perceiving certain things more positively than we should or less positively than we should, for example, unattractive people are more likely to be found guilty of a crime than are attractive people.

The halo effect as it applies to managers, and the way that managers and firms are written about, is the subject of a book by Philip Rosenzweig (2007). He gave the example of the Lego corporation, which at the time was doing poorly, with its CEO recently sacked. All the news reports about Lego were negative – everything it did seemed to be rather dumb and ill-conceived – to business writers, at least. But Rosenzweig noted that these news reports were written by people who *knew* Lego was doing poorly, and so that coloured their perception of everything about the company. It could actually be that many of the specific strategies Lego was employing were quite sensible (indeed quite similar to many other businesses) but because Lego was failing, the halo effect meant they were interpreted as bad. The problem for managers is that they can read things about a company that make it sound like 'strategy X is a poor or bad thing to do, look how Lego did that and it's lost money and sacked its CEO'. They conclude, 'oh let's not do strategy X!' But there might not be anything wrong with doing X. Maybe Lego might have been worse off if it hadn't done it.

We also see the halo effect at play in what is called the 'excellence' literature. This name is from a famous book by Peters and Waterman called *In Search of Excellence* (1982). These authors identified 20 high-performing US companies, then went to them to find out what made them excellent. They concluded there were eight attributes of excellence – things like: a bias for action, being close to the customer, allowing autonomy and entrepreneurship, productivity through people, 'hands-on, value driven' and so on. The unfortunate problem with this work – and the many similar attempts that have followed – is all the conclusions are influenced by the halo effect. Imagine you go into a company you know is performing extremely well at the time. You are going to conclude what they do must be good! Let's say you notice a company has a strange ritual, that every Monday morning they do jumping jacks and turn to each other and say, 'Nanu Nanu'. You know the company is very successful. You'll be tempted to think, 'interesting, this ritual must help the employees and managers bond, so it is a manifestation of a close culture'. This might then prompt you to look for a close culture in other businesses you have pre-identified as successful. Now imagine you went into the same company, but you knew it was doing very poorly. You notice that same strange ritual, but this time you'll think, 'how stupid is this, the company has a problem in that managers force employees to do mindless rituals – a manifestation of rigidity or authoritarianism'. Therefore, the same phenomena in both instances would be considered good or bad, based on other information that was readily available – which is the classic halo effect.

Management Implication

First and most simply, managers need to be aware their judgements and decisions about things are not necessarily logical, and they might not know they are not logical. Hiring a new staff member? Judgements about their ability might be biased by appearance or other easily visible cues. Deciding on a new advertising agency? Perhaps this choice will be affected by the same effect. Did our most recent campaign work? The business is going well, so it must have. Or, the business isn't going well, so it didn't work – but perhaps the two things have separate causes.

There is no easy solution to avoid being hoodwinked by the halo effect. But being aware that our decisions are often influenced by it is a start, at least. One possible way to handle halo effects is to decide on the criteria by which you would make a decision beforehand. For example, decide on what criteria you would judge something (like a marketing initiative) 'worked' before it happened, not afterwards. This approach tends to force more logical choices.

THE NARRATIVE FALLACY

The narrative fallacy is one in which people believe a storyline or account of some phenomenon because it matches a narrative with intuitive sense. For example, we might wish to know why a particular businessperson has been so successful. We read a story in which we learn how the young person watched his father take exceptional care in making furniture, then later found out the man who he thought was his father wasn't his biological father. This combination of the absorption of the principle of taking extreme pride in work, as well as the trauma of finding out he was adopted, drove him to have an extreme penchant for detail, a great need to prove himself and an almost messianic zeal in pushing his big ideas. Sound reasonable? It wasn't actually true, it was a book and movie plot about a real person (Steve Jobs), but it was largely invented. But we'd accept it as true because the narrative made sense. The narrative fallacy is linked to our desire to understand why things occur. Why did that brand become so successful? Ah, because its clever owners harnessed the power of social media. Sounds very plausible. But maybe there were other brands that had a lot of work done on their social media profile that didn't become as successful. We don't think of the less obvious factors – maybe a bit of luck, maybe it was good timing, perhaps it was hard work behind the scenes for several years as well.

Kahneman (2011: 202) summed this issue up nicely:

> Stories of how businesses rise and fall strike a chord with readers by offering what the human mind needs: a simple message of triumph and failure that identifies clear causes and ignores the determinative power of luck and the inevitability of regression. These stories induce and maintain an illusion of understanding, imparting lessons of enduring value to readers who are all too eager to believe them.

Of course, if we read stories of successful people or brands they often feature a description of the hard work and sacrifice made to accomplish that success. And this part of the book is not meant to trivialise the fact that success does usually involve hard work. It's unlikely a management team can build a good brand or make a business successful without hard work. But it's also worth noting that there are many businesses or brands that are not particularly successful, yet an awful lot of hard work went into them. The point is, the narrative fallacy can imply – because the stories based on it are usually about success – that hard work does always pay off. Of course, the narrative might be about something else – such as, a firm was struggling until it 'hit on the right advertising ingredient – humour'.

Management Implication

When you read a story about a person or business that attempts to explain the reason why they are successful, reflect on whether the storyline is actually a narrative fallacy. Is the implicit 'lesson' or explanation for the success rather too convenient? Could it be that other people or businesses have done exactly the same thing and been far less successful?

SELECTION BIAS

Selection bias is the effect in which some element of the sampling that is used to identify a phenomenon biases it, so that it is different from the broader population that the researcher is interested in. To illustrate: suppose we want to do some market research about mobile phones, and we do some intercept surveys in a busy shopping mall during the week. We might find a large number of people surveyed have inexpensive phones and cheap plans. But that could be a selection effect because we're less likely to be talking to people who work full time – they're at work during the week, not in shopping malls.

I once experienced an issue with selection bias doing some market research. We surveyed people who had enquired (but not yet enrolled) about studying with a particular university, about two months after they had enquired. We asked them if they had enquired with, or were considering enrolling with, a competitor university. We found that around 70 per cent said yes they had either enquired with, had enrolled with, or were going to enrol with the competitor. I was initially shocked by this result! Such a huge proportion of people who had enquired with our university were going to go to a competitor! What had gone wrong? Fortunately, I realised after some thinking that this result was entirely due to selection bias. Of course, among those who had enquired with our university and months later had not yet enrolled, a large proportion would *now* have enquired, considered or gone to a competitor. And this proportion would grow over time. If we had surveyed the sample only a week after they had enquired, the proportion would have been much smaller – they hadn't necessarily had time to also enquire/consider a competitor, but as time goes on the proportion who enquire with one university but don't enrol – and then go to a competitor – must increase. This is simply a selection effect, or selection bias.

One more example of selection bias is of a firm that surveys its own customers. It asks them about how much of its product they buy, and how much they buy from competitors. It finds, to its delight, that its customers seem more loyal to it than to the competition. But this is an artefact, a selection effect from surveying one's own customers. Among your own customers, some are solely loyal to you but among your customers, none of them can be solely loyal to competitors. Therefore, you will have a biased sample and those sorts of results are inaccurate.

A Type of Selection Bias – Survivor Bias

A particular type of selection bias is called attrition or survivor bias. It can lead to overoptimism, because failures are ignored. For example, if we look at the performance of companies in an investment fund over 10 years, we might note that they earn an average 10 per cent rate of return on invested capital. But this would ignore the businesses that perhaps went bankrupt over the period: they are not counted because they don't exist anymore. Another example is that we notice old buildings in a city like Amsterdam or Brussels and marvel at their beauty, and we could conclude all buildings hundreds of years ago were very beautiful and very well built. But the ones we like to look at today are the surviving buildings, we don't know about all the poorly built and ugly buildings from hundreds of years ago (from looking now) because they don't exist anymore. We might notice MMA fighters seemingly able to absorb punishing blows to the head and body in a cage fighting match, and conclude, punches to the head in a fight could be absorbed. But this is survivor bias – only a small subset of humans who have a particular resilience to head and body blows (and they have a freakish ability to move their head to partially deflect a blow) can hope to stay in the sport long enough to compete in MMA events that are shown on television.

Confirmation bias is related to selection bias. It occurs when people seek confirmation of an existing idea they have, rather than trying to determine if that idea is correct or not. For example, if a manager thinks their new brand campaign should be heavily based on social media then they will tend to look for information that supports their idea, and they will find it, because they're looking for it and not looking for dissonant information. So, they will merely reinforce their initial thoughts, which might lead to a poor decision.

Management Implication

Be aware that various sorts of claims or opinions or market research results might be influenced by selection bias. For important decisions based on research, particularly if the results seem surprising, query the source of the information to ensure it is not subject to this effect. Is the sample being discussed a random sample, or a subset of a larger population and so is different from it in some way? If that's the case, there is a good chance the result is due to a selection effect.

STATUS QUO BIAS

Status quo bias is where people largely prefer what they already have to what they could change to – 'a preference for the current state of affairs'. This bias is closely related to and perhaps sometimes confounded with inertia, which is that people largely prefer to do nothing about an issue than do something about it. An example of the status quo bias is about residents in a European town that had a terrible road system, due to it being designed hundreds of years ago, before the advent of cars and rail. This meant travelling around in the town was very inefficient. The residents were presented with a plan by which they would all be moved to a beautiful new town with new houses re-creating their old ones, and a very efficient road system. The vast majority voted for the status quo – they said no to the change.

An example of status quo bias that I experienced while doing a research project for a client was a name change. Two financial institutions had merged, and it was necessary to decide on the name of the new institution. A series of new names were given to clients along with an option to keep the name the same. A large proportion voted to keep the name the same (which was bad news for the business as senior managers really wanted to change it). Fortunately, we suggested it was to be expected that a large number would vote to keep the same name, not because they were really wedded to it, but simply due to a tendency to 'keep things the same'. The name was changed, and it turned out that there were no real problems among the client base regarding the new name.

Management Implication

Managers should be aware that their clients and customers would generally like things to stay as they are, rather than changing. Likewise, many of their staff if presented with a plan for change might not be enthusiastic about it. This reaction may not necessarily reflect badly on their plan, but simply reflect a human tendency to like things the way they are.

REGRESSION TO THE MEAN

Regression to the mean is an effect whereby if we observe unusually low or high observations for some object (person, brand, company) at one point in time, the next time we observe it, those unusual observations will have changed, or trended, towards their mean average figure. The classic example is a test with a bunch of true/false questions that a class of students takes on one day. Some do extremely well, some do poorly and many do 'just OK'. Then the students take the test two days later. On average the students who did very badly the first time do better the second time, and on average the students who did very well the first time don't do quite as well the second time. This effect occurs because there was some random element in the performance in both tests. Some students were a little lucky, or a little unlucky, the first time and that luck 'averaged out' a bit in the second test. Note I'm not suggesting there is no difference in ability between the students, some will consistently score better because they're smarter and/or study harder. If we had a large sample, we could look within the groups of high-ability and low-ability students and still see a tendency to regress upward or downward towards a longer-term within-group average level.

Another example is from my marketing planning class. I get students to toss coins ten times and record the number of heads. Those who get three or less heads are identified as the 'bad' performers and eight or more are 'good performers'. We toss the coins again. And what happens is, the bad performers tend to do better next time and the good performers do worse.

Regression to the mean sounds like an obscure trifle in statistics but it's quite important for marketers to know about. For example, suppose we observe consumers in a period of time like a quarter or a year. We note some are light buyers, some medium and some are heavy. Then when we observe them again (a quarter or year later) and on average, the lights are heavier and the heavies are lighter! Without knowing this is simply regression to the mean we could come to all sorts of wrong conclusions. For example, suppose we had done some direct response advertising to the light buyers – ha ha, it worked so well! Actually, sales would have gone up for light buyers, on average, anyway. Or we enrolled the heavy buyers in a loyalty programme – oh no, their purchasing declined on average when we next looked! Actually, it would have declined anyway – because of regression to the mean. A report once claimed that US brands were 'losing loyalty' because about 50 per cent of their heavy buyers weren't heavy the following year! (Pointer Media Network, 2009). Again, this is explainable as regression to the mean. Heavy buyers can't really get much heavier, and some of them simply bought a bit more than usual in one year so they just have to down-weight somewhat in the second year.

Now let's turn back to the halo effect, and the idea of identifying excellent companies to learn their principles for success. Follow-up studies showed many of the excellent companies were quite ordinary performers five years later. This, too, is explainable from regression to the mean. Some companies do indeed perform better than others, – and some are run better or have better resources, capabilities or strategies than others. But if we select a group that are extremely high performing, they are bound to not do as well later because success has *some* element of luck or randomness. This means some that perform super well at initial observation will have regressed back to their average level later. The same can occur for people – perhaps we hire someone and in their first week they seem absolutely amazing. Don't expect them to necessarily be so amazing in another week or two.

Management Implication

Suppose a manager learns that some collection of entities – such as buyers (or businesses, or employees) – has a particular characteristic that appears to be quite prominent or high on some measure, or quite low on some measure. For example, a staff member's sales performance, a firm's revenue growth in the past 12 months, or that some buyers buy an awful lot and others hardly buy at all. It might the case that next time those staff, or firms, or buyers are observed, they aren't extreme observations anymore. And it might not be due to any particular reason, it could just be they have regressed back to their longer-term mean level. Consider that in the meantime a manager has mounted an intervention to get those really light buyers to buy more – they could falsely interpret the intervention as a success when perhaps a lot of the change could have happened anyway (non-buyers, for instance, can't buy less in the future than they do now). Knowing how or when to discern between actual change over time and regression to the mean is an important skill for an intelligent manager or analyst.

THE PLANNING FALLACY

It might seem incongruous to have a section called the planning fallacy in a marketing planning book. It's not the case that plans are inherently fallacious. But evidence shows when decision makers try to estimate the cost and difficulty of undertaking a project – building a brand, achieving an ambitious sales objective, implementing a new way of doing things – they tend to underestimate the time, cost or difficulty of doing so – often by a lot. There are many examples that can be used to illustrate this point. The Sydney Opera House was originally estimated to take six years and $7 million (in 1960's dollars). It actually took 16 years and over $100 million. Another example is the HS2 high-speed railway project in the UK. It was originally costed at £56 billion and after commencement is presently now estimated to cost £106 billion. These are incredibly big mistakes! Understanding why they happen should be valuable knowledge.

The fallacy seems to exist in many different situations. Kruger and Evans (2004) investigated the planning fallacy in a series of experiments involving shopping, preparing for a date, assorted editing tasks and meal preparation. They found participants in these studies invariably underestimated the time or effort it would take to do the task.

Flyvbjerg (2007) identified that the planning fallacy is pervasive in large transportation infrastructure projects, but pointed out it applies in other types of large projects as well. He examined 258 projects across 20 countries and found the average cost overrun was between 20 to 50 per cent. Moreover, this tendency to underestimate cost had not improved over a 70-year period! This is surprising considering computers and access to more information should make for more accurate managerial estimates. Some specific examples given by Flyvbjerg were that the Denver Airport redevelopment cost 200 per cent more than estimated ($5 billion), and the Channel tunnel cost 80 per cent more than its budget.

Why Does the Planning Fallacy Exist and What Should Be Done to Reduce Its Effect?

One explanation for the planning fallacy is simply optimism and hope – planners or managers want their project to go ahead and succeed, so they unconsciously minimise the likely barriers. A second, related explanation is 'strategic misrepresentation' – managers want their project to go ahead because it will make them look good, or they are competing for funds or support against other managers or other projects. This might mean they deliberately misrepresent the likely cost and time (thinking the rewards will come sooner and someone else can perhaps cope with the problems). The third explanation is simply that decisions may not be based on adequate data or that it is simply very difficult to forecast the future.

Flyvbjerg (2007) suggested the big culprit is strategic misrepresentation. He put forward many examples of projects in which expert's assessment of cost, time or likely demand were asked to be re-assessed by their superiors in order to make the project more attractive, to 'get it over the line' of an approval process.

A solution to the planning fallacy, according to Flyvbjerg (2007) is to use 'reference class forecasting' – simply to explicitly use information on a class of similar project. For building a tunnel under a harbour, for example, one would assemble information on the costs and time involved in constructing similar projects. Then look at the distribution of those costs and time periods for the reference projects and decide where in that distribution this current project would sit (i.e. at the lower end, the middle or the higher end). This approach might sound intuitively sensible but is obviously not often done because of the prevalence of underestimation cited above. Unfortunately, this method is not necessarily suitable for projects in which information is not publicly available such as implementing a marketing plan, successfully launching a new product and so on. For those sorts of projects, a method called 'unpacking' is appropriate. This approach, as its name suggests, involves unpacking a large project into its parts, estimating the cost and time for each part separately. Kruger and Evans (2004) found this approach led to more realistic estimates. The reason it works is probably because the act of unpacking highlights all the components of a project, some of which managers or decision makers simply don't recall or consider if they just think about the project in total (without unpacking it). For a particular project or task within a marketing plan, therefore, the manager should ask their team to generate a list of all the specific things required for it to occur (not in fine detail, but enough detail to consider their magnitude). Then estimate the cost and time of each component and sum the total. To illustrate, suppose the marketing plan for a homebuilder included new colour brochures showing high-quality pictures of interiors and exteriors. To do this, one would need to find and hire a professional photographer, arrange the photo shoot (assuming the home details which the manager wants in the brochures are actually in existence), select the best pictures, find a graphic designer, brief them on the requirements, review drafts, agree on the final design, find a printing firm and order the brochures. At first glance the idea of something simple like organising brochures might be thought to take a couple of weeks, but considering all these steps, it might actually take two months or more since each step would likely take a week or longer and each needs to happen before the next.

Management Implication

It is quite likely a manager planning a major task or project will underestimate how long or difficult it is likely to be. A simple approach – called reference class forecasting, basically involves unpacking the big task into parts and estimating the cost/time of each – appears to be a promising method to reduce this problem.

ASSUMING 'WHAT'S IMPORTANT' TO BUYERS IS THE PANACEA

It is very common for marketing people to want to know what's important to buyers. They feel that if they get insights into what's important or what buyers want, then obviously if they then offer those features or benefits it could make them more popular among buyers. And doing this can work. Take, for example, a business that sells ceramic tiles, tile glue, grout and tiling tools – it sells to professional tilers and builders who order via phone, email, through sales reps or a web order interface. One thing they really want is that their order is ready when they arrive to pick it up, otherwise they are standing around waiting for their order to be packed and losing time they could be spending on the work site, earning money. And suppose a firm's performance is somewhat patchy on this important service feature. Therefore, asking customers what's important could yield a very definite piece of information about orders being ready, which the business should make an absolute priority to improve on. This might not necessarily provide a route to growth for the company, but it arguably addresses an aspect of physical availability, making the business easier to buy from and ensuring it is on par at least with its competitors. So far, this idea is not contentious and fits in with the general idea of the 'marketing concept', which is that a business should try to think about customer needs and wants as a part of creating its offerings.

But there's a caveat to asking customers or intending buyers what is important. What people say is important to them might not actually be important. It could simply be that they think it 'makes sense' that a certain factor is important. Second, people do not necessarily notice what affects their behaviour – and so some aspect of marketing can actually be important to the business, but buyers don't necessarily realise or know it's important. Therefore, asking them about it can give misleading results. Two examples explain these points. First, there has been a stream of news reports that say things like '71 per cent of consumers say they will support brands with a good social conscience' or similar. We infer that a social conscience is important to buyers. But these sorts of reports are a manifestation of response bias or social desirability bias – it's easy to agree that it's good for a brand or business to have a good social conscience or support good causes – who wouldn't agree! But of course, whether these good things can actually influence purchases is not the same as people agreeing they are important in a survey. This sort of thing has been proved time and again with 'buy local' campaigns, when consumers are surveyed and asked 'do you support buying local goods and services' a vast majority say 'yes', but when they do buy, the vast majority of what they buy is not local goods and services. In part this can be because they don't know they're local. Another issue is that while people will say they want to support brands or businesses that do good things – it is another matter entirely for people to know they do those good things. Imagine you are buying a power drill or a refrigerator – which brand does more good things for the environment or society? Hardly anyone would know.

It might also be the case that asking what's important yields information that certain things are not considered to be important to buyers but nevertheless strongly influence their behaviour. A classic example is advertising – imagine if you were asked how important these aspects of a brand are to you: product quality, competitive price and good advertising. Hardly anyone will say good advertising is important as a purchase criterion. Based on survey results asking about importance, then, a business might conclude it should not advertise, which would be a poor decision!

Management Implication

Be cautious about basing strategies around what buyers say is important to them. Be careful not to over-interpret surveys of buyers that ask about important buying factors.

Self-test Questions

1. A company has been struggling to grow for quite a few years and has had a series of senior management changes, as one CEO left after the other. Finally, the company settles on an experienced insider, Graham Ireland. Ireland knows the recycling business backward and forward and has brought a much-needed cool head to the troubled company. Finally, ScrapStream is growing and analysts are rating the stock a good buy.

   Comment on this scenario, based on what you've read in this section of the book.
2. We notice that many of our highly loyal buyers from last year were not so loyal this year.

   Consider this statement: is this a problem, or is there a simple explanation?
3. After a lot of planning, we determined that a targeted advertising campaign across social media with an emphasis on our brand purpose was the best approach. So far, research is indicating this strategy is working spectacularly well.

   Comment on this statement, based on what you've read in this section of the book.

References

Abesamis, A. (2019). Exclusive: Krispy Kreme is opening a 24-hour flagship store in NYC's Times Square. Available at: www.forbes.com/sites/abigailabesamis/2019/06/10/exclusive-krispy-kreme-is-opening-a-24-hour-flagship-store-in-nycs-times-square/ (accessed 9 March 2021).

Ali, Z. (2020). The world's 100 largest banks. Available at: www.spglobal.com/marketintelligence/en/news-insights/latest-news-headlines/the-world-s-100-largest-banks-2020-57854079 (accessed 9 March 2021).

Anderson, E. W., Fornell, C., & Mazvancheryl, S. K. (2004). Customer satisfaction and shareholder value. *Journal of Marketing*, 68(4): 172–185.

Anesbury, Z., Winchester, M., & Kennedy, R. (2017). Brand user profiles seldom change and seldom differ. *Marketing Letters*, 28(4): 523–535.

Ansoff, H. I. (1957). Strategies for diversification. *Harvard Business Review* (Sept–Oct): 113–124.

Anthony, S. (2019). Banks must now publish their own customer satisfaction figures. Available at: www.bankrate.com/uk/current-accounts/banks-must-now-publish-their-own-customer-satisfaction-figures/ (accessed 9 March 2021).

Armstrong, J. S. (1982). The value of formal planning for strategic decisions: Review of empirical research. *Strategic Management Journal*, 3: 197–211.

Armstrong, J. S., & Brodie, R. J. (1994). Effects of portfolio planning methods on decision making: Experimental results. *International Journal of Research in Marketing*, 11: 73–84.

Armstrong, J. S., & Collopy, F. (1996). Competitor orientation: Effects of objectives and information on managerial decisions and profitability. *Journal of Marketing Research*, 33(May): 188–199.

Armstrong, J. S., & Green, K. (2007). Competitor-oriented objectives: The myth of market share. *International Journal of Business*, 12(1): 117–136.

Bain, J. S. (1965). *Barriers to New Competition* (Competition edn). Cambridge: Harvard University Press.

Bain, J. (1967). Market structures: Degree of product differentiation within industries, *Industrial Organization* (2nd edn). New York: Wiley, pp. 223–250.

Bain, J. S. (1968). *Industrial Organization*. New York: John Wiley & Sons.

Banelis, M., Riebe, E., & Rungie, C. (2013). Empirical evidence of repertoire size. *Australasian Marketing Journal*, 21(1): 59–65.

Bemmaor, A. C., & Mouchoux, D. (1991). Measuring the short-term effect of in-store promotion and retail advertising on brand sales: A factorial experiment. *Journal of Marketing Research*, 28(2): 202–214.

Bennett, D. (2008). Brand loyalty dynamics – China's television brands come of age. *Australasian Marketing Journal*, 16(2): 39–50.

Bird, M., Channon, C., & Ehrenberg, A. (1970). Brand image and brand usage. *Journal of Marketing Research*, 7(3): 307–314.

Bird, M., & Ehrenberg, A. (1970). Consumer attitudes and brand usage. *Journal of the Market Research Society*, 12(4): 233–247.

Blankson, C., Kalafatis, S., Cheng, J. M.-S., & Hadjicharalambous, C. (2008). Impact of positioning strategies on corporate performance. *Journal of Advertising Research*, 48(1): 106–122.

Boden, A. (2020). Learning to fly. Starling Bank blog. Available at: www.starlingbank.com/blog/starling-2019-year-in-review (accessed 3 March 2021).

Bolton, R. N. (1989). The relationship between market characteristics and promotional price elasticities. *Marketing Science*, 8(2): 153–169.

Bronnenberg, B. J., Kruger, M. W., & Mela, C. F. (2008). The IRI marketing data set. *Marketing Science*, 27(4): 745–748.

Browne, R. (2018). Europe's banks brace for a huge overhaul that throws open the doors to their data. Available at: www.cnbc.com/2017/12/25/psd2-europes-banks-brace-for-new-eu-data-sharing-rules.html (accessed 3 March 2021).

Bruce, N. I., Becker, M., & Reinartz, W. (2020). Communicating brands in television advertising. *Journal of Marketing Research*, 57(2): 236–256.

Bunge, J., & Kendall, B. (2020). Six chicken-industry officials are indicted in price-fixing probe. Available at: www.wsj.com/articles/six-chicken-industry-officials-are-indicted-in-price-fixing-probe-11602085637 (accessed 9 March 2021).

Butler, S. (2020). Ikea to buy back unwanted furniture for up to half original price. Available at: www.theguardian.com/business/2020/oct/13/ikea-buy-furniture-price-uk-ireland-black-Friday (accessed 9 March 2021).

Buzzell, R. D., & Gale, B. T. (1987). *The PIMS Principles*. New York: The Free Press.

Campbell, D., Edgar, D., & Stonehouse, G. (2011). *Business Strategy: An Introduction* (3rd edn). Basingstoke: Palgrave Macmillan.

Chad, P. (2013). Extending the use of market orientation: Transforming a charity into a business. *Australasian Marketing Journal*, 21(1): 10–16.

Choi, H., Kim, S.-H., & Lee, J. (2010). Role of network structure and network effects in diffusion of innovations. *Industrial Marketing Management*, 39(1): 170–177.

Chung, H. (2020). McDonald's Q1 global same-store sales tumble 3.4% amid COVID-19. Available at: https://uk.finance.yahoo.com/news/mcdonalds-q1-2020-earnings-covid-coronavirus-110003076.html (accessed 9 March 2021).

Collis, D. J., & Montgomery, C. A. (1995). Competing on resources: Strategy in the 90s. *Harvard Business Review*, 73(4): 118–128.

Colombo, R., Ehrenberg, A., & Sabavala, D. (2000). Diversity in analyzing brand-switching tables: The car challenge. *Canadian Journal of Marketing Research*, 19: 23–36.

Colombo, R., & Sabavala, D. (2013). Approaches to analyzing brand switching matrices. *Journal of Empirical Generalisations in Marketing Science*, 14(1).

Competition and Markets Authority (2020). Latest banking customer satisfaction results published. Available at: www.gov.uk/government/news/latest-banking-customer-satisfaction-results-published (accessed 9 March 2021).

Corkindale, D., Balan, P., & Rowe, C. (1996). *Marketing: Making the Future Happen* (2nd edn). Melbourne: Thomas Nelson Australia.

Cossor, B. (2019). Starling Bank: How they did it. Available at: https://thephagroup.com/starling-bank-how-they-did-it/ (accessed 9 March 2021).

Current Account Switch Service (2020). A smooth switch for you. Available at: www.currentaccountswitch.co.uk (accessed 3 March 2021).

Danenberg, N., Kennedy, R., Beal, V., & Sharp, B. (2016). Advertising budgeting: A re-investigation of the evidence on brand size and spend. *Journal of Advertising*, 45(1): 139–146.

Dawes, J. (2008). Regularities in buyer behaviour and brand performance: The case of Australian beer. *The Journal of Brand Management*, 15(3): 198–208.

Dawes, J. (2009). Brand loyalty in the UK sportswear market. *International Journal of Market Research*, 51(4): 449–463.

Dawes, J. G. (2014). Patterns in competitive structure among retail financial services brands. *European Journal of Marketing*, 48(5–6): 7.

Dawes, J. G. (2016a). Brand growth in packaged goods markets: Ten cases with common patterns. *Journal of Consumer Behaviour*, 15(5): 475–489.

Dawes, J. G. (2016b). Testing the robustness of brand partitions identified from purchase duplication analysis. *Journal of Marketing Management*, 32(7): 695–715.

Dawes, J. (2020a). Do customer satisfaction scores link to business revenue over time? *Social Science Research Network*. Available at : https://papers.ssrn.com/sol3/papers.cfm?abstract_id=3657826 (accessed 23 March 2021).

Dawes, J. (2020b) The natural monopoly effect in brand purchasing: Do big brands really appeal to lighter category buyers? *Australasian Marketing Journal (AMJ)* 28(2): 90–99.

Dawes, J., Romaniuk, J., & Mansfield, A. (2009). Generalized pattern in competition among tourism destinations. *International Journal of Culture, Tourism and Hospitality Research*, 3(1): 33–53.

Dawes, J. G., & Trinh, G. (2017). Category and brand purchase rates (still) follow the NBD distribution. *Social Science Research Network*. Available at: https://papers.ssrn.com/sol3/papers.cfm?abstract_id=3042332 (accessed 23 March 2021).

Deighton, J., Henderson, C. M., & Neslin, S. A. (1994). The effects of advertising on brand switching and repeat purchasing. *Journal of Marketing Research*, 31(February): 28–43.

De Jong, M. G., Lehmann, D. R., & Netzer, O. (2012). State-dependence effects in surveys. *Marketing Science*, 31(5): 838–854.

Department for Communities and Local Government (2007). *Outdoor Advertisements and Signs: A Guide for Advertisers*. Available at: https://assets.publishing.service.gov.uk/government/uploads/system/uploads/attachment_data/file/11499/326679.pdf (accessed 9 March 2021).

Ehrenberg, A (1974). *Data Reduction*. Chichester: Wiley. Available at: www.empgens.com/article/data-reduction/ (accessed 23 March 2021).

Ehrenberg, A. (1991). Politicians' double jeopardy: A pattern and exceptions. *Journal of the Market Research Society*, 33(1): 347–353.

Ehrenberg, A. (2000). Repeat-buying: Facts, theory and applications. *Journal of Empirical Generalisations in Marketing Science*, 5(2): 392–770.

Ehrenberg, A., & England, L. R. (1990). Generalising a pricing effect. *Journal of Industrial Economics*, 39: 47–68.

Ehrenberg, A., Goodhardt, G., & Barwise, T. P. (1990). Double Jeopardy revisited. *Journal of Marketing*, 54(3): 82–91.

Ehrenberg, A., Uncles, M. D., & Goodhardt, G. G. (2004). Understanding brand performance measures: Using dirichlet benchmarks. *Journal of Business Research*, 57(12): 1307–1325.

Ely, J. W., Graber, M. L., & Croskerry, P. (2011). Checklists to reduce diagnostic errors. *Academic Medicine*, 86(3): 307–313.

Fingas, R. (2017). UK's mobile-only Starling Bank adds Apple Pay support. Available at: https://appleinsider.com/articles/17/07/18/uks-mobile-only-starling-bank-adds-apple-pay-support (accessed 9 March 2021).

Flyvbjerg, B. (2007). Policy and planning for large-infrastructure projects: Problems, causes, cures. *Environment and Planning B: Planning and Design*, 34(4): 578–597.

Fornell, C. (1995). The quality of economic output: Empirical generalizations about its distribution and relationship to market share. *Marketing Science*, 14(3): G203–G211.

Gelzinis, A. (2017). What happens when brands stop advertising? Documenting long-term sales trends. Unpublished Masters, University of South Australia Australia.

Gilligan, C., & Wilson, R. (2009). *Strategic Marketing Planning*. Abingdon: Routledge.

Gordon, J., Grüntges, V., Smith, V., & Staack, Y. (2016). New insights for new growth: What it takes to understand your customers today. McKinsey & Company, 23 September. Available at: www.mckinsey.com/business-functions/marketing-and-sales/our-insights/new-insights-for-new-growth-what-it-takes-to-understand-your-customers-today# (accessed 23 March 2021).

Hammett, E. (2019). John Lewis, Ikea and M&S top UK brand health rankings. Marketing Week, 20 August. Available at: www.marketingweek.com/john-lewis-ikea-ms-top-brand-health-rankings/ (accessed 23 March 2021).

Hammond, K., Ehrenberg, A., & Goodhardt, G. J. (1996). Market segmentation for competitive brands. *European Journal of Marketing*, 30(12): 39–49.

Hansen, F., & Bech Christensen, L. (2005). Share of voice/share of market and long-term advertising effects. *International Journal of Advertising* 24(3): 297–320.

Heffernan, M. (2013). What happened after the Foxconn suicides. CBS News, 7 August. Available at: www.cbsnews.com/news/what-happened-after-the-foxconn-suicides/ (accessed 23 March 2021).

Hollensen, S. (2010). *Marketing Planning A Global Perspective* (2nd edn). London: McGraw Hill.

ideaconnection (2012). Nivea co-creates with the crowd to eliminate stain problem. Available at: www.ideaconnection.com/open-innovation-success/Nivea-Co-Creates-with-the-Crowd-to-Eliminate-Stain-Pr-00365.html (accessed 23 March 2021).

IKEA Canada (2020). IKEA Canada to launch alternative Black Friday campaign to inspire more sustainable living. Available at: www.ikea.com/ca/en/this-is-ikea/newsroom/alternative-black-friday-campaign-pub5ad13df0 (accessed 23 March 2021).

Ikea Group (2014). People & Planet Positive-IKEA Group Sustainability Strategy for 2020. Delft, Netherlands: IKEA Group.

Intersoft Consulting (2020). Rights of the data subject. Available at: https://gdpr-info.eu/chapter-3/ (accessed 23 March 2021).

Jacobson, R., & Obermiller, C. (1990). The formation of expected future price: A reference price for forward-looking consumers. *Journal of Consumer Research*, 16(March): 420–432.

Jones, J. P. (1995a). Does advertising produce sales today or sales tomorrow? *Journal of Marketing Communications*, 1(1): 1–11.

Jones, J. P. (1995b). We have a breakthrough: Single-source data is the key to proving advertising's short term effects. *Admap* (June): 33–35.

Kahneman, D. (2011). *Thinking, Fast and Slow*. New York: Farrar, Straus and Giroux.

Keiningham, T. L., Cooil, B., Andreassen, T. W., & Aksoy, L. (2007). A longitudinal examination of net promoter and firm revenue growth. *Journal of Marketing*, 71: 39–51.

Kotler, P., Brown, L., Adam, S., Burton, S., & Armstrong, G. (2007). *Marketing* (7th edn). Frenchs Forest: Pearson Education Australia.

Kruger, J., & Evans, M. (2004). If you don't want to be late, enumerate: Unpacking reduces the planning fallacy. *Journal of Experimental Social Psychology*, 40(5): 586–598.

Kumar, V., Petersen, J. A., & Leone, R. P. (2007). How valuable is word of mouth? *Harvard Business Review*, October: 139–146.

Lam, D. (2006). Applicability of the duplication of purchase law to gaming. *UNLV Gaming Research & Review Journal*, 10(2): 55–62.

Lee, K. S., & Ng, I. C. L. (2007). An integrative framework of pre-emption strategies. *Journal of Strategic Marketing*, 15(4): 327–348.

Lees, G., & Wright, M. (2009). Does the duplication of viewing law apply to radio listening? Paper presented at the Proceedings of the Australian & New Zealand Marketing Academy Conference, Melbourne, Australia.

Levitt, T. (1960). Marketing myopia. *Harvard Business Review*, 38(July–August): 45–56.

Loewentheil, H. (2017). 13 mind-blowing facts about buying wine and liquor at Costco. BuzzFeed. Available at: www.buzzfeed.com/hannahloewentheil/xx-secrets-for-buying-wine-and-liquor-at-costco (accessed 23 March 2021).

Lynn, M. (2013a). Lessons from duplication of purchase data. *Cornell Hospitality Report*, 13(3): 4–16.

Lynn, M. (2013b). The target market misapprehension: Lessons from restaurant duplication of purchase data. *The Center for Hospitality Research*, 13(3): 6–15.

Macaulay, T. (2018). Starling Bank CIO John Mountain reveals plans to challenge big banks. Available at: www.cio.com/article/3525730/starling-bank-cio-john-mountain-reveals-plans-to-challenge-big-banks.html (accessed 9 March 2021).

Mansfield, A. (2004). *How Do Tourism Destinations Compete? An Analysis of the Duplication of Purchase Law*. Adelaide: University of South Australia.

Mansfield, A., & Romaniuk, J. (2003). How do tourism destinations compete? An application of the duplication of purchase law. Paper presented at the EMAC, Glasgow.

Manthrop, R. (2018). What is Open Banking and PSD2? *WIRED explains*. Available at: www.wired.co.uk/article/open-banking-cma-psd2-explained (accessed 3 March 2021).

McCarthy, J. (2019). Starling Bank turns to TV to lead brand building strategy to become a household name. Available at: www.thedrum.com/news/2019/10/14/starling-bank-turns-tv-lead-brand-building-strategy-become-household-name (accessed 9 March 2021).

McDonald, M., & Wilson, H. (2011). *Marketing Plans: How to Prepare Them, How to Use Them*. Chichester: John Wiley & Sons.

Mouzas, S. (2006). Efficiency versus effectiveness in business networks. *Journal of Business Research*, 59(10–11): 1124–1132.

Mulhern, F. J., Williams, J. D., & Leone, R. P. (1998). Variability of brand price elasticities across retail stores: Ethnic, income, and brand determinants. *Journal of Retailing*, 74(3): 427–446.

Murphy, P. E., Laczniak, G. R., & Harris, F. (2017). *Ethics in Marketing: International Cases and Perspectives* (2nd edn). London: Routledge.

Nagle, T., & Holden, R. (2003). *The Strategy and Tactics of Pricing: A Guide to Profitable Decision Making* (3rd edn). New Jersey: Prentice-Hall.

Narver, J. C., & Slater, S. F. (1990). The effect of a market orientation on business profitability. *Journal of Marketing*, 54(4): 20–35.

Nenycz-Thiel, M., Dawes, J., & Romaniuk, J. (2018). Modeling brand market share change in emerging markets. *International Marketing Review*, 35(5): 785–805.

Nenycz-Thiel, M., Romaniuk, J., & Sharp, B. (2016). Building physical availability. In J. Romaniuk, & B. Sharp (eds), *How Brands Grow: Part 2*. Melbourne: Oxford University Press, pp. 145–172.

Neubaum, D. O., Pagell, M., Drexler Jr., J. A., Mckee-Ryan, F. M., & Larson, E. (2009). Business education and its relationship to student personal moral philosophies and attitudes toward profits: An empirical response to critics. *Academy of Management Learning and Education*, 8(1): 9–24.

PBS (2004). *The Persuaders*. USA: PBS Broadcasting Corporation.

Peters, T. J., & Waterman, R. H., Jr. (1982). *In Search of Excellence – Lessons from America's Best-Run Companies*. New York: Harper & Row, Publishers.

Pew Research Center (2016). A wider ideological gap between more and less educated adults. Available at: www.pewresearch.org/politics/2016/04/26/a-wider-ideological-gap-between-more-and-less-educated-adults/ (accessed 23 March 2021).

Pointer Media Network (2009). Losing loyalty: The consumer defection dilemma 14. St Petersburg, FL: Pointer Media Network, The Chief Marketing Officer (CMO) Council.

Pollack, A. (2015). Drug goes from $13.50 a tablet to $750, overnight. *New York Times*, 20 September. Available at: www.nytimes.com/2015/09/21/business/a-huge-overnight-increase-in-a-drugs-price-raises-protests.html (accessed 23 March 2021).

Porter, M. E. (1979). How competitive forces shape strategy. *Harvard Business Review*, 57(March–April): 137–145.

Porter, M. E. (1985). *Competitive Advantage: Creating and Sustaining Superior Performance*. New York: Free Press.

Reichheld, F. F. (2003). The one number you need to grow. *Harvard Business Review* (December): 46–54.

Richardson, A. (2004). Estimating individual values of time in stated preference surveys. 26th Conference of Australian Institutes of Transport Research (CAITR). Melbourne.

Robinson, S. (2016). *The Practice of Integrity in Business*. London: Springer Nature.

Romaniuk, J. (2003). Brand attributes – 'distribution outlets' in the mind. *Journal of Marketing Communications*, 9(June): 73–92.

Romaniuk, J. (2013). Modeling mental market share. *Journal of Business Research*, 66(2): 188–195.

Romaniuk, J. (2016). Building mental availability. In J. Romaniuk, & B. Sharp (eds), *How Brands Grow: Part 2*. Melbourne: Oxford University Press, pp. 62–86.

Romaniuk, J. (2018). Creating distinctive brand assets. In J. Romaniuk (ed.), *Building Distinctive Brand Assets*. South Melbourne, Victoria: Oxford University Press, pp. 5–14.

Romaniuk, J., Dawes, J., & Nenycz-Thiel, M. (2014). Generalizations regarding the growth and decline of manufacturer and store brands. *Journal of Retailing and Consumer Services*, 21(5): 725–734.

Romaniuk, J., & Ehrenberg, A. (2012). Do brands lack personality? *Marketing Theory: An International Review*, 12(3): 333–339.

Romaniuk, J., & Gaillard, E. (2007). The relationship between unique brand associations, brand usage and brand performance: Analysis across eight categories. *Journal of Marketing Management*, 23(3): 267–284.

Romaniuk, J., & Sharp, B. (2004). Conceptualizing and measuring brand salience. *Marketing Theory*, 4(4): 327–342.

Romaniuk, J., & Sharp, B. (2016). *How Brands Grow: Part 2*. South Melbourne: Oxford University Press.

Romaniuk, J., Sharp, B & Ehrenberg, A. (2007). Evidence concerning the importance of perceived brand differentiation. *Australasian Marketing Journal*, 15(2): 42–54.

Rosenzweig, P. (2007). *The Halo Effect*. New York: Free Press.

Roser, M., & Oritz-Ospina, E. (2020). Tertiary education. Available at: https://ourworldindata.org/tertiary-education (accessed 23 March 2021).

Rubin, J. D. (2012). Fairness in business: Does it matter, and what does it mean? *Business Horizons*, 55(1): 11–15.

Schwepker Jr, C. H., & Good, D. J. (2007). Exploring the relationships among sales manager goals, ethical behavior and professional commitment in the salesforce: Implications for forging customer relationships. *Journal of Relationship Marketing*, 6(1): 3–19.

Scriven, J., & Ehrenberg, A. (2004). Consistent consumer responses to price changes. *Australasian Marketing Journal*, 12(3): 21–39.

Seiders, K., Voss, G. B., Grewal, D., & Godfrey, A. L. (2005). Do satisfied customers buy more? Examining moderating influences in a retailing context. *Journal of Marketing*, 69(4): 26–43.

Shapiro, B. T., Hitsch, G. J., & Tuchman, A. E. (2020). Generalizable and robust TV advertising effects. NBER Working Paper. Available at: www.nber.org/system/files/working_papers/w27684/w27684.pdf (accessed 23 March 2021).

Sharp, B. (1995). Brand equity and market-based assets of professional service firms. *Journal of Professional Services Marketing*, 13(1): 3–13.

Sharp, B. (2010). *How Brands Grow*. South Melbourne, Australia: Oxford University Press.

Sharp, B., & Sorensen, H. (2017). Physical availability, retailing, shopping. In B. Sharp (ed.), *Marketing: Theory, Evidence, Practice*. Melbourne: Oxford University Press, pp. 330–356.

Shaw, R. (2008). Opinon piece: Net promoter. *Journal of Database Marketing and Customer Strategy Management*, 15(3): 138–140.

Silverman, E. (2020). For the first time, drug makers and PBMs must jointly face an insulin price fixing lawsuit. *STAT News*, 30 September. Available at: www.statnews.com/pharmalot/2020/09/30/insulin-texas-price-fixing-conspiracy-lilly-sanofi-pbm/ (accessed 23 March 2021).

Simpson, G. (2018). Starling Bank's mobile-first marketing opens more accounts: Campaign of the Month. Available at: www campaignlive.co.uk/article/starling-banks-mobile-first-marketing-opens-accounts-campaign-month/1459246 (accessed 9 March 2021).

Sinarski, M., Fellner, M., & Varju, M. (2020). Measuring business outcomes in biopharmaceutical digital healthcare marketing. *Journal of Digital & Social Media Marketing*, 7(4): 306–313.

Srivastava, R. K., Shervani, T. A., & Fahey, L. (1997). Driving shareholder value: The role of marketing in reducing vulnerability and volatility of cash flows. *Journal of Market-Focused Management*, 2(1): 49–64.

Srivastava, R. K., Shervani, T. A., & Fahey, L. (1998). Market-based assets and shareholder value: A framework for analysis. *Journal of Marketing*, 62(1): 2–18.

Starling Bank (2019). Starling Bank pledges to transform banking for small businesses as it is awarded £100 million grant. Available at: www.starlingbank.com/news/rbs-cif-funding-feb2019 (accessed 3 March 2021).

Statista (2021). Share of adults who own a smartphone in the United Kingdom (UK) in 2008 and 2019, by demographics. Available at: www.statista.com/statistics/956297/ownership-of-smartphones-uk/ (accessed 3 Mach 2021).

Strickler, L. (2019). Purdue Pharma offers $10–12 billion to settle opioid claims. NBC News, 27 August. Available at: www.nbcnews.com/news/us-news/purdue-pharma-offers-10-12-billion-settle-opioid-claims-n1046526 (accessed 23 march 2021).

Swift, J. (2020). Share of search: The new most important brand metric? Available at: www.contagious.com/news-and-views/share-of-search-the-new-most-important-metric-for-brands-google (accessed 23 March 2021).

Taylor, J., Kennedy, R., & Sharp, B. (2009). Is once really enough? Making generalizations about advertising's convex sales response function. *Journal of Advertising Research*, 49(2): 198–200.

Tellis, G. (1988). The price elasticity of selective demand: A meta analysis of econometric models of sales. *Journal of Marketing Research*, 25(4): 331–341.

Uncles, M. D., & Ellis, K. (1989). The buying of own labels. *European Journal of Marketing*, 23(3): 47–70.

Uncles, M., Kennedy, R., Nenycz-Thiel, M., Singh, J., & Kwok, S. (2012). In 25 years, across 50 categories, user profiles for directly competing brands seldom differ: Affirming Andrew Ehrenberg's principles. *Journal of Advertising Research*, 52(2): 252–261.

Valentin, E. K. (2001). SWOT analysis from a resource-based view. *Journal of Marketing Theory and Practice*, 9(2): 54–69.

Vieceli, J., & Sharp, B. (2001). The inhibiting effect of brand salience on recall. Paper presented at the ANZMAC, Auckland.

Vieceli, J., & Sharp, B. (2002). Salience effects on recall. British Academy of Management Conference, London.

Vigen, T. (2020). *Spurious Correlations*. New York: Hachette.

WARC (2017). *Advertising–Sales Ratios, US*. New York: World Advertising Research Centre.

Westwood, J. (2005). *The Marketing Plan Workbook*. London: Kogan Page.

Wilson, A. L., Nguyen, C., Bogomolova, S., Sharp, B., & Olds, T. (2019). Analysing how physical activity competes: A cross-disciplinary application of the Duplication of Behaviour Law. *International Journal of Behavioral Nutrition and Physical Activity*, 16(1): 1–13.

Index

Page numbers in *italics* refer to figures; page numbers in **bold** refer to tables.